T0319889

Biodiversity, Conservation and Sustainable Development

NEW HORIZONS IN ENVIRONMENTAL ECONOMICS

Series Editors: Wallace E. Oates, *Professor of Economics, University of Maryland, USA* and Henk Folmer, *Professor of General Economics, Wageningen University and Professor of Environmental Economics, Tilburg University, The Netherlands*

This important series is designed to make a significant contribution to the development of the principles and practices of environmental economics. It includes both theoretical and empirical work. International in scope, it addresses issues of current and future concern in both East and West and in developed and developing countries.

The main purpose of the series is to create a forum for the publication of high quality work and to show how economic analysis can make a contribution to understanding and resolving the environmental problems confronting the world in the twenty-first century.

Recent titles in the series include:

Biodiversity, Conservation and Sustainable Development

Principles and Practices with Asian Examples

Clem Tisdell
Professor of Economics
The University of Queensland
Australia

NEW HORIZONS IN ENVIRONMENTAL ECONOMICS

Edward Elgar
Cheltenham, UK • Northampton, MA, USA

Published by
Edward Elgar Publishing Limited
The Lypiatts
15 Lansdown Road
Cheltenham
Glos GL50 2JA
UK

Edward Elgar Publishing, Inc.
William Pratt House
9 Dewey Court
Northampton
Massachusetts 01060
USA

Reprinted 2003

This book has been printed on demand to keep the title in print.

A catalogue record for this book is available from the British Library

Library of Congress Cataloguing in Publication Data
Tisdell, Clem
        Biodiversity, conservation, and sustainable development:
principles and practices with Asian examples / Clem Tisdell.
        (New horizons in environmental economics)
        1. Nature conservation—Economic aspects. 2. Sustainable
development—Environmental aspects. 3. Biological diversity
conservation—Economic aspects. 4. Nature conservation—Economic
aspects—Asia—Case studies. 5. Sustainable development—
Environmental aspects—Asia—Case studies. I. Title. II. Series.
QH75.T57 1999
33.95'16—dc21   98–30464
                                                       CIP

ISBN 978 1 85898 735 4

Printed and bound in Great Britain by
Marston Book Services Limited, Didcot

Contents

PART IV   CONCLUDING OBSERVATIONS

Figures

Tables

Preface

Those who value the conservation of nature highly and want to preserve biological diversity for its own sake need to be aware of the economic issues and problems involved in sustaining nature conservation and biodiversity. Those who take a more instrumentalist economics-type attitude towards nature also need to be aware of such issues and should know of the role which nature conservation can play in sustainable development. Both groups of readers should find this book of interest.

This book concentrates mainly, but not exclusively, on wildlife conservation (including conservation of biodiversity) and the integration of wildlife conservation with policies for sustainable development. It considers, amongst other things, the significance of biodiversity conservation in relation to different concepts of sustainable development, the value of biodiversity in providing ecological and productive stability, economic use of wildlife as a means for conserving biodiversity and the impact of the global economic system on nature conservation. Issues involved in obtaining and allocating financial support for protected areas, and the role which ecotourism can play in providing funds for nature conservation, are discussed.

After considering the general principles raised by the above-mentioned issues and policies, experiences and cases from Asia involving conservation are reviewed. Initially, an overview of Asian economic growth and its impact on natural environments is provided. Then the focus shifts to problems and features of nature conservation in Xishuangbanna Prefecture in Yunnan, China, a region rated as rich in biodiversity. Although this may seem to be a rather specific area of focus, the lessons to be learnt from this region carry over to other regions in Asia, and to other developing countries. Topics addressed include the benefits and costs to China of Xishuangbanna State Nature Reserve; problems and policies for reconciling economic development, nature conservation and local communities; the role of tourism development in conservation in this prefecture; problems raised by the presence of agricultural pests from protected areas and some strategies adopted to deal with these problems; and difficulties involved in financing nature reserves in Xishuangbanna and China generally. Conservation problems in north-east India provide an additional case study. These studies illustrate general problems and raise matters of interest beyond the particular localities considered.

Material in this book has benefited from presentations (seminars or lectures) in China (Southwest Forestry College, Kunming), in India (North East Hills University, Aizawl Campus, Mizoram), Brazil (Federal University of Pernambuco, Recife), Britain (York University), Canada (Queen's University), Germany (Duisburg University; Kiel University; and the Science Centre, Berlin), Sweden (Göteborg University and the Swedish University of Agricultural Sciences, Uppsala), and USA (University of California, Riverside), as well as from presentations within Australia, in Brisbane, Canberra and Sydney. International conferences held in Australia, Hong Kong, India, Thailand, the UK, the USA, and Venezuela provided further feedback on work reported here.

I would like to thank those who have played a relatively direct role in the production of this book. In particular, I would like to thank Zhu Xiang of the Ministry of Forestry, Beijing for his assistance with material which is reported in Chapters 10-14. These chapters are an outgrowth of our research co-operation, made possible by a research grant from the Australian Centre for International Agriculture Research (Project No. 40: *Economic Impact of Rural Adjustments to Nature Conservation (Biodiversity) Programmes: a Case Study of Xishuangbanna Dai Autonomous Prefecture, Yunnan, China*. This co-operation commenced when Zhu Xiang was at the Southwest Forestry College, Kunming and Chapters 10-14 draw upon articles which we published jointly, as reported in the acknowledgments.

I would also like to take this opportunity to thank the Australian Centre for International Agriculture Research (ACIAR) for its small research grant, and a travel grant which was instrumental in enabling the case studies to be completed in Asia. In this respect, I am grateful in particular to Drs K. Menz and P. Lal of ACIAR for their support.

Chapters 6 and 7 are based upon presentations which I made originally at the IVth World Congress on National Parks and Protected Areas held in Caracas, Venezuela in 1992. I wish to thank IUCN (World Conservation Union) for funding my participation in this Congress, and Dr Jeffrey McNeely for inviting me to present a paper in a plenary session.

In north-east India, I am especially grateful to the staff at the North East Hills University (Aizawl Campus) for their assistance to me, especially Professor K.P. Nath, members of the Economics Department, and Professor K. Jha, Professor of Forestry. Without their help, Chapter 15 would be of lesser value. Timely information from Professor P.J. Ramakrishnan of Jawaharlal Nehru University was also of help. Nevertheless, none of the persons mentioned above is responsible for any shortcomings in this book.

Jeannine Fowler, assisted by Averil Ström and other secretaries from time to time, have completed the production of the typescript. My sincere thanks to them for their efforts over the last year or so. I am also grateful to Edward Elgar and associated staff for their interest in the book and their essential contribution to its production. Finally, I wish to thank my wife, Mariel, and my family, for tolerating one who always seems to be writing or going on field trips.

Clem Tisdell
Brisbane

Acknowledgements

The Chapters listed draw to some extent on my previously published articles as specified below. In most cases, considerable changes or additions have been made to these articles. I am grateful to the appropriate editors and/or publishers for their permission to draw on, or reproduce, these works.

Chapter	Article
5	'Keynote Address: Does the Economic Use of Wildlife Favour Conservation and Sustainability', Ch. 15 in G.C. Grigg, P.T. Hale and D. Lunney (eds), *Conservation Through Sustainable Use of Wildlife,* Centre for Conservation Biology, The University of Queensland, 1995, pp. 86–91.
6	'Conservation, protected areas and the global economic system: how debt, trade exchange rates, inflation and macroeconomic policy affect biological diversity', *Biodiversity and Conservation,* **3**: 419–436, 1994.
7	'Environmental economic guidelines – inter-country and inter-regional requests for financial support for protected areas', *Parks,* **4**(2): 13–21, 1994.
8	'Ecotourism, economics and the environment: observations from China', *Journal of Travel Research,* **34**(4): 11–9, 1996.
9	'Asian development and environmental dilemmas', *Contemporary Economic Policy,* **13**: 38–49, 1995.
10	(With Xiang Zhu) 'Economics, Gains and Costs of Biodiversity Conservation in China', Ch. 19 in G.C. Grigg, P.T. Hale and D. Lunney (eds), *Conservation Through Sustainable Use of Wildlife,* Centre for Conservation Biology, The University of Queensland, 1995, pp. 110–6.
11	(With Xiang Zhu) 'Reconciling economic development, nature conservation and local communities: strategies for

biodiversity conservation in Xishuangbanna, China', *The Environmentalist,* **16**: 203–11, 1996.

12   (With Xiang Zhu) 'Tourism development and nature conservation in Xishuangbanna, Yunnan: a case study', *TigerPaper*, **23**(2): 20–8, 1996.

13   (With Xiang Zhu) 'Protected areas, agricultural pests and economic damage: conflicts with elephants and pests in Yunnan, China', *The Environmentalist*, **18** (in press).

14   (With Xiang Zhu) 'Financing nature reserves in China: a case study', *TigerPaper*, **24**(4): 21–6, 1997.

15   'Biodiversity, conservation and sustainable development: challenges for Northeast India in context', *Indian Journal of Quantitative Economics*, **11**(1): 1–17, 1996.

PART I

An Overview

1. Economics, Nature Conservation and Sustainable Development: An Overview

INTRODUCTION

Nature is under continuing threat from mankind and the world's biodiversity continues to decline at an alarming rate (Barbier *et al.*, 1994, Ch. 1; Pearce and Moran, 1994, Ch. 1) due to economic growth and inadequate socio-economic mechanisms to protect nature. Biodiversity decline may eventually imperil the economic welfare of mankind and may well lead to a less satisfactory universe than many of us desire. Losses in nature and in biodiversity can result in unsustainable development which economically injures future generations. We need to be concerned about the issues involved, whether we take a purely anthropocentric view of the world (the view that only the wishes of humankind are to count) or whether we accord intrinsic rights to other living things and believe that this imposes some obligations on humans to care for other species and nature. Economics will clearly be of central importance if one takes an anthropocentric point of view, but it is also important if one adopts a more ecocentric stance. In the latter case, it is important (1) to know to what extent economic mechanisms and economic growth are compatible with nature conservation, and (2) to search for 'least-cost' mechanisms which promote targets for nature conservation. At least one should be in a position to reject socio-economic mechanisms which are demonstrably more costly than others in achieving the same nature conservation goals. Financing the management of nature and protected areas also involves many economic questions in itself. Hence, it can be seen that economics relates to this subject from several different points of view.

However, nature conservation and sustainable development are not entirely a matter for economics. Ecology must also be a major consideration. So the subject is one of central importance for ecological

3

economics. Nevertheless, many other disciplines and considerations will
have a bearing on it, such as sociology and politics.

THE ECONOMIC VALUE OF NATURE CONSERVATION

Whether or not it is possible to separate the economic value of nature
conservation from the conservation of biodiversity is a moot point. Yet,
until recently, most economic evaluations of nature concentrated on the
value of conserving particular species and natural areas. For this
purpose, methods such as contingent valuation, hedonic pricing, travel
cost methods and so on have been used. Biodiversity as such is only a
secondary consideration in such studies, if it is a consideration at all.
Pearce and Moran (1994, pp. 86–93) tabulate the findings of a large
number of these studies and, in their Chapter 5, review the methods used
for such economic valuation. However, such assessments are not
evaluations of the precise value of biodiversity.

Modern economic studies of the value of species, ecosystems and
natural areas, emphasize the importance of providing a *total* economic
valuation of these. It is certainly important not to confine economic
valuation solely to direct-use benefits of such resources, or only to
tangible benefits. Nevertheless, much controversy exists over the
reliability of estimates of total economic valuation and, in some quarters,
the ethical or moral status of such valuations, because they are made on
the basis that nature is solely an instrument for the satisfaction of human
desires; a point of view likely to be rejected by deep ecologists and those
who assign some independent moral worth to the existence of living
things other than human beings.

Regarding the above, it may be worth bearing in mind the injunction of
Pigou (1932) that economic valuation is *not complete* valuation; it is
merely an ingredient to be considered in making a final policy decision.
In making that decision, other values and evaluations should also be
taken into account by the policy-maker. This means that total economic
valuation of nature, even if accurate, is not complete valuation, but one
suspects that some practitioners lose sight of this. This is not to deny that
total economic valuation should be an important consideration in policy-
making.

How should one decompose the total economic value of a species,
natural area, and so on, in order to measure it? Pearce and others
(Pearce and Moran, 1994; Pearce *et al.*, 1989) separate it into direct

economic value in use, plus indirect-use value, plus non-use value. This is not the only way in which it may be decomposed. It could for example be divided into tangible plus intangible benefits, direct and indirect; or material plus non-material benefits. In the case of a protected area, benefits could be divided into off-site and on-site benefits.

The direct use from a protected area may include, for example, its use for tourism and recreation or, in some less developed countries, its use for gathering products in the wild, such as medicinal plants like wild ginger in Yunnan. Indirect-use benefits could include reduced soil erosion and less variable water supplies to nearby farms and sequestration of carbon dioxide. Pearce and Moran (1994) include option values, bequest and existence values under non-use values. However, in the case of both option and bequest values, these would appear to depend on potential future use. Therefore, blurring can be present between the components if the above decomposition is used.

Furthermore, the total economic value of a protected area cannot be obtained by simple addition of the value of its components. The value of the whole in some circumstances is greater than the sum of its parts. This is not to suggest that the concept of total economic valuation of nature is worthless. In fact, one of its merits is to emphasize that the economic value of nature consists of much more than the value of material production or of tangibles, and involves much more than its direct-use value. Nevertheless, we can decompose and consider total value in a variety of ways. The appropriateness of each alternative is likely to alter with the task to be done.

It is difficult to determine just how important biodiversity is in relation to the economic value of nature and for economic sustainability. This is not to say that it is of little significance, but it must be considered critically. It cannot be assumed that greater biodiversity always provides greater economic value, or that it makes for heightened economic sustainability or for greater chances of species or ecosystem survival. This is one of the matters taken up in this book. Some ecosystems which make use of nature do not appear to depend heavily on biodiversity for their economic value.

Some modern agroecosystems, forest plantations and types of aquaculture depend upon lack of *local* biodiversity for their economic value. Monocultures reduce competition between species in the field and allow economic specialization but, at the same time, do not take advantage of mutualism. Their economic productivity is, as a rule, relatively unstable and depends heavily on human management and external inputs of resources; many of these are not renewable, such as hydrocarbons. Such systems, though they possess little biodiversity may, depending upon the exact system involved, provide a number of environmental services beyond their direct-use value. For example, forest plantations help to sequester CO_2, agroforestry may reduce soil erosion and help regularize stream flows, and so on. It is even possible for man-made rural landscapes which reduce biodiversity to be pleasing to humans.

Again, the dependence of outdoor recreation and tourism on biodiversity varies despite nature being an important ingredient in the attractiveness of such activities. For some activities, merely green grass and shade from trees suffices, with the occasional bird. Biodiversity is not an essential part of the outdoor experience in such a case, though nature may be essential to it.

SUSTAINABLE DEVELOPMENT, SUSTAINABILITY AND NATURE

Despite everything, a number of ecosystems which are lacking in biodiversity, such as some agricultural systems, may require conservation of biodiversity for their sustainability. This may involve the provision of a gene bank to draw on, to counteract diseases and pests which could otherwise threaten the continued existence of such systems. Yet in some circumstances, it seems necessary to concede that a reduction in biodiversity may sustainably increase human welfare; the elimination of smallpox is a good example.

From an instrumentalist perspective, much of the living material giving rise to biodiversity must be regarded as contributing to the stock of natural capital. Its destruction reduces this stock. Loss of biodiversity through such reduction can therefore eventually threaten the economic welfare of mankind (Tisdell, 1997).

At the same time, not all systems which make use of nature rely on biodiversity at the local level for their sustainability. In fact, many from a human perspective appear to be more efficient when they are less diverse. They may be sustained because humans are willing to expend effort to do this. Systems involving little biological diversity need not collapse if humans maintain environments favourable to the species involved. The use of algae to treat wastewater is one example.

We may, however, be interested in the maintenance of biodiversity, not only for its ability to sustain human welfare, but because our goal is to sustain biodiversity *per se* in certain areas, such as those under special protection. In these cases, it is important to study the socio-economic conditions and policies which support or impede this goal. Much of the coverage in this book, (for example in relation to protected areas in Yunnan), is motivated by such a consideration; that is, how the chances of conserving biodiversity in protected areas can be improved through economic and related changes. This also requires the identification of socio-economic problems which arise in nature conservation.

BIODIVERSITY –
SOME BACKGROUND CONSIDERATIONS

Preservation of biodiversity is an important aspect of nature conservation and it has also become a significant consideration in relation to sustainable development and the sustainability of ecosystems. The sustainability of ecosystems has implications for the sustainability of any economic benefits (or disbenefits) obtained from such ecosystems, and for the retention of economic options. The retention of biodiversity keeps open future economic options, both of a use and of a non-use type. However, in a few cases, conservation of some forms of living things may pose hazards or possible future hazards to human beings. Even though these cases may be rare, we are obliged to consider the whole picture.

Although the economic importance of biodiversity conservation has received considerable emphasis in recent times, it is not commonly appreciated how complex the concept of biological diversity is, and how difficult biodiversity is to measure quantitatively, both in theory and in practice. There are so many biological forms, biological complexes and parameters of diversity (or variation) that can be measured. Owing to such complexity, measures of biodiversity indicate only a few aspects of it. Even when a measure is agreed upon, specifying it in practice may be difficult or impossible. For example, we do not know the number of species on Earth because most organisms appear not to have been catalogued.   Estimates of existing species differ by millions (most estimates range between 5–30 million, but some are higher) and only about 1.4 million living species (at the most about 35 per cent) have been described (Pearce and Moran, 1994, p. 4).

Some of the varied ways in which biodiversity can be specified include the extent of genetic variation within species; the number of species present (but one may also consider higher order genera); and ecosystem biodiversity which itself may be specified in terms of a number of different characteristics.

Pearce and Moran (1994, p. 5) point out that 'ecosystem diversity relates to the variety of habitats, biotic communities and ecological processes in the biosphere as well as diversity within ecosystems'. Within ecosystems diversity may be described (1) by functional diversity, the abundance of functionally important but different organisms, (2) the diversity of the communities involved (patchiness) and (3) landscape diversity.

In short, elements which may form a part of most biodiversity assessments are indicated in Table 1.1. The situation is, however, more complex than this table indicates.

Table 1.1 Elements in the assessment of biodiversity

---

1. *Intra-species diversity.* Extent of genetic variation within species.

2. *Diversity of species.* For example, as measured by number of species. However, this measure does not take account of the extent of difference between species, for example, whether they are in the same genus or not.

3. *Ecosystem diversity.* May be described in terms of functional diversity, patchiness and landscape variety

---

As appropriately pointed out by Pearce and Moran, (1994, p. 4) and as suggested in this book, there is no simple relationship between the extent of biodiversity present in an ecological system and its ability to provide economic services and sustain this supply. Nor are ecosystems with greater diversity necessarily more resilient or sustainable. The situation is much more complex.

Note that apart from the types of biodiversity mentioned in Table 1.1, we might also want to consider additional locational aspects. For example, is local biodiversity valuable or is global biodiversity more important? Considerable global biodiversity (the existence of many species globally, for instance) could in principle be compatible with the existence of few species at each local level. The spatial distribution of biodiversity has implications for its economic value and for the sustainability of ecosystems.

Such considerations could be important for assessing the relationship between biodiversity and tourism (especially ecotourism) and between it and outdoor recreation. To what extent are ecotourists attracted by considerable biodiversity in particular locations, for example, to regions of megadiversity, like Xishuangbanna in Yunnan, or coral reef environments? To what extent does global tourism depend on rare living species, such as whale sharks, which may not be present in biodiversity-rich local environments? There is much more to be discovered about this. We know that biodiversity is not essential for the enjoyment of some types of outdoor recreation or tourism utilising natural living environments, for example, picnic spots. In other pursuits, such as bird watching, it is a very important part of the outdoor experience.

Biodiversity is not always essential for pollution control, but sometimes polluted environments show a marked reduction in biodiversity, for example, nitrogen/phosphate enriched waters and waters in which oxygen availability is severely reduced usually support little biodiversity. The loss of marker species and their replacement by others can be a useful indicator of environmental change, so that biologically diverse environments can be valuable providers of information for environmental control.

In agriculture, the value of biodiversity at the local or micro-level varies, depending upon whether the cultivated species exhibit mutualism, commensalism or competition. But in a broader context, conservation of biodiversity is important up to a point, for the sustainability of agricultural production. Biodiversity conservation helps to provide backstop species and genetic material of possible future use to mankind, particularly as erosion occurs in the value of existing genetic material already being used commercially (Swanson, 1997). This erosion comes about as commercial varieties of plants and animals become less resistant to existing pests and diseases, or as new types of pests evolve, to which existing commercial varieties show little or no resistance.

As pointed out by Swanson (1997) in relation to agriculture, it may be economically advantageous in such cases to have diverse varieties in the field or *in situ* rather than *ex situ*, for example in seed banks. The former may be more likely to generate information about which varieties (not commercially used or used on a large scale) are resistant to the pest in question and to allow a more effective response. Genetic diversity in the field can have extra economic value as a provider of information and it may be worthwhile to subsidise its conservation up to a point.

Biodiversity can also give rise to commodities of economic value as yet unimagined, for example, cures for unknown diseases, new possibilities for biotechnologies. Therefore, biodiversity conservation can have precautionary and option values beyond those indicated earlier. It may also have bequest and pure existence values.

Regrettably, markets (both actual and the theoretically perfect) cannot be relied on to protect nature and conserve biodiversity. This is also true of non-market mechanisms. Actual markets fail because of externalities, of the public good aspects involved, of socially unsuitable rates of discounting the future, and of limitations of the way in which risk and uncertainty is taken into account (Tisdell, 1991, pp. 43–61). In some cases, government policies further undermine the ability of markets to preserve biodiversity.

Even in a perfect market system, conservation of nature and of biodiversity can be endangered, as discussed in Chapter 5. As Clark (1976) shows, in certain cases, it is economic to eliminate slow-growing species. The greater the perfection of the market system, the greater the likelihood of such elimination. That is not to say that all market reforms are unfavourable to the conservation of nature and biodiversity, but some are (see Chapters 5 and 6).

Furthermore, the creation of private property rights is not by any means a complete solution. This is partly for the reasons given above, but also because transaction costs often make it uneconomic to create private property rights in nature. Nevertheless, private property rights in nature can be created up to a point, and changes in existing regimes of property rights can sometimes help to promote the conservation of nature. As the case studies in this book indicate, institutional factors have major influences on the conservation of nature.

COVERAGE OF THIS BOOK

Environmental and resource economics can play a significant role in effective planning for sustainable development and in devising measures for fostering nature conservation and retaining biodiversity. The character of its possible contribution is indicated in Chapter 2. Chapter 3 considers the importance of biodiversity conservation for a sustainable development by linking it with several different concepts of sustainable development. It also points out that the diversity of biological resources is a part of the stock of natural capital, and therefore gains significance in those models of sustainable development which stress the importance of conserving the stock of natural resources.

The sustainability of ecosystems can be important from the point of view of sustainable economic development as well as for those who place weight upon nature conservation in its own right. While biodiversity conservation can be important for the sustainability of some ecosystems, its significance may well have been exaggerated. Certainly, some ecosystems containing great biological diversity appear not to be very sustainable, whereas others with little diversity seem to be very much so. Factors other than diversity are important for the sustainability of ecosystems and species, such as their adaptability, degree of biological tolerance and mobility. Furthermore, the concept of resilience of ecosystems is found to be inadequate as an indicator of the sustainability of ecosystems. It needs to be supplemented by other concepts, which are discussed, such as robustness.

Biodiversity conservation may require disturbance of habitats. There is some evidence that biodiversity tends to be high in disturbed habitats. In considering the subject, we really need to examine the dynamics of ecological systems. However, as pointed out in Chapter 4, it does not follow that humankind, by disturbing more and more natural habitats, will increase global biodiversity. Furthermore, the impact of human disturbance in a locality depends on the nature and severity of that disturbance.

A few biologists and some economists see the extension of private property rights, and greater economic use and sale of wildlife products and services as favourable to the conservation of wildlife and biodiversity. However, it is argued in Chapter 5 this is not necessarily so and that it may even distort the composition of the surviving biological stock. Furthermore, in Chapter 6 it is argued that the global economic system and the extension of markets are often unfavourable to the conservation of nature, as are the type of economic structural adjustment policies supported by the World Bank and the IMF. The matter is quite complex. Apart from considering the likely influence of the international economic system on biodiversity conservation, this chapter considers the impact of macroeconomic policy upon it and international externality and public good aspects of nature conservation.

On a world scale, obtaining finance and distributing it on behalf of nature conservation is an important activity for many donors. Chapter 7 explores factors which should be taken into account by donors in allocating the money, and the economics of raising such funds.

Sustainable development and conservation are always easier to achieve when they bring positive economic benefits to communities affected by these endeavours. Ecotourism is frequently seen as a promising method of reconciling nature conservation with economic benefits to local communities, and to countries possessing the living resources on which such ecotourism depends. In Chapter 8, features of ecotourism are discussed and factors favourable to its economic success or otherwise are outlined. Attention is also drawn to dangers and difficulties involved in developing ecotourism for nature conservation purposes.

Part III of this book draws on experiences and cases from Asia, to illustrate the difficulties and challenges which economic growth poses for the conservation of nature and biodiversity. It considers some of the ways in which these challenges are being met, particularly in China. Although economic growth and economic globalization raise problems for nature conservation, they may also provide new opportunities for it, for example through the expansion of tourism.

Many environmental changes and impacts on nature have occurred in Asia as a result of economic growth. These are considered generally in Chapter 9; this study then concentrates on case material from Xishuangbanna Prefecture in Southern Yunnan, an area of high biodiversity. Chapter 10 assesses the costs and benefits of nature conservation in the Xishuangbanna State Nature Reserve. Chapter 11 concentrates on issues involved in Xishuangbanna in trying to reconcile possible conflicts between economic development, nature conservation and local communities. Chapter 12 concentrates on the role of tourism in Xishuangbanna in fostering the conservation of nature and local communities. Protected areas do not always yield a 'win-win' situation for everyone. Protected areas often harbour pests from the point of view of nearby agriculturalists, and Xishuangbanna State Nature Reserve is no exception; elephants from this reserve sometimes do considerable damage to agricultural crops. This issue is discussed in Chapter 13. Most developing countries are short of finance for managing their protected areas and China has this problem too. Financial realities affect the management of protected areas and the strategies adopted by their managers, and this in turn impacts on the biological diversity actually protected. Features of this are discussed in Chapter 14 in relation to Xishuangbanna State Nature Reserve, but the political economy and public finance issues involved are not peculiar to this reserve.

The penultimate chapter concentrates on North-east India. Like Yunnan, it is a region of rich biological diversity. However, this biodiversity is under considerable threat and a number of current economic activities in this region, such as slash-and-burn agriculture, are becoming unsustainable. There are many reasons for this; some have to do with institutional rigidities, such as failures to modify property rights in land (lack of co-evolution), as well as an increasing population, rising income aspirations, and the scarcity of local economic alternatives to natural resource utilisation. Serious biodiversity loss is in fact associated with the type of unsustainable economic change which is occurring in the area. Although this large region is peripheral to India, it is nevertheless one rich in biodiversity and it contains many different cultures. For these reasons it is worthy of global attention. The dynamics of its situation and the character of its human-natural environment interaction could also provide useful insights into other developing regions undergoing similar changes.

MEANS TO AN END

It will be pleasing if this book helps to make readers more sensitive to the role of biodiversity and nature conservation in sustainable development, and more aware of the challenges and difficulties involved in achieving such conservation, particularly in developing countries. Both those who take a purely anthropocentric attitude to nature, and those who accord conservation of nature and biodiversity standing in its own right, should find material in this book of relevance to them.

The subject matter is approached in a critical fashion in order to provide a secure foundation for the results, and the temptation to offer easy solutions or 'quick policy-fixes' is avoided. In fact, the case studies indicate the complexity of interactions and relationships between humankind and natural environments, particularly in dynamic situations in developing countries undergoing economic growth and change. In such a situation, the path of co-evolution of human institutions and practices and the state of nature environments is likely to be disrupted and their co-variation can become quite uncertain. Difficult as it is to take a holistic rather than a reductionist approach to studying the issues considered in this book, effective theory and policy require the wider approach when considering nature conservation.

REFERENCES

Barbier, E.G., J.C. Burgess and C. Folke (1994), *Paradise Lose? The Ecological Economics of Biodiversity*, London: Earthscan Publication.
Clark, C.W. (1976), *Mathematical Bioeconomics*, New York: John Wiley.
Pearce, D., A. Markandya and E.B. Barbier (1989), *A Blueprint for a Green Economy*, London: Earthscan Publications.
Pearce, D. and D. Moran (1994), *The Economic Value of Biodiversity*, London: Earthscan Publications.
Pigou, A.C. (1932), *The Economics of Welfare*, 4th ed., London: Macmillan.
Swanson, T. (1997), 'The management of genetic resources for agriculture: ecology and information, externalities and policies', mimeo; Biodiversity Programme CSERGE, University College, London. A paper prepared for XXIII meeting of International Association of Agricultural Economists, Sacramento, California, August 1997.

PART II

General Principles and Policies

2. Environmental and Resource Economics: Its Role in Planning Sustainable Development

INTRODUCTION

With mounting public concern about environmental degradation and natural resource depletion, environmental economics and natural resource economics have attained increased prominence in economics and in policy formulation and planning (Harrison and Tisdell, 1994). This is reflected at university level by the widespread introduction of courses in these areas, and in government by the rise of new institutions for policy-formulation, which partly draws on the theory of environmental and resource economics (ERE) in its decision-making. Existing public policy institutions, such as the Industries Commission in Australia (which is now incorporated in the Productivity Commission), have also been required to pay increasing attention to ERE. Furthermore, ERE has become important at the international and global level. It is increasingly recognised that many environmental and natural resource problems have international ramifications and that several have global impacts. Therefore, the planning of sustainable development is not only a matter for individual nations but also one that has to be addressed by the international community. Official aid-giving bodies are devoting greater attention to ERE by providing support for developing countries.

Given the likely impact of ERE in policy formulation and widespread community interest in planning for sustainable development, it is important to have an adequate appreciation of ERE and particularly the philosophies which underlie it. Furthermore, economic concepts of sustainable development and their implications for planning need to be considered.

THE NATURE AND EVOLUTION OF ENVIRONMENTAL AND RESOURCE ECONOMICS

By the end of the eighteenth century, economists had recognised three factors of production (land, labour and capital) as important determinants of the level of production and the wealth of nations. By the end of the nineteenth century, an additional productive element, entrepreneurship, was also recognised. In economics, 'land' refers to all gifts of God or nature, not just soil or spatial area. In effect, it covers all natural resources – soil, minerals, fish in the ocean, natural forests, water and so on. Hence, the whole of the natural environment can be considered to fall within the subject area covered by land economics or as it now more commonly called, natural resource economics.

Environmental economics is also concerned with the natural environment, but not exclusively so. For example, man-made and cultural or social environments may also be a part of the subject matter of environmental economics. Economic discussions of the relationship between humans and their surroundings are the main focus of environmental economics. It was not until early in the 20th century that the possible economic importance of such relationships, particularly those involving externalities or environmental spillovers, came to be recognised. Pigou (1932) was the first economist to give prominence to such effects, although many economists continued to regard them as being of trivial importance. However, many of the examples given by Pigou did not relate to natural resources, for example, the case of sparks from coal-fired trains increasing the risk of fires on properties near the rail line. Today much more emphasis is placed on the importance of externalities and several important externalities have been recognised in relation to natural resources. These arise from both the use of such resources to produce material goods and their use as sinks and receptors for waste from industry and domestic activities. For example, the use of water in one place for irrigation may affect its availability and quality elsewhere, and give rise to an unfavourable externality in production. The use of the air to dispose of gases and waste products from the combustion of materials used in industry may give rise to acid rain and to global effects such as those attributed to greenhouse gases. In an increasingly interdependent world, there is a need to ensure that greater account is taken of the real social costs of such activities.

Another area of considerable interest in environmental and natural resource economics is the subject of limits to growth. To what extent, if any, does the availability of natural resources limit economic growth? It may prove impossible to sustain economic production because natural resources are depleted by their use in production processes or because these resources (for example, air and water) are no longer able to absorb wastes from economic production and consumption, without imposing severe economic and other penalties on communities which use them. Economic growth may falter because of loss of natural resources, and because of diminishing marginal productivity arising as a result of intensification and extension of natural resource use; a possibility recognised by Ricardo (1817) in extending and clarifying the theory of Malthus (1798). By the early 1970s, three main possible limits to sustaining economic growth were recognised: (1) natural resource depletion; (2) 'pollution' of natural resources; and (3) diminishing marginal productivity with intensification and extension of natural resource use.

Two factors have played a major role in enabling economic growth to be achieved despite natural resource constraints. These are: (1) scientific and technological progress; and (2) the accumulation of man-made capital.

A central question is whether these factors are likely to continue to reduce natural limits to economic growth. Technological optimists argue that technological progress and capital accumulation are likely to be sufficient to overcome resource constraints. In their view, achieving economic sustainability is not a major problem.

Nevertheless, not all technological optimists suggest that we can continue with 'business as usual'. Many accept the view that environmental externalities are important in the modern world and that those economic agents generating adverse environmental effects should pay the full costs involved in their activities. This is highlighted in the 'polluter-pays' principle. The application of such a principle is likely to assist in sustaining economic production and/or economic welfare by ensuring that all costs, including environmental costs, are taken into account by responsible parties.

However, the extension of knowledge is not without cost nor is the production of man-made capital. Both may be at the expense of natural resource stocks. To what extent is it desirable to keep adding to human/man-made capital if this is at the expense of natural capital? This substitution is under debate, particularly in relation to the distribution of income between generations (Tisdell, 1997a,b; and special issue of *Ecological Economics*, 22(3), 1997).

Environmental and resource economics has many dimensions –

growth, equity and allocative efficiency implications. But as it is currently practised, the sole focus of ERE is on human welfare. It is anthropocentric (Cf. Cobb, 1990, p. 110). Environments and other creatures have value only in so far as they have value to human beings. The sole objective is to manipulate these or use them as instruments for human satisfaction.

In operational economic models, it is usually assumed that the net value of retaining an environment can be measured by the amount of money those favouring its retention would be willing to pay for this, less the amount of money needed to compensate those disadvantaged by its retention. However, this assumes that those destroying the environment or nature have a right to do so. In reality, much can depend on how property rights are assigned, and the assignment of property rights is not purely an economic matter. If property rights run in the opposite direction, those destroying or using the environment will need to be able to compensate those who wish to conserve it. This test may result in a net benefit being assigned to conservation whereas a net disadvantage may be suggested by the first test (Cf. Knetsch and Sinden, 1984; Knetsch, 1990; Hohl and Tisdell, 1997). On the other hand, both tests could give the same result, depending on the circumstances. But no matter which of these tests are adopted, the approach is purely an anthropocentric one.

It should also be observed that this method cannot be applied in relation to future generations since they are not alive to express their preferences. But present generations can act, up to a point, as guardians of the assumed interests of future generations by, for example, including bequest values in their own preferences.

ECONOMIC CONCEPTS OF SUSTAINABLE DEVELOPMENT

Several economic concepts of sustainable development exist (see Tisdell 1991, Ch.11; 1992) but only the most prominent one will be considered here, namely that type of development which sustains inter-generational economic welfare. Tietenberg (1988, p. 33) states that 'the sustainability criterion suggests that at a minimum, future generations should be left no worse off than current generations'. The World Commission on Environment and Development (1987, p. 43) assumed that 'sustainable development is development that meets the needs of the present without compromising the ability of future generations to meet their own needs'.

Tietenberg's definition suggests that the real income per head of future generations or their standard of living should be no lower than that of present generations. It leaves open the question whether these should be higher. Certainly those in less developed countries might hope that the incomes or the standards of living of their people would be higher in the future.

The question then arises of how this criterion relates to conservation of natural resources and strategies for economic development. The view may be taken that natural resources are held by current generations in trust for future generations. Depletion of natural resources by current generations can reduce (though it need not) the ability of future generations to meet their needs. Pearce *et al.*, (1989, p. 3) suggest as a general principle that 'future generations should be compensated for reductions in the endowment of resources brought about by the actions of present generations'. They suggest, for example, that an increase in man-made capital, especially an increase in scientific and technological knowledge, might be used to compensate future generations. The question then is: how adequate is man-made capital as a substitute for natural capital or as compensation for a reduction in natural resource stocks? Furthermore, to what extent is this substitution possible without endangering the ability of future generations to sustain income levels in an equitable manner?

IMPLICATIONS OF THE ABOVE CONCEPT FOR THE NATURE OF ECONOMIC DEVELOPMENT

Given the above concept of sustainability, the onus is on those who wish to use natural resources and reduce natural resource stocks to show that future generations will be adequately compensated for the loss of these stocks. Given this view, there would be no objection to a less developed country, such as Indonesia, logging its rainforests unsustainably if future generations of Indonesians could be compensated by a larger stock of man-made capital. Similarly, there would be no objection to the elimination of a species by present generations if future generations of humans could be compensated from an increased supply of man-made capital.

Those favouring the traditional economic growth approach might argue that, in reality, such compensation has taken place in the past. Present generations have benefited from the economic growth impulses and sacrifices of previous generations. They might then go on to extrapolate and suggest that this would also be the best strategy for the future.

However, this overlooks the fact that it may no longer be so easy to ensure rising standards of living for future generations (or maintain current income levels) by continuing to substitute man-made capital for natural resource stock (Tisdell, 1997). As resource stocks dwindle, the comparative productive value of remaining natural stocks may rise. Second, with greater demands on the natural environment, it is necessary to take more account of the real costs of using natural resources such as air and water for waste-disposal purposes. Such usage should be priced. Third, it must be recognised that standards of living do not depend on material or marketed goods alone; unpriced environmental goods may also have economic value and add to the quality of life. Fourth, we cannot always be sure of the consequences for future generations of depletion of natural resource stocks. In this case Pearce *et al.*, (1989) suggest that it behoves us to be cautious and to try to keep economic options open. This may require greater conservation of natural resources, including biodiversity, than otherwise (Cf. Dragun and Jakobsson, 1997).

CONCLUDING COMMENT

The economic criterion of sustainability outlined above does not imply that conservation of natural resources is a virtue in itself. But rather it suggests that from a practical point of view, greater attention to such conservation is necessary, compared to the past, if the standard of living of future generations is to be at least as high as that of current generations. One could also add that current generations might, in addition, obtain a rise in their standard of living as a result of more attention being given to the economic value of conserving environmental and natural resources.

However, it should be observed that some individuals believe that conservation of special environments and of natural resources, particularly living resources, is a virtue in itself. These views have been expressed by Aldo Leopold (1933, 1966). Mankind is seen as having a stewardship role in relation to nature. This suggests that humanity should accept some constraints on man-centred economic growth or development in order to maintain or sustain other species' natural living systems. This view is now more widely accepted than in the past.

While economic concepts of sustainable development are more precise and operational than many of the alternatives which have currency at present, because of uncertainties, conceptual problems and disagreements about appropriate values and ethics, they are not a straightforward means for planning development. Furthermore, economic concepts may be too narrow in their focus (Tisdell, 1990, Ch. 3; 1991, Ch. 11; 1992). Nevertheless, economic concepts of sustainable development raise important philosophical and other issues that might otherwise be overlooked and are fostering the development of techniques which are likely to enhance their operational value.

REFERENCES

Cobb, J.B. (1990), 'An index of sustainable economic welfare', *Development*, 3/4, 106–11.

Dragun, A.K. and K.M. Jakobsson (1997), *Sustainability and Global Environmental Policy: New Perspectives*, Cheltenham, UK: Edward Elgar.

Harrison, S.R. and C.A. Tisdell (1994), 'Resource economics and the environment', *Review of Marketing and Agricultural Economics*, 62, 399–413.

Hohl, A. and C.A. Tisdell (1997), 'Ethics in modern economic thought and their consequences for environmental conservation, land and resource-use', *Humanomics*, 13(2), 1–37.

Knetsch, J.L. (1990), 'Environmental policy implications of disparities between willingness to pay and compensation demanded measures of value', *Journal of Environmental Economics and Management*, 18, 227–37.

Knetsch, J.L. and J.A. Sinden (1984), 'Willingness to pay and compensation demanded: experimental evidence of an unexpected disparity in measures of value', *Quarterly Journal of Economics*, 99, 507–21.

Leopold, A. (1933), *Game Management*, New York: Scribner.

Leopold, A. (1966), *A Sand Country Almanac: with other Essays on Conservation from Round River*, New York: Oxford University Press.

Malthus, T.R. (1798), *An Essay on the Principle of Population as it affects the Future Development of Mankind*, London: J. Johnson.

Pearce, D., A. Markandya and E.B. Barbier (1989), *Blueprint for a Green Economy*, London: Earthscan Publications.

Pigou A.C. (1932), *Economics of Welfare*, 3rd edn, London : Macmillan.

Ricardo, D. (1817), *The Principles of Political Economy and Taxation*. London.

Tietenberg, T. (1988), *Environmental and Natural Resource Economics*, 2nd edn, Glenview, Illinois: Scott, Foresman and Company.

Tisdell, C.A. (1990), *Natural Resources, Growth and Development : Economics, Ecology and Resource – Scarcity*, New York: Praeger.

Tisdell, C.A. (1991), *Economics of Environmental Conservation*, Amsterdam and New York: Elsevier Science Publishers.

Tisdell, C.A. (1992), 'The nature of sustainability and of sustainable development', *The Middle East Business and Economic Review*, 4(1), 21–5.

Tisdell, C.A. (1997a) 'Weak and strong conditions for sustainable development', *Paper FS11 98–402*, Berlin: WZB, Science Center Berlin.

Tisdell, C.A. (1997b), 'Capital/natural resource substitution: the debate of Georgescu Roegan (through Daly) with Solow/Stiglitz', *Ecological Economics*, 22(3), 299–302.

World Commission on Environment and Development (1987), *Our Common Future*, New York: Oxford University Press.

3. Conservation of Biodiversity: Most Important Aspect of Sustainable Development?

INTRODUCTION

Several different concepts of sustainable development exist in the literature (Tisdell, 1993, Ch. 9). However, it seems that no matter which of these concepts is adopted, conservation of biological diversity is necessary for its achievement, even though there is room for argument about the amount and type of biodiversity that should be preserved.

In order to decide how important biodiversity is for sustainable development, consider its significance in relation to five commonly-used concepts of sustainability:

(1) The intergenerational equity concept of sustainability, as commonly used in economics, requires economic growth or change to be such that future generations are at least as well off as the current generation, from an economic point of view. Alternatively, in a less strong form, as expressed in the Brundtland Report (World Commission on Environment and Development, 1987), the current generation should try to ensure that the economic needs of future generations can be met with the stock of resources bequeathed to them.

(2) Survival of the human species for as long as possible. This concept of sustainability involves the avoidance of the human species being forced into premature extinction by man-induced environmental or related economic change.

(3) Maintenance of the resilience (stability and robustness) of productive systems, especially economic systems such as agricultural ones dependent on ecological and environmental relationships.

(4) Sustainability or maintenance of community. This refers to the maintenance of satisfactory sociological interrelationships in human communities.

(5) The maintenance of the 'web of life' with its variety of life forms, as suggested by those favouring the 'land ethic'.

In one way or another, biological diversity can be linked to all these concepts. Conservation of biological diversity may be necessary to meet the needs of future generations; to maximise the span of existence of the human species, to contribute to the stability and robustness of many economic and ecological systems. In addition, some might even argue that if individuals have more opportunities to commune with nature in varied forms that this will strengthen communal life. Finally for those who subscribe to the 'land ethic', biodiversity conservation is an integral requirement of this ethic. Let us consider the relationship between the above concepts of sustainability and biodiversity in detail.

INTERGENERATIONAL EQUITY

Maintenance of biological diversity seems necessary for ensuring intergenerational equity from at least three points of view:

(1) The maintenance of the productivity of economic activities relying primarily on living resources (such as agriculture, aquaculture and forestry) is dependent upon the preservation of adequate gene banks or reserves. Productivity based on existing genetic material which is utilised can rarely be sustained, for example due to the occurrence or evolution of new diseases (Cf. Swanson, 1997); we need to maintain a much larger stock of genetic material than that in current commercial use in order to provide flexibility.

(2) Preservation of biodiversity is necessary to keep options open for future generations for example, a new use may be found for an organism previously regarded as useless or as a pest. Furthermore, not all organisms are yet known to mankind, so maintaining biodiversity through conservation, for the time being, will afford the chance of discovering new organisms and learning more about their properties.

(3) Individuals may obtain intangible benefits from the existence of other species via non-consumptive use, for example, curiosity value, non-destructive recreational value, existence value. Reducing

biodiversity can deprive future generations of non-consumptive benefits and this can involve a considerable loss. However, the loss is hard to measure. For example, Australians may feel deprived by the disappearance of the Tasmanian tiger, but it is not apparent that they feel deprived by the disappearance of dinosaur-like species.

Pearce *et al.*, (1989) have suggested that in order to achieve sustainability in the sense of ensuring intergenerational equity, it is necessary to preserve the existing natural resource or environmental stock. They in fact suggest that all project appraisal should be subject to this constraint. They are therefore wary of the substitution of man-made capital for natural capital, including the natural capital embodying biological diversity. However, Pearce *et al.*, (1989) concede that in some circumstances, it may be allowable to reduce the natural resource stock for an increase in the stock of knowledge.

Intervention to preserve the existing stock of natural resources is believed to be necessary because of failure of the market mechanism. Even under relatively ideal conditions, the market mechanism does not ensure the optimal balance between the conservation of natural resource stock and the conversion of natural resources into man-made commodities, from the point of view of sustaining incomes (See Daly, 1997).

According to Locke's principle, each generation should leave 'enough and as good for others' that follow on. Apart from the imprecision of Locke's rule, this raises the question of whether there should be 'betterment' for future generations. If incomes are low and poor socio-economic conditions prevail, economic 'betterment' of future generations would seem appropriate. If economic growth or development did not occur in a very poor society, living in some sort of a stationary state with nature, income might be sustainable. However, the society might be vulnerable to natural disasters, at the mercy of nature to some extent and the prevailing economic conditions could be undesirable, a situation facing our ancestors in the past. What one needs to attain and sustain from an anthropocentric point of view, is a satisfactory standard of living. Once this is achieved, there is no reason why future generations should have a higher one.

In order to achieve a minimum satisfactory standard of living in society, it will probably be necessary to exploit natural resource stocks and in some cases reduce biodiversity; for example, to eliminate populations of slow-growing species in order to generate sufficient surplus income to enable additions to the stock of knowledge and man-made capital. Nevertheless, such depletion is not necessarily sufficient to transform all societies from low-income ones to those with a higher sustainable satisfactory level of per capita income (Tisdell, 1994).

The above point has policy implications for those who believe in Malthusian low-level equilibrium trap theories (Cf. Todaro, 1981, Ch. 7). Attempts to escape from the trap too early by drawing on natural resources may be counterproductive and destructive of biodiversity. Delay may sometimes improve the chances of sustainable escape (Tisdell, 1994).

However, as biodiversity declines, the marginal opportunity cost of removing more diversity is likely to increase and do so at an increasing rate. At the same time, uncertainty about the ecological impact of eliminating further species may escalate. Therefore, the importance of applying the precautionary principle and conserving biodiversity may increase because the economic value of retaining remaining options may rise. Consequently, the application of safety-oriented rules such as the safe minimum standard approach to species conservation, may obtain increasing support. However, as pointed out by Hohl and Tisdell (1993), these cannot be applied in a simple mechanical fashion.

SURVIVAL OF THE HUMAN SPECIES FOR THE LONGEST TIME POSSIBLE

Fears have been intermittently expressed that the impacts of human beings on environmental and natural resources could be enough to extinguish the human species prematurely. Pollution from economic activities and depletion of stocks of non-renewable resources have been seen as recipes for such a disaster, as expounded in the predictions of the Club of Rome (Meadows *et al.*, 1972). Basically, this approach predicted the demise of humanity as resulting from depletion of non-living resources such as non-renewable energy resources. Georgescu-Roegen (1971) has provided a sophisticated exposition of this problem using the Law of Entropy. Whereas the Club of Rome predicted the possibility of a cataclysmic global collapse, Georgescu-Roegen sees a slower, irreversible run-down of non-renewable resource stocks, which nevertheless could result in the premature end of the human species.

His suggestion is to adjust human population levels and economic activity to levels which can be supported by relying solely on the sustainable use of renewable resources.

One may debate whether such a restriction is really necessary to ensure the survival of the human species for as long as possible. No intrinsic merit is involved in leaving non-renewable resources in the ground, and their limited use will enhance human welfare without serious impacts on the living environment. Nevertheless, Georgescu-Roegen's theory does highlight the possible long-term significance of biodiversity for human survival and welfare. As non-renewable resources become increasingly depleted, mankind is likely to become more dependent on living resources as substitutes for non-renewable resources. Therefore, biodiversity assumes greater economic importance and the conservation of biodiversity may become essential for the long term survival of the human species.

The above theories basically see the premature end of the human species brought about as a result of non-renewable resource depletion. However, there have also been warnings that loss of living resources could similarly result in this fate. A view has been expressed that the existence of species is interdependent. The loss, therefore, of some of them could lead to the loss of many more. Ultimately, the loss of some species, especially keystone species, is believed to threaten the survival of all through a chain of extinctions. As Randall (1986) points out, if one believes in the extreme version of this theory, the only policy choice regarding human-induced extinctions would be concerning the speed with which the process to ultimate extinction of all species takes place, since some have already been extinguished.

However, there is little evidence that all species are so closely interdependent that the extinction of one (or even a sizeable set) will result in the eventual extinction of all. Nevertheless, important interdependence between sets of species often exists, and it is true that the removal of one species can set in train a chain-reaction leading to the extinction of others. One of the difficulties is that such interdependence is not always fully understood and that keystone species are not always obvious. Therefore, the impact of extinction of a single species is very uncertain.

According to Young (1992, p. 38), 'A related proposition of interest to a significant number of ecologists is the GAIA hypothesis. The idea behind the GAIA is the proposition that the world is one single complex living entity, arranged in a hierarchy of mutually interdependent components which, through collective interaction, maintain a stable self-organising and self-regulating system'. Furthermore, it is believed that as a result of economic growth, mankind is destroying components of this system, including biological diversity, and consequently threatening the survival of all life.

RESILIENCE – ECOLOGICAL SUSTAINABILITY AND STABILITY

To some extent we have already touched on the resilience of systems or lack of it, particularly their susceptibility to irreversible collapse. However, let us consider the matter at a more micro-level. There appears to be a widespread view that ecological systems are more resilient and sustainable if they possess greater genetic diversity, even though the evidence in this regard is not conclusive (Perrings *et al.*, 1995, p. 5). In reality, however, the most sustainable ecological systems could be those which contain few species, whereas the least sustainable may be those that contain many (see Chapter 4).

In the temperate zone, there are few species but they are very adaptable to changing environmental conditions. In the tropics, there are many species but they are not very adaptable or tolerant – each tends to make use of a narrow niche and each has a narrow range of tolerance to a change in environmental conditions. Under these conditions, it can be argued that greater sustainability is associated with the least diverse and least specialised ecological system.

Despite the above, it is necessary to recognise that the loss of species from a particular ecosystem may threaten the functioning of the system as whole, depending upon the paths of interdependence between species. However, whether this loss is likely to create greater impairment to the functioning of ecosystems with less diversity than those with greater diversity, is unclear. For example, is the loss of species in a temperate zone more likely to impair the operation of an ecosystem than a loss of similar magnitude in a tropical zone? Nevertheless, as the diversity of species in a region is decreased, the sustainability of ecosystems in the region, and the services provided by ecosystems, are likely to be increasingly impaired.

SUSTAINABILITY OF COMMUNITY

The ideal of sustaining human community, a satisfactory set of sociological relationships, has been stressed by a number of writers as an important social objective even though views often differ about what constitutes a satisfactory community. One view is that small democratic communities, in which all individuals have a chance to interact in social decision-making, are ideal. Such communities are considered cohesive and they are likely to be fostered by appropriate technologies involving small scale operation, particularly in a rural context (Schumacher, 1973). The idea is to overcome the alienation of individuals from nature and from one another, largely brought about by the advent of impersonal competitive market economies, involving extreme specialisation of labour and very often large-scale economic operations. The need for mankind to preserve the natural environment and nature are stressed in a number of expositions of this approach (Schumacher, 1973). It is believed that when mankind has the opportunity to commune with nature and achieves a harmonious relationship with it that this leads to more harmonious and stable communal relationships. Supporters of the community concept of sustainability usually favour the preservation of biodiversity.

There is another sense in which sustainability of community and biodiversity may be interrelated. Norgaard (1992) and others (Gowdy, 1994) believe that human societies, and their technologies and cultures, evolve along with nature. There is co-evolution. Significant disruption to the evolving natural world can threaten the societies that have evolved in parallel with it. These societies could be rendered unsustainable by a rapid loss of species, particularly if this threatens, directly or indirectly, species on which the community depends for its livelihood.

MAINTENANCE OF THE 'WEB OF LIFE' – THE LAND ETHIC

Aldo Leopold (1966) in particular has stressed non-anthropocentric reasons for conserving species. His view is that mankind has a moral obligation not to destroy the web of life; life in all its diversity involving myriad interconnections should be preserved. Thus this is a moral imperative for conserving biodiversity, which contrasts with those arguments in favour of biodiversity which mainly stress human benefits as the rationale. Leopold's emphasis is on the desirability of conserving the whole system, including species considered by many to be pests to man.

In more recent times, authors such as Rolston (1988), Calicott (1989), Rolston (1989) and Sagoff (1988, 1994) have been critical of moral anthropocentrism in relation to nature conservation.

CONCLUDING COMMENTS

If one believes in the 'land ethic' then conservation of biodiversity is the most important aspect of ecologically sustainable development. It requires that economic development be consistent with preserving the diversity and integrity of nature. Given the land ethic, ecological values constrain man-centred ones. Furthermore, it seems that if one believes in maximising the possible span of human existence, maintenance of biodiversity is one of the most important requirements. If economic development is to be consistent with intergenerational equity, in the senses previously defined, conservation of biodiversity is an important prerequisite. Furthermore, such conservation is important to maintain the resilience of particular ecosystems. Without resilience they may fail to perform their economic functions adequately. Even in relation to the maintenance of human community (closely knit harmonious communities), conservation of nature can play an important role.

The 'bottom line' as far as sustainability is concerned, is that *homo sapiens* is a higher order animal – the survival of the human species depends upon other species and ultimately on the conservation of ecological systems of value to mankind (Tisdell, 1991, Ch. 1). To the extent that any loss of biodiversity threatens the continued existence of such systems or their productivity, it must remain an important social concern in relation to sustainable development. At this stage in economic development, it is appropriate to regard conservation of biodiversity as one of the most, if not the most, important prerequisite for sustainable development.

REFERENCES

Calicott, J.B. (1989), *In Defence of the Land Ethic*, New York: State University of New York.

Daly, H. (1997), 'The Contribution of Nicholas Georgescu-Roegen', Special Issue of *Ecological Economics*, 22(3), 171–306.

Georgescu-Roegen, N. (1971), *The Entropy Law and the Economic Process*, Cambridge, Mass: Harvard University Press.

Gowdy, J. (1994), *Coevolutionary Economics*: Boston, Kluwer Academic Publishers.

Hohl, A. and C.A. Tisdell (1993), 'How useful are environmental standards in economics? The example of safe minimum standards for the protection of species', *Biodiversity and Conservation*, 2, 168–81.

Leopold, A. (1966), *A Sand Country Almanac: with Other Essays on Conservation from Round River*, New York: Oxford University Press.

Meadows, D.M., Ronders, J. and W. Behrens (1972), *The Limits of Growth: A Report from the Club of Rome's Project on the Predicament of Mankind*, New York: Unwin Books.

Norgaard, R.B. (1992), *Development Betrayed*, London: Routledge.

Pearce, D.W., Markandya, A. and E.B. Barbier (1989), *Blueprint for a Green Economy*, London: Earthscan Publications.

Perrings, C.A., K-G Mäler, C. Falke, C.S. Holling and B.-O. Jansson (1995), *Biodiversity Conservation: Problems and Policies*, Dordrecht: Kluwer Publishers.

Randall, A. (1986), 'Human Preferences, Economics and the Preservation of Species' in B.G. Gordon (ed.) *The Preservation of Species: The Value of Biological Diversity*, pp. 79–109, New York: Princeton University Press.

Rolston, H. (1988), *Philosophical Aspects of the Environment*, Philadelphia: Temple University Press.

Rolston, H. (1989), 'Philosophical Aspects of the Environment', in H. Rolston (ed.) *Philosophy Gone Wild*, New York: Prometheus.

Sagoff, M. (1988), *The Economy of the Earth*, Cambridge: Cambridge University Press.

Sagoff, M. (1994), 'Should preference count', *Land Economics*, **70**, 127–44.

Schumacher, E.F. (1973), *Small is Beautiful: A Study of Economics as if People Mattered*, London: Blond and Briggs.

Swanson, T. (1997), 'The management of genetic resources for agriculture: ecology and information, externalities and policies', mimeo; London: University College London. Paper prepared for XXIII meeting of the International Association of Agricultural Economists, Sacramento, California, August 1997.

Tisdell, C.A. (1993), *Environmental Economics: Policies for Environmental Management and Sustainabile Development*, Aldershot, UK: Edward Elgar.

Tisdell, C.A. (1994), 'Population, Economic, Development and Enviornmental Security', in N. Polunin and M. Nazim (eds), *Population and Global Security*, Geneva: The Foundation for Environmental Conservation, pp. 63–84.

Tisdell, C.A. (1991), *Economics of Environmental Conservation*, Amsterdam: Elsevier Science Publishers.

Todaro, M.P. (1981), *Economic Development in the Third World*, 2nd edn, New York: Longmans.

World Commission on Environment and Development (1987), *Our Common Future*, London: Oxford University Press.

Young, M.D. (1992), *Sustainable Investment and Resource Use: Equity, Environmental Integrity and Economic Efficiency*, Cornforth, UK: Parthenon Publishing Group.

4. Biodiversity, Stability and Sustainability: An Appraisal

INTRODUCTION

As mentioned in the previous chapter, several authors stress the importance of biological diversity for the sustainability of ecosystems and individual species and, therefore, for the maintenance of the stream of services (economic and otherwise) which they provide, and for the continuing satisfaction of values which some individuals espouse. Given that biodiversity is an important natural asset, it is worthwhile exploring the extent to which species survival and ecosystem functioning is dependent on the presence of biodiversity. In the previous chapter, the naive GAIA principle was rejected, but nevertheless it was suggested that biodiversity is an important part of natural capital and plays a pivotal role in sustaining economic production and human welfare. Yet we should not accept the idea completely without subjecting it to critical scrutiny. The purpose of this chapter is to engage in such scrutiny.

It involves a brief discussion of agricultural systems and biodiversity; the dependence of the resilience of ecological systems on biodiversity; introduction of the view that resilience is not a sufficient indicator of the sustainability of ecosystems and biological species or varieties and that other factors, such as robustness, must be taken into account; and a discussion of the role of disturbance and variations of ecological stress in the preservation of biodiversity.

SUSTAINABILITY/STABILITY OF AGRICULTURAL SYSTEMS AND BIODIVERSITY

In assessing alternative agricultural ecosystems, Gordon Conway (1985, 1987) supposes that four characteristics are important:

(1) their impact on the level of income or yield (the magnitude of economic benefit provided);
(2) the variability of this level;
(3) their ecological sustainability;
(4) their consequences for the distribution of income in the community.

He is of the opinion that traditional agricultural systems are likely to be more favourable in relation to the last three characteristics than modern agricultural ecosystems; but he proposes that modern agriculture is superior in relation to the first mentioned characteristic. It is not intended to debate here the merits or otherwise of this point of view (see Tisdell, 1993, Ch. 11, especially pp. 173–174) but to use Conway's approach as an introduction to the complex issues involved in considering the sustainability and variability of ecosystems.

Conway considers the sustainability of agriculture ecosystems in terms of their resilience; their ability to return to homeostasis, that is to their original equilibrium or stationary state, after having been subjected to ecological stress or shock with the stress being subsequently withdrawn. He considers this for agricultural systems in terms of their ability to sustain economic returns or yields, see Figure 4.1.

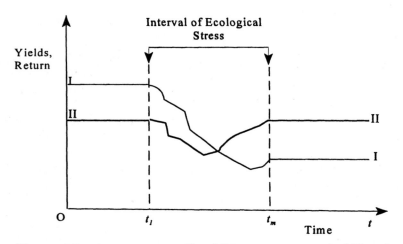

Figure 4.1   Agroecosystem II exhibits greater sustainability than agroecosystem I according to Conway because it is more resilient

In Figure 4.1, agrosystems I and II are compared in terms of the sustainability of their yields or returns. When system I is subjected to ecological stress in the internal $t_1 \leq t \leq t_m$, its yield plummets and after the stress is withdrawn in t_m, yields do not return to their previous level. The system therefore is relatively unsustainable in terms of yields. On the other hand, in the case of agrosystem II, while yields are depressed by the same ecological stress, they return to their previous level when the stress is withdrawn. Thus in Conway's terminology, agrosystem II is relatively sustainable. This is a binary model of ecological stress, it is either on or off but presumably the nature of the stress could take many different forms with different response functions applying depending on its form or origin.

In considering Conway's resilience property however, we should not only take account of whether or not a system returns to its original equilibrium, but we should also consider how long it takes to return to that equilibrium, and its actual path during disequilibrium. For example, a system which is in disequilibrium for a very long period and which can be deflected far from its equilibrium may be inferior from a human perspective to one which returns to an equilibrium more promptly, albeit an inferior equilibrium value to the original. Paths, not just their stationary values, are of significance.

Conway assumes a binary model, but ecological stress may be continuous and we may wish to explore how ecosystems behave in this case. Furthermore, the ecological stress may be variable or take alternative forms with the passage of time. It may be that the system

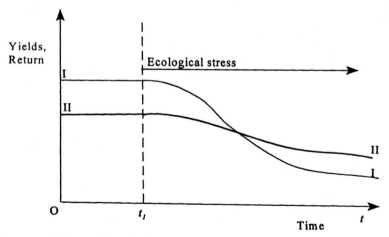

Figure 4.2 Hypothetical performance of two alternative agroecosystems under continual ecological stress

does not attain a stationary state if subjected to continuous stress, although it is conceivable that it could eventually come into a new equilibrium which accommodates this stress. In Figure 4.2, two alternative agrosystems are illustrated, which are subject to continual stress from period t_1 onwards. Yields from system II showed less depression than for system I and this technique II appears to give a more sustainable outcome than technique I.

Much more research is needed to define the responses of ecosystems when subjected to ecological stress and to explore their responses to different types and patterns of ecological stress.

It is possible for two ecosystems to be sustainable but for one to show greater variability than the other with varying environmental conditions. For example, in Figure 4.3, the production function for a modern crop variety as a function of an environmental condition – moisture – shown by the peaked curve, ABC, whereas for a traditional variety, it is shown by the 'flat' curve DFEG. The modern variety is not very tolerant to variation in the environmental condition. If it is to yield well, humans must manage the environmental condition so that it remains within a narrow range. Although the traditional variety is incapable of providing such high yields as the improved variety, it shows greater environmental tolerance. Thus, it is less dependent on human control for its survival and capable of giving less variable yields with less human effort (Cf. Tisdell, 1983a, b; Tisdell and Alauddin, 1989).

The above discussion does not highlight all important aspects of

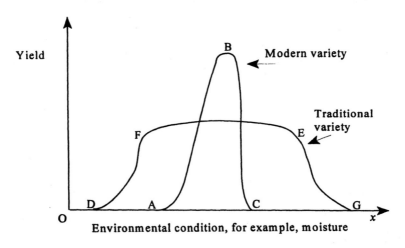

Figure 4.3 Tolerance of agricultural varieties

traditional agricultural systems compared to modern monocultural ones. Some traditional systems appear to be compatible with greater biodiversity and this may be conducive to their sustainability and their resistance to perturbations. For example, they may have the following features:

(1) greater biodiversity at the field and farm level and nearby;
(2) use of species or varieties with greater tolerance to environmental variation;
(3) dependence on a wider range of varieties (for example, between districts) and species than in modern agriculture, that is a wider genetic base.

This is not to say that all traditional agricultural systems are sustainable. In many parts of the world, population increases and demands for cash and market exchange goods (as well as appropriation of forested land) has made shifting slash-and-burn agriculture unsustainable. These socio-economic pressures have been associated with reduced fallow periods, falling productivity, accelerated loss of biodiversity and mounting environmental problems, such as higher rates of soil erosion and degradation. While the slash-and-burn system is highly sustainable for long fallow periods, it becomes unsustainable when fallow periods become short.

Agricultural systems based on principles of ecological balance can be relatively sustainable, as are a number of the integrated farming systems developed in Asia. These involve greater biodiversity than Western monoculture systems, and the recycling of wastes. The latter reduces possible adverse environmental spillovers from agriculture.

On the whole, agriculture has been very destructive of biodiversity (Swanson, 1994). While it may have stimulated some new forms of genetic diversity, it has converted much natural habitat into farmland. This loss of habitat has been a major one in extinction of species in modern times, although not the only one (Swanson, 1994).

In addition, modern market-based agriculture and globalisation has increased the dependence of agriculture on a narrow band of varieties. Many local varieties and land races have therefore been lost. There has been a major displacement effect and this is also reducing the genetic pool available to agriculture.

The dependence of agriculture on improved strains means that the dominant strain at any one time, because its population is so large, has a high chance of coming into contact with some variant of a potentially fatal pathogen or pest. Therefore, the economic life of such varieties tends to be short, around 5–10 years (Swanson, 1997). Thus, there is a continual genetic race – plant and animal scientists must anticipate such problems and be looking constantly for new varieties which will be resistant. The race becomes more difficult for scientists as the wild genetic bank is eroded, the stock of land race and village-based varieties disappears and as the proportion of 'exposed' (utilised) genetic stock in relation to the total genetic stock, rises. The danger appears to be increasing, that modern agricultural systems will no longer be able to sustain their agriculture yields because of loss and erosion of their genetic base. It has been argued that there is a case for adopting measures which help to preserve agricultural biodiversity; for example, by subsidising some traditional forms of agriculture and other forms of *in situ* conservation, and providing some public support for seed banks and other forms of *ex situ* conservation (Swanson, 1997).

While a convincing case can be made out along these lines, we are not entitled to conclude that ecosystems which contain greater biodiversity are more sustainable and less subject to variation than those that contain less biodiversity. Let us consider this.

TOLERANCE, RESILIENCE AND SURVIVAL OF SPECIES AND ECOSYSTEMS

There is a general idea that ecological systems are more resilient and sustainable if they possess greater genetic diversity. For example, Barbier et al., (p. 27) maintain, 'The principal ecological importance of biodiversity must therefore be its role in preserving ecosystem resilience'. In reality, however, the most sustainable ecological systems could be those which contain few species whereas the least sustainable may be those that contain many species.

In the temperate zone, there are few species but they are very adaptable to changing environmental conditions. In the tropics there are many species but most are not very adaptable – each tends to make use of a narrow niche and each has a narrow range of tolerance to a change in environmental conditions. Under these conditions, it can be argued that greater sustainability is associated with the less diverse and less specialized ecological system.

The above observation can be illustrated by Figures 4.4 and 4.5. In Figure 4.4, the biological tolerance curves for three species, identified by

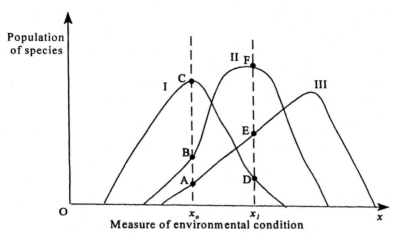

Figure 4.4   The species in this ecosystem show a high degree of biological tolerance. Although the ecosystem is not very diverse, it is relatively sustainable should environmental conditions alter

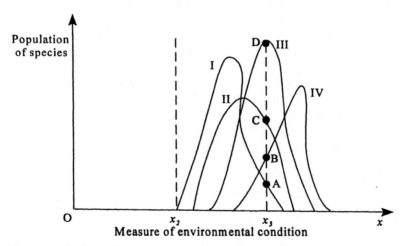

Figure 4.5   Even if a system is very diverse, it will lack environmental stability if species show little environmental tolerance

I, II and III, are shown and we suppose these to be representative of one ecosystem in a temperate zone. Figure 4.5, shows the tolerance zones for a group of many species (only a few, I–IV, indicated) each of which has a low tolerance to environmental change; this represents a tropical ecosystem. In this case, the less diverse system appears to be more sustainable than the highly diverse one because the species in the first system are much more tolerant or adaptable to environmental changes than in the latter.

Suppose that initially a relevant environmental condition (for example, of an environmental variable such as air temperature) is distributed over a region so that all of the species with the tolerance functions shown in Figures 4.4 and 4.5 can survive there. Suppose for example, that the distribution is initially centred on x_1 with a finite range for the region with low diversity. Subsequently, suppose that the whole distribution shifts, with its range remaining the same or reducing, so that it becomes centred on x_0. In this case shown in Figure 4.4, no species disappear. This is not so for the case shown in Figure 4.5, if the environmental variable shifts from x_3 to x_2.

This supposes that species can exist independently of one another. Of course, in reality, not all species can and the situation is far more complicated. The ability of species to survive depends on much more than the biodiversity of ecosystems. Factors of significance for the survival of a species include the degree of biological tolerance of the species and its mobility, particularly its ability to move to avoid adverse environmental conditions. Biological adaptability, mobility and geographical dispersion would all seem favourable traits for the survivability of a species. If environmental changes are occurring slowly over a long period of time, the ability of species to adapt by evolutionary means would also be important for the survival of a species.

This accords with Grant's observation that, 'A narrowly specialized organism is more vulnerable to extinction during a change in the environment, other factors being equal. If one type of food were to disappear, koalas would become extinct, whereas raccoons would not. Vulnerability is a weakness inherent in narrow specialization' (Grant, 1991, p. 371). It is another dimension of lack of adaptability of a species.

If evolutionary trends favour speciation (Grant, 1991, Chs 23, 31) and thereby greater biodiversity, biological systems could become increasingly threatened if species become even *more* specialised to fill even more specific ecological niches. The consequence would be increasing loss of adaptability of living species and an increasing threat to their survival from widespread environmental change, especially macro-environmental change, such as a sudden change of climate, whether from an asteroid impact (Gould, 1990) or other episodic physical events. In the past, changes in climate and the physical environment seem to have been the main cause of mass extinctions of species and of the higher orders of living things (Grant, 1991, p. 493). While evolutionary processes under relatively stationary (but not constant) environmental conditions may favour increased specialisation, at the same time a number of adaptable, opportunistic species may continue to survive. Whether these adaptable species will survive an episodic environmental event will depend on the nature of the event and the range of their tolerance. It is even feasible that such an event creates an environment which favours a highly specialised species inflexibly adapted to a particular niche, because it creates the environment peculiar to that niche on a wide scale. Thus, both adaptability and varied specialisations across a wide range of environmental niches could play a favourable role in survivability of species, under conditions of chance variations in the environment. Nevertheless, survival and evolution may still be influenced by contingency factors (Gould, 1989, p. 51, Ch. 5).

Despite the above, it is still necessary to recognise that the removal of keystone species from an ecosystem may threaten the functioning of the system as whole, depending upon the nature of interdependence between species. Whether this loss is likely to create greater impairment to the functioning of ecosystems with less diversity rather than ones having more diversity is unclear. For example, is the loss of species in a temperate zone more likely to impair the operation of an ecosystem than a similar loss in a tropical zone, given that the former exhibits less biodiversity than the latter? It is still possible that as the diversity of species in a region is decreased, that the sustainability of ecosystems in the region is likely to be increasingly impaired.

THE IMPACT OF HUMAN DISTURBANCE OF NATURAL ENVIRONMENTS ON BIODIVERSITY

Controversy exists about the impact on biodiversity of human disturbances on natural environments. On the one hand, there are those who believe that it leads to reduced biodiversity whereas others believe that it is associated with an increase. Smiet (1992) found a greater variety of trees per hectare on sites disturbed by human use in Java than on undisturbed sites. Similar results have been reported elsewhere.

However, one must be careful in drawing inferences about biodiversity from such observations. It would, for example, not be appropriate to conclude that by increasing the land area disturbed by humans that global biological diversity would be increased.

It is true that some ecosystems depend for their continuance on disturbances, either man-made or natural. Biodiversity is likely to be reduced if they are protected from these disturbances and they are unable to complete their stages of ecological succession. For example, 'Some natural disturbances, such as events triggered by fire, wind and herbivores, are an inherent part of internal dynamics of ecosystems and in many cases set the timing of successional cycles, (Holling, *et al.*, 1994). If they are not allowed to enter the ecosystem, it will become ever more over-connected, and thereby even larger perturbations will be invited with the risk of massive and widespread destruction'.

The extent of biodiversity on a global scale seems to depend upon the variety of environments available to species. The more varied the available environments, the greater the range of species supported, as a rule. If human disturbance adds to the range of environments available, it could add to biodiversity in the long term. Some species such as the Rufous hare wallaby, *Lagorchestes hirsutus*, may have evolved to take advantage of environments created by the land-use patterns of Australian aborigines. With the decline of those patterns of aboriginal land-use involving fire-burns, this species is now threatened with extinction (Van Oosterzee and Morrison, 1991, p. 100).

Even if greater variety of species exists in some human-disturbed environments, it does not follow that global biological diversity will be increased by disturbing all natural environments in a similar manner, because, compared to a situation where some natural environments are disturbed and some are not, the overall variety of habitats is reduced. Thus, a universe consisting of a mixture of disturbed and non-disturbed habitats is likely to support more biodiversity than one consisting only of undisturbed or disturbed habitats. Much, however, depends upon the nature of the human disturbances.

Empirical evidence suggests that ecological systems, at least regionally, are much more stable than suggested by the GAIA principle. Significant loss of endemic species can occur and yet ecological systems seem able to survive and function. The Pacific islands have been given as an example of this (Ash, 1992; Thaman, 1992). Many have had their ecological systems severely disturbed over a long period of time. The same could also be said of Europe and China.

COMPLETE SYSTEMS AND SUSTAINABILITY

Despite concern that concepts of sustainability have proliferated, it can be argued that more rather than fewer such concepts are needed. Surprisingly, economists do not seem to have developed holistic concepts of sustainability based upon the functioning of interdependent parts of systems, even though input-output analysis and general equilibrium analysis have become part of the standard fare of economics. How sustainable or resilient is a system in relation to possible losses of its parts, or to a reduction in their ability to function? If a system loses any of its parts, or if these are impaired, can it continue to perform its 'essential functions'? If it is able to perform well with substantial loss or impairment, then it would appear to be relatively robust and sustainable.

To develop this concept we may need to consider two characteristics: (1) the susceptibility of the system to loss of parts (or their impairment) and (2) the ability of the system to function (in some essential respects) subject to loss or impairment of parts. Four broad cases are identified in Table 4.1. A system with low susceptibility to loss or impairment of parts and good ability to function should such loss or impairment occur is clearly very sustainable (Case 1). In the opposite case (Case 4), the system is lacking in sustainability characteristics. Cases 2 and 3 involve a mixed situation – they involve one favourable and one unfavourable sustainability characteristic. Where systems involve at least one unfavourable characteristic from a sustainability point of view, it may be possible to manipulate them to improve their sustainability properties. This could at least provide a useful focus for policy purposes.

Table 4.1 Factors affecting the sustainability of systems as a whole

Case	Susceptibility of system to loss or impairment of parts	Ability of the system to function with such loss
1	Low	Good
2	Low	Poor
3	High	Good
4	High	Poor

Ecological systems involve complex networks and interdependencies. Nevertheless, we have some knowledge, though not complete, about their operation. We can examine the effects in a system of removal of species which provide food for others, for example, parasites; the situation where commensalism occurs; where competition and mutualism exists between species, and so on (Grant, 1991, p. 215). Our predictors are unlikely to be perfect, but they should provide us with insights into the sustainability of ecological systems when some species are removed or some added.

NEED TO FURTHER SUPPLEMENT THE CONCEPT OF RESILIENCE IN CONSIDERING SUSTAINABILITY

While the concept of resilience is most commonly used in considering the sustainability of ecosystems, it not only needs to be supplemented in the way discussed above (so as to consider the consequences for the operation of a system of loss of parts of it, or impairment of its parts) but it also needs to be supplemented in other ways. Resilience refers to the ability of a system to bounce back to an original state after disturbance. Yet, the reference state involved, given a human perspective, may be restricted to one providing particular services wanted by human beings. From some perspectives, this will be too limited.

Furthermore, a defect of the resilience concept of sustainability is that it leaves out of account the proneness of a system to disturbance. Some systems may be very prone to disturbance and others may be very resistant to being placed into disequilibrium. Let us call systems that are resistant to disequilibrium, 'robust'. Clearly a system which is robust and resilient would seem more desirable than one that is not, given that the system provides a desired service. Table 4.2 provides four indicative possibilities for systems, taking this view into consideration.

Table 4.2 Four systems differing in robustness and resilience

System 1	Robust	Resilient
System 2	Not Robust	Resilient
System 3	Robust	Not Resilient
System 4	Not Robust	Not Resilient

Even these supplements to the concept of sustainability (the ability of the system to continue to carry out its desired functions in the presence of disturbance) still enables only a partial picture to be drawn. We should also consider further properties of the systems once they are thrown into disequilibrium or disarray. Is the disequilibrium likely to be restricted to a small region or will it be large scale? For how long will it last? This means, for example, that some robust systems (those resistant to disequilibrium) may experience major disequilibrium once their robustness is overcome and they may only slowly return to equilibrium. They are highly resistant to disequilibrium, but once the resistance barrier is crossed, they succumb overwhelmingly to ecological stress. One can manufacture other possibilities from the above elements. The main point, however, is that from a sustainability point of view the resilience of systems must be supplemented by other concepts.

CONCLUDING COMMENTS

Relationships between sustainability, biodiversity and stability of environmental processes and systems are complex. The simplistic notion was questioned, that greater biodiversity of ecosystems makes for their greater sustainability because one needs not only to consider the diversity of species but also their adaptability either as individuals or as groups.

It is suggested that one should be cautious in drawing inferences from the empirical findings of some ecologists, that biodiversity tends to be greater in environments disturbed by humans than in undisturbed ones. Certainly, if humans disturb all environments it does not follow that biodiversity will be increased. Nevertheless, in some environments ecological disturbance is necessary for the survival of some species – they depend on disturbed environments for their regeneration and survival.

An extension in the range of sustainability and related concepts would be useful and a sustainability concept related to the functioning of systems as a whole is suggested for further development. In extending this concept, we need to consider the impact of the loss or impairment of parts of the system (for example, species) on the functioning of the whole system. The consequences of losses in biodiversity for the sustainability of ecosystems and productivity may be best considered in such a context. In addition, the resistance of systems to disequilibrium (their 'robustness') and disequilibrium characteristics additional to resilience must be considered.

REFERENCES

Ash, J. (1992), 'Vegetation ecology Fiji: past, present and future perspectives', *Pacific Science*, **46**, 111–27.

Barbier, E.B., J.C. Burgess and C. Folke (1994), *Paradise Lost? The Ecological Economics of Biodiversity*, London: Earthscan.

Conway, G.R. (1985), 'Agroecosystem analysis', *Agricultural Administration*, **20**, 31–55.

Conway, G.R. (1887), ' The properties of agroecosystems', *Agricultural Systems*, **24**, 95–117.

Gould, S.J. (1989), *Wonderful Life: The Burgess Shale and the Nature of History*, New York: Norton.

Gould, S.J. (1990), *The Individual in Darwin's World*, Edinburgh: Edinburgh University Press.

Grant, V. (1991), *The Evolutionary Process: A Critical Study of Evolutionary Theory*, 2nd ed., New York: Columbia University Press.

Holling, C.S., D.W. Schindler and B.W. Walker (1994), 'Biodiversity in the Functioning of Ecosystems: An Ecological Primer and Synthesis', in C. Perrings, K.G. Mäler, C. Folke, C.S. Holling and B.O. Jansson (eds), *Biodiversity Loss: Ecological and Economic Issues*, Cambridge: Cambridge University Press.

Smiet, A.C. (1992), 'Forest ecology on Java: human impact and vegetation on mountain forest', *Journal of Tropical Ecology*, **8**, 129–52.

Swanson, T. (1994), *The International Regulation of Extinction*, New York: New York University Press.

Swanson, T. (1997), 'The management of genetic resources for agriculture: ecology and information, externalities and polices', mimeo; Biodiversity Programme CSERGE, University College, London. A paper prepared for XXIII meeting of International Association of Agricultural Economists, Sacramento, California, August 1997.

Thaman, R.R. (1992), 'Vegetation of Nauru and the Gilbert Islands: case studies of poverty, degradation, disturbance and displacement', *Pacific Science*, **46**, 128–58.

Tisdell, C.A. (1983a), 'The optimal choice of a species for variable environmental conditions', *Journal of Agricultural Economics*, **34**, 175–85.

Tisdell, C.A. (1983b), 'The biological law of tolerance, average biomass and production in a variable uncontrolled environment', *The International Journal of Ecology and Environmental Sciences*, **9**, 99–109.

Tisdell, C.A. (1993), *Environmental Economics*, Aldershot, UK: Edward Elgar.

Tisdell, C.A. and M. Alauddin (1989), 'New crop varieties: impact on diversification and stability of yields', *Australian Economic Papers*, **28**, 123–40.

Van Oosterzee, P. and R. Morrison (1991), *The Centre: The Natural History of Australia's Desert Regions*, Balgowlah, N.S.W.: Reed Books.

5. Does the Commercial Use of Wildlife Favour Conservation of Biodiversity?

INTRODUCTION

For whatever reason, there is often a desire to conserve biological diversity. An important issue is what socio-economic mechanisms can be used to foster this objective. Traditional methods have included provision of protected areas by the state, and legislation to prohibit the killing of selected species or destruction of nature on private land.

Restrictions on the killing of wild species on native land do little to prevent habitat destruction, one of the main reasons for biodiversity loss.

Wild species in many western countries and their former colonies belong to the crown or the state, even when they occur on privately owned land. Owners have little or no interest in protecting such wildlife, except incidentally. Some biologists argue that if land owners could be given property rights to wildlife occurring on their land that this would be beneficial for nature conservation, owing to the fact that the wildlife concerned has some commercial value. However, this is only a partial solution to the conservation of biodiversity because (1) it may fail to conserve fugitive species of high commercial value which become effectively 'open-access' property, and (2) it is only likely to result in selected conservation of species of low mobility; namely conservation of those with higher commercial value at the expense of those with lower commercial value or none at all. Therefore, it is not a complete solution to the conservation of biodiversity.

Economic use of wildlife can be consumptive or non-consumptive, commercial or non-commercial. As a rule, the total economic value of a species usually exceeds its commercial value, that is, the value which can be obtained through market exchange. Given the economic preoccupation of virtually all modern societies, wildlife of commercial value or use is favoured for conservation. However, does the commercial use of wildlife favour its conservation? This depends largely on whether private property rights exist and are enforceable. If property rights can be economically established and commercial use of a species is profitable, a strong force exists for preservation of the wildlife concerned. On the other hand, if private property rights do not exist and there is open-access to commercially valuable wildlife, the tragedy of the commons is liable to occur and species may be driven to extinction by commercialism. Farming of a wildlife species is one form of commercial use, but it does not necessarily favour conservation of biodiversity. Nevertheless, commercial farming of some species may be environmentally more favourable than others, for example, farming of kangaroos rather than sheep or cattle in parts of Australia. Commercialisation and choice based on economic value has selective impacts on the populations of living things. It changes the composition of species. It therefore alters the natural web of life and is bound to be unacceptable to followers of Aldo Leopold who saw virtue in the land ethic. The general tendency of commercialisation is to reduce biodiversity and thereby sustainability, even though it may save some species from early extinction.

Emphasis in policy formulation on using economic incentives and mechanisms to sustain biodiversity has increased. When the World Conservation Strategy (IUCN, 1980) was drawn up in 1980, use of economic incentives as a means of conserving wildlife and biological diversity generally was not stressed, even though the importance of sustainable development for conservation was recognised. When this strategy was revised in 1991, much more emphasis was placed on the use of economic mechanisms and incentives (IUCN-UNEP-WWF, 1991; Tisdell, 1993, Ch. 16). More recently, the Convention on Biological Diversity (5 June, 1992), agreed to at the United Nations' Conference on Environment and Development held in Rio de Janeiro, gave prominence to economic incentives for conservation. Article 11 states 'Each Contracting Party shall, as far as is possible and as appropriate, adopt economically and socially sound measures that act as incentives for the sustainable use of components of biological diversity'.

The purpose of this chapter is to discuss the extent to which the greater economic use of wildlife favours nature conservation and sustainability. But before doing so, it may be useful to discuss the nature of the economic use of wildlife. Economists distinguish between consumptive and non-consumptive use of wildlife; the former involves the physical consumption of wildlife, for example, kangaroos for meat and hides, whereas the latter involves non-physical use, as in the traililng of wildlife for viewing or photography. The former involves the killing of wildlife and the latter does not. However, both types of economic use of wildlife can reduce wildlife population. For instance, tourists may disturb wildlife and reduce their rate of reproduction, or lead to their capture for display in zoos, thereby possibly depleting wild populations.

Economic use of wildlife may be for commercial market-related economic activities or for subsistence purposes. In the modern world, there is considerable emphasis on the commercial aspect of economic activity. Consequently, if economic use is to provide an incentive for the conservation of wildlife or nature, those responsible for its conservation must also be able to make a profit or economic gain from it. Whether they can do so will be influenced by their property rights in wildlife.

PROPERTY RIGHTS, ECONOMICS AND WILDLIFE CONSERVATION

The owner of private property has the power to exclude others from its use, and from using its product, yield or output, and the right to transfer its ownership. Thus exclusivity and transferability are features of private property (Cf. Tietenberg, 1992, Ch. 3). This means that any use of such property by non-owners can be made subject to a payment and payment may be obtained for conservation, investment or improvement of property (an asset) when it is transferred. Thus private property provides a mechanism for economic reward.

However, the fact that private property legally exists does not necessarily make it possible or economic to enforce private property rights. The economic costs of exclusion may, for example, exceed the economic benefits. For instance, in a remote national park with several access routes, the cost of enforcing entrance fees may exceed the cost of employing rangers to enforce these. The creation of property rights is largely an economic question (Demsetz, 1967; North, 1981). As techniques or methods of exclusion improve, or as the profitability of exclusion rises, economic incentives to create private property rights rise also. The extension, for example, of the exclusive fishing zone from 3 miles to 200 kilometres is partly a consequence of improved methods for enforcing exclusion.

In relation to the conservation and utilisation of wildlife, although private property rights sometimes exist they are often too partial to encourage conservation. This is the case where there is open-access to harvesting of wildlife but the harvest becomes the private property of the harvester on capture. No individual has an incentive to conserve wildlife in this case because he/she cannot appropriate the benefit from it when all others are free as a result of open access (common access) to reap the rewards of that individual's conservation effort (Tisdell, 1991, Ch. 6). Furthermore, under open-access, the rising economic value of a wildlife species results in its increased rate of exploitation and may result in its being rendered extinct. So in this case, the market system with limited property rights, results in a perverse economic reaction and has the opposite result to that occurring when a more complete system of private property rights exists. This is an example of the tragedy of the commons.

This tragedy may, however, occur not only because there is common (open) access to the 'output' of an ecological system but also if there is open access to its 'inputs'. Open access to habitat valuable for sustaining wildlife may result in its destruction if components of the habitat have economic value or marketability.

The answer to the problem of nature conservation may appear to be one of extending private property rights. However, it is sometimes very costly to enforce such rights and the private property solution becomes then uneconomic. Thus, control of resources as communal or state property may then be the most viable economic solution; but sometimes there may be no viable economic alternative to tolerating open-access. This implies that no single type of property right (such as private property) is the best for all situations.

Even when a relatively comprehensive system of private property rights exists, there may still be difficulties in appropriating all benefits from conserving wildlife because of the existence of environmental externalities or spillovers (Tisdell, 1991, Ch. 3). Those, for example, conserving suitable habitats for migrating or mobile birds, may confer benefits on bird-lovers beyond the confines of the habitats preserved. There may be no economic mechanisms for the conservationists to be fully compensated for their preservation of habitats and some political intervention may be necessary to support their co-operation.

It should be noted that even when complete private property rights can be established in a species, they do not ensure its conservation. Even if the species has market value, it may pay to eliminate it, for example, when the rate of growth of the biomass of a species is slow and its economic value is not expected to rise substantially (Cf. Clark, 1976). Suppose that by the optimal conservation and utilisation of a species, a maximum return of 2 per cent can be obtained, but that by replacing the species by another a maximum return of 8 per cent can be achieved. The owner of the former species has an economic incentive to eliminate it and replace it by the latter. For example, owners of properties containing slower-growing species of trees often harvest these and replace them by faster-growing species. Alternatively, if the going rate of interest on capital is in excess of 2 per cent, it may pay to harvest the stock of the slow-growing species completely, sell the harvest and invest the capital sum obtained at the going rate of interest. In either case, one species is eliminated. Hence, full private property rights, even in economically valuable species, do not ensure their conservation or survival. They must be sufficiently valuable, otherwise alternatives to their conservation will be chosen if economics determines the decision.

This is not to say that private property rights and marketing of wildlife cannot assist conservation of particular species or natural areas. However, they are not a panacea.

THE USER OR BENEFICIARY PAYS FOR WILDLIFE

In line with the increased emphasis on an economic means to support wildlife conservation, the 'user pays' or 'beneficiary pays' principles have been promoted (McNeely, 1988; Young, 1992, Ch. 3). It is possible for the user or beneficiary to be forced to pay for use of wildlife if exclusion is possible. Then, use of the wildlife or access to wildlife resources can be made dependent on a payment. However, one needs to consider the economics of collecting the charge, that is the cost of policing and enforcing payment. If this is too costly, collection of fees will not be economic (Cf. Tisdell, 1995).

When resources are able to earn income, administrators and government officials generally take a more favourable view towards conserving them than when their management is a drain on the public purse. So if national parks and protected areas are able to earn income, this is likely to be considered a positive feature by governments. They may for example be able to raise revenue by entrance fees, camping fees and the sale of concessions to businesses, such as shops and providers of accommodation within the park. However, to set user charges so as to maximise profit or net returns is not socially optimal as a rule. Because national parks or protected areas have some uniqueness, the demand curve for visits is likely to be downward sloping and a partial monopoly exists (Tisdell, 1972). According to economists, the exploitation of a monopoly situation by 'charging what the traffic will bear' is not usually in the public interest. Sometimes, charges may also be influenced by

conservational considerations – a high fee may be charged intentionally
to reduce visitor numbers so as to reduce their load on the environment.

A modest fee has been introduced for visits to the Great Barrier Reef
Marine Park (GBRMP) to defray some of the costs of operating the
GBRMP Authority. The fee is so low as not to be a significant deterrent
to visits or to constitute a monopoly price.

EXAMPLES OF ECONOMIC USE ASSISTING CONSERVATION

In South Africa, national parks and protected areas are largely self-
financing. For example, Kruger National Park obtains finances from:

(1) the culling of wildlife (mainly elephant and cape buffalo) and the
    operation of a processing plant for this purpose;
(2) entrance fees paid by visitors;
(3) income from accommodation and shops within the Park.

Culling of some species of large animals is considered necessary
because their seasonal movement has been restricted by the Park area
and their numbers tend to increase beyond the carrying capacity of the
Park unless they are culled.

It is interesting to note that both South Africa and Zimbabwe opposed
the ban on international trade in ivory introduced in October 1989 under
CITES (The Convention on International Trade in Endangered Species)
(Barbier, 1991, p. 407). Both countries engage in harvesting of elephants
within their national parks and sell the produce. Furthermore, elephant
populations are not endangered in either country (Barbier, 1991, p. 407).
There is, however, often discussion of whether the elephant cull is too
greatly influenced by commercial rather than biological considerations.

Selective culling of wildlife or habitat modification may be undertaken
in protected areas to adjust the composition of certain species in order to
match tourist demands for viewing. This increases tourisism to such
areas. Although culling is economically motivated, there is room for
debate about whether the influence is positive from a conservation
viewpoint.

An interesting case of nature conservation and economic use occurs in
the Otago Peninsula, located near Dunedin in New Zealand. The royal
albatross, *Diomedea epomophoran*, nests on Taiaroa Headland which is
only accessible to humans by a narrow neck of land. In the past, this

nesting ground was threatened by human disturbance and invading pests. It is now under the protection of the Otago Peninsula Trust which earns income from visitors' fees, paid for viewing the albatross colony from a viewing station. The colony is maintaining its own. Commercial conditions for conservation of the royal albatross colony are good for the following reasons which I have also mentioned elsewhere:

(1) The amount of land that has had to be set aside for conservation is relatively small. The opportunity cost of keeping the colony is correspondingly small.

(2) Exclusion from the site is relatively easy, so the service of conserving species on the site for viewing can be sold to the public via entry fees. The service can be marketed, as with most private goods. Nevertheless, it is possible to see flying albatross from boats or from outside the enclosure without paying.

(3) Since the Otago Peninsula Trust, as authorised by the Department of Conservation, has a monopoly (is the only operator able to sell rights to see royal albatross colonies in the area), it can charge a monopoly price for entry.

(4) Because a high proportion of young albatrosses born in the colony return to breed on reaching adulthood, there is a close connection between attempts to conserve young in the colony and future populations of royal albatross there.

(5) The site is easily accessible in virtually all weather conditions.

(6) Not only albatross but also breeding colonies of shags can be seen as a rule, and there is the added interest of a magnificent view across the harbour, including Aramoana Spit. (Tisdell, 1990, p. 89).

Another example to consider is one of animal conservation *ex situ*. Lone Pine Koala Sanctuary in Brisbane claims to have the largest population of *ex situ* koalas in the world and operates as a commercial enterprise. It is reliant on income from visitors fees and appears to be a profitable undertaking. Does it assist the conservation of koalas? By making the public more aware of koalas, it may make them more supportive of such conservation. Displays at the Sanctuary indicate that it has supported research into koalas and this may indirectly assist their conservation. Furthermore, eucalypt plantations have been commenced to provide food for the koalas in the Sanctuary, rather than continuing to rely on collection of leaves from trees occurring naturally.

The keeping of wild animals in commercial zoos has often been controversial from a conservation point of view. One fear is that zoos may provide an economic incentive for the capture of rare animals from the wild and endanger their populations. On the other hand, there have been occasions when zoos have been instrumental in saving species which have become extinct in the wild; and have provided a source for the re-introduction of wildlife species to their original habitat.

FARMING AS A MEANS OF 'WILDLIFE' CONSERVATION

Biologists have sometimes seen farming of particular species as a practical way of saving them from extinction. This has been suggested, for example, for turtles, giant clams and crocodiles. In Africa, a number of private wildlife farms have been established to rear wildlife for sale for hunting, for the meat and for trade. For farming to be practical, it must be economical to confine the animals concerned and for the owner to be able to exclude others from making use of them, except on his/her terms.

When farming of a species is profitable, it will undoubtedly provide a strong incentive for conservation of that particular species. However, it does not necessarily follow that farming is favourable to the maintenance of biological diversity.

When the farming of a species is profitable, there is a tendency to select only the most economic varieties of it for farming. Other varieties and breeds are liable to be allowed to die out or are extinguished. Hence, natural genetic diversity is reduced. While this may be compensated for to some extent by artificial breeding programmes, general evidence is that agriculture and the livestock industries are relying on an ever-diminishing genetic base as a result of private economic selection.

There is a second way in which farming is liable to reduce genetic diversity. Where a species is farmed, habitat favoured by wild populations may be appropriated for farming and wild populations may be extinguished within this geographical range (Cf. Swanson, 1994). This is also likely to lead to reduced genetic diversity.

Furthermore, farming generally leads to habitat modification and destruction of any wild animals liable to compete with farmed animals. Farming, if widespread, results in greater uniformity of environments. Both of these elements can reduce genetic diversity. Sometimes it is even claimed that farming leads to greater demand for remaining wild members of species and actually increases the harvesting of them (Tisdell, 1991, Sec. 6.4).

Thus (even ignoring the last-mentioned possibility) in the longer-term, farming is liable to lead to reduced genetic diversity. Indeed, it could reduce gene banks of significance for sustaining agricultural productivity to low levels which may make it difficult or impossible to sustain some types of farming in the long-term. Efforts to sustain genetic diversity outside the farming sector could therefore be important for the sustainability of farming itself.

This does not imply that previously unfarmed species should not be farmed. Farming is bound to continue as an economic activity. It may well be that some existing wild species are environmentally more suitable for farming purposes than those animals currently farmed. For example, kangaroo farming in parts of Australia may be environmentally more suitable than sheep or cattle grazing. Currently, one of the impediments to such farming is the difficulty of confining kangaroos to an individual property.

A related issue is whether the assignment of hunting, harvesting and other rights of economic use of wildlife awarded to private property owners, will enhance or reduce nature conservation compared to a situation in which wildlife is state property and its private use is prohibited or regulated by the state. The answer seems to be that it may do either depending on the circumstances. It may reduce nature conservation if the species concerned are highly mobile (fugitive) and of considerable economic value. The situation here is akin to the open-access case. Furthermore, even if the species has commercial value, it may also do damage as a pest, for example, agricultural damage by elephants. If commercial losses exceed the traded value of the species, it may be rapidly eliminated. Furthermore, private owners of wildlife are likely to be selective about the species conserved, the selection depending on net commercial value. The CAMPFIRE programme in Zimbabwe has been designed to assign rights in wildlife to local communities and is therefore an innovative property-rights approach to the problem of nature conservation. However, it is not free of the above problems.

DISCUSSION AND CONCLUSION

Economic use of wildlife, particularly commercial use of a species, may be favourable to survival of wildlife but need not be. This depends upon the nature of property rights and the economic profit that can be obtained from using a species commercially. Under open-access, economic use of a species is not favourable to its conservation and measures to control its utilisation are usually required. While the creation of private property rights in wildlife may lead to its conservation, this is sometimes insufficient to ensure the survival of a commercially valuable species because alternative economic options to conserving the species are more profitable. Furthermore, it has not always been economic to establish private property rights in wildlife species.

Commercial use of species, in a system designed to reflect economic values fully, is selective. It favours survival species and varieties of greatest commercial value, to the detriment of those of smaller or of no apparent economic value. Interference in natural systems is designed solely with commercial ends in mind. Such an approach to nature conservation is likely to be at odds with the land ethic, the ethical responsibility of humankind to conserve ecosystems as a whole (Leopold, 1966). One would expect followers of Leopold (1966) to reject conservation solely for commercial or utilitarian ends and to be increasingly alarmed by policy reforms which fostered this approach.

Even those taking a less ecocentric view may feel that the appropriate course of action is a middle course, namely that some, but definitely not all, wildlife conservation should be determined by economic use or values. They may do so because:

(1) They are favourably disposed to the land ethic to some extent. They are neither completely anthropocentric or ecocentric in their value system.

(2) Considerable uncertainty exists about future values, including economic values, of particular species and ecosystems and conservation of nature is a rational means of allowing for such uncertainties. This is an application of the precautionary principle (Young, 1992, p. 67).

(3) The economic costs of conserving many remaining natural ecosystems may be low, on average, and the economic benefit of transforming them to their currently most economically valuable state may be slight. Therefore there may be no case for the latter economic action, when it is possible that such transformation could result in a significant economic loss in the more distant future, perhaps due to extinction of species of possible future economic value (Ciriacy-Wantrup, 1968; Bishop, 1978). This view suggests that the only wise course of action is to allow current (or currently perceived) economic values to determine conservation of wildlife in a restricted spatial area, reserving other areas for holistic

conservation or with this as the prime aim. Of course, this leaves open the question of the size of restricted areas or of the area to be reserved for holistic conservation of nature.

At the opposite extreme to the ecocentric view is the anthropocentric one that ideally all wildlife conservation should be determined by economic values, and that systems should be developed so that the conservers of economically valuable wildlife can be fully rewarded. Ethically, I prefer the middle path of valuation based on a combination of anthropocentric and ecocentric values. However, it is accepted that sometimes greater realisation of economic values will foster nature conservation and support the cause of conservationists. Nature conservationists are not necessarily inconsistent when on some occasions they support, and on other occasions they oppose, greater reliance on commercial or economic use as a means of supporting wildlife conservation. Conservationists need to be selective in their support of economic incentives and values for wildlife conservation if their main goal is to preserve biodiversity. This is the main message of this chapter.

REFERENCES

Barbier, E.B. (1991), 'Managing trade and environment: the demand for raw ivory in Japan and Hong Kong', *The World Economy*, 14 (1), 407–30.

Bishop, R.C. (1978), 'Endangered species and uncertainty. The economics of a safe minimum standard', *American Journal of Agricultural Economics*, 60, 10–8.

Clark, C.W. (1976), *Mathematical Bioeconomics*, New York: John Wiley.

Ciriacy-Wantrup, J.V. (1968), *Resource Conservation: Economics and Policies*, Division Agricultural Economics, Davis: University of California.

Demsetz, H. (1967), 'Towards a theory of property rights', *American Economic Review*, 57, 347–59.

IUCN (1980), *World Conservation Strategy*, Gland, Switzerland: IUCN.

IUCN-UNEP-WWF (1991), *Caring for the Earth: A Strategy for Sustainable Living*, Gland, Switzerland: IUCN.

Leopold, A. (1966), *A Sand Country Almanac: with Other Essays on Conservation from Round River*, New York: Oxford University Press.

McNeely, J.A. (1988), *Economics and Biological Diversity: Developing and Using Economic Incentives to Conserve Biological Resources*, Gland, Switzerland: International Union for the Conservation of Nature and Natural Resources.

North, D.C. (1981), *Structure and Change in Economic History*, New York: Norton.

Swanson, T. (1994), *The International Regulation of Extinction*, New York: New York University Press.

Tietenberg, T. (1992), *Environmental and Natural Resource Economics*, 3rd edn, New York: Harper Collins.

Tisdell, C.A. (1972), 'Provision of parks and preservation of nature – some economic factors',

Australian Economic Papers, **11**, 154–62.

Tisdell, C.A. (1990), *Natural Resources, Growth and Development*, New York: Praeger.

Tisdell, C.A. (1991), *Economics of Environmental Conservation*, Amsterdam: Elsevier Science Publishers.

Tisdell, C.A. (1993), *Environmental Economics*, Aldershot, UK: Edward Elgar.

Tisdell, C.A. (1995), 'Investment in ecotourism: assessing its economics', *Tourism Economics*, **14**, 375–87.

Young, M.D. (1992), *Sustainable Investment and Resource Use*, Carnforth: UNESCO, Paris and The Parthenon Publishing Group.

6. Conservation, Protected Areas and the Global Economic System

INTRODUCTORY OVERVIEW

The previous chapter considered how extension of the commercial use of wildlife might effect the conservation of biodiversity. It was argued that such extension is not always effective in protecting wildlife and that even in cases where it may be considered to be effective, it is usually selective in its conservation of species and variety. Therefore, it is likely to be inadequate in conserving biodiversity and the webs of life so dear to Aldo Leopold (1996). Private property rights and commercialisation of wildlife do not provide a complete answer to the conservation of biodiversity; protected areas need to be provided to ensure a more acceptable level of biodiversity conservation. A related economic matter poses the question: what effects do the extension of the market system and the process of economic globalisation have on the conservation of nature, including its biodiversity? This is taken up in this chapter.

The world is increasingly subject to economic globalisation. The global economic system is characterised by international specialisation in production, massive amounts of production and trade in goods and services, and the presence of international flows of finance, capital and technology. The system is bound together by the use of money and markets which rely on and foster self-interested production and the exchange of commodities. To some extent, the system is supplemented by international movements of labour and by official and unofficial aid. Major decision-makers in the global system include private traders and financiers, multinational corporations, national (centralised) governments and international public service bodies, such as the United Nations and its agencies.

The system results in the replacement of ecosphere communities by biosphere communities, and depersonalises social, economic and environmental relationships. It places great pressure on natural resources, results in the increased loss of natural areas and of biodiversity and adds to global pollution. Its major consequence is the much greater externalisation of environmental effects of economic activity. The system is a threat to the sustainability of production in the long run, despite its economic advantages in the short- to medium-term such as reduced economic scarcity as a whole.

Natural areas in isolated, or relatively isolated, economies are at particular risk when these economies are drawn into the global system, particularly if significant economic growth is achieved. In such cases, natural areas must increasingly be officially protected or set aside as national parks if irreversible genetic loss is to be avoided. At this time, aid from developed countries for nature protection may be crucial. Once a country becomes 'developed' and integrated into the global economic system, conservation of nature, and therefore biodiversity, becomes heavily dependent on government maintenance and protection of natural areas. In turn, such protection relies substantially on political processes, including lobbying by conservation groups.

It has been claimed that free trade, for example, implementation of WTO (World Trade Organization) regulations, can be expected to foster greater nature conservation, as will the structural adjustment policies recommended by the IMF (International Monetary Fund) and World Bank to debtor countries. These call for freer markets and smaller government sectors. But these policies do not ensure greater conservation and can reduce biodiversity. The position is complex, but the safest approach is to target policies specifically to maintain biodiversity and natural areas. So, if the above policies are pursued they should be supplemented by specific policies aimed at protecting natural areas. As far as biodiversity is concerned, it is dangerous to rely on broad generalisations about the beneficial effects on conservation of the above-mentioned policies, especially if the meaning of 'greater conservation' remains undefined, as is common.

Modern economic systems involve a serious employment-conservation conflict. They depend for the maintenance and expansion of employment on the growth of economic production. The 'need' for economic growth for employment-creation is especially apparent where the population is increasing, labour-saving technological progress is occurring, when real wages (income) are inflexible downwards or creep upwards, and when reduction of hours of work or sharing of jobs by the employed with the unemployed, is not an option. The global economic system continues to be locked into economic growth as a creator of employment. Reduced consumption in this system can be expected to result in growing unemployment and lack of income for the unemployed. Thus, it is difficult to implement neo-Malthusian recommendations of reducing consumption levels in developed countries and achieving steady-state economies. Even less radical conservation policies are often thwarted by this issue, which is still largely unresolved politically.

The global economic system is subject to fluctuation and instability. In an economic recession or with a sudden deterioration in the economic situation of a country (for example, due to balance of payment problems), there is a temptation to draw on natural resources, like logging forests more intensely, and to engage in unsustainable harvesting of living natural resources, to tide the country over its difficulties. This can be a source of considerable loss of genetic diversity and of natural areas. Furthermore, exports of living natural resources can be used to finance economic growth. This can obviously be a threat to genetic diversity and is of dubious value if the economic growth proves to be unsustainable.

International capital and technology flows, multinational enterprises, devaluation of national currencies, foreign loans and aid can all have an impact on the conservation of natural areas and the maintenance of biodiversity. As discussed previously, they can assist or hinder conservation, depending on the circumstances.

Debt-for-nature swaps have been much publicised as a means of easing the foreign debt burden of less developed countries and ensuring greater conservation of nature. But debt-for-nature swaps do have some shortcomings. These swaps and environmentally-dependent aid policies raise the question of who gains from conservation in less developed countries. How are benefits distributed between aid donors and recipients, that is between the developed and the less developed world? Some recipients of environmentally sensitive foreign aid claim that they are being disadvantaged. This possibility and others are examined, using a matrix of alternative international distributions of gains and losses from nature conservation.

The spread and the development of the global economic system has increased and is increasing the need for more officially protected areas. Economic globalization is a threat to nature conservation and biodiversity. Policies to encourage the spread of this system (such as freer markets, structural economic adjustments, replacement of subsistence communities by cash and market-oriented ones) are likely to accelerate the disappearance of species, unless they are combined with policies targeted specifically at ensuring greater conservation of nature, such as increasing the protection of existing natural areas and the quantity of natural areas officially protected. In this context, greater attention should also be given to economic mechanisms designed to finance and promote nature conservation.

THE GLOBAL ECONOMIC SYSTEM: ITS BASICS

Nowadays environments in most parts of the Earth and the lives of virtually everyone are affected by the global economic system. These effects arise from international trade in goods and services, from international capital flows and factor movements, from technology transfer and from expanded international communication, as well as direct environmental spillovers from economic activities. Scientific and technical developments in transport and communication have widened the scope for international exchange of commodities and for the operation of market systems.

The global economic system is characterised by:

(1) international specialisation in production by countries and regions;
(2) greater specialisation by individuals and economic agents in productive and economic activities than formerly;
(3) heavy dependence on capital-intensive technologies which rely for their operation on the use of non-renewable resources, such as fossil fuels, and on mechanical-chemical technologies and increasingly electronic technologies, even in agriculture;
(4) enormous and increasing levels of economic production which tax the environment, both in terms of the provision of raw materials for this production and in terms of its ability to assimilate wastes and pollutants generated by the production.

To function and maintain its viability the global economic system requires exchange of commodities on a gigantic scale. This exchange (which makes specialisation in production and economic activity possible) is facilitated:

(1) by the use of monetary systems (in which cash actually now plays only a small part);
(2) by the extension of market systems.

The use of market and monetary systems can (and in fact has) alter relationships between humanity, nature and the environment in ways which will be discussed below. Efforts are continually being made to extend and perfect these systems further, for example, by urging countries to remove or reduce restrictions on international trade (through WTO), by encouraging subsistence and semi-subsistence communities to become more cash-, monetary-, and exchange-oriented, and by exhorting previously centrally planned socialist countries to extend the operation of markets. It is usually argued that such developments will reduce economic scarcity and increase economic welfare. While these developments can have economic and social benefits, they can also have environmental and social costs and there is a risk that any economic benefits or scarcity-reduction may be impermanent or unsustainable. They do not guarantee economic Utopia. They can result in one set of problems being replaced by another.

At the same time as market and monetary systems have been extended globally, other institutional developments and changes have occurred. These include the rise of centralised states and centralised monetary and banking systems, the emergence of large companies and business organisations, including multinational enterprises, and the development of relatively large public sectors and international bureaucracies, including bodies such as the United Nations, World Bank and IMF. As a result, the control of local communities over their own affairs has been reduced. The control of individuals over their economic circumstances has increased in some respects but has been reduced in others because of their growing dependence on others, but in the abstract or impersonally. Furthermore, in those areas where 'economic development' has proceeded furthest, most individuals lack direct access to the means of production and basically, most sell their labour to survive. For example, as 'economic development' proceeds landlessness becomes more common, thus depriving people of direct access to an important means of subsistence. All of these changes are occurring against a background of considerable wealth and income inequality between developed and less developed nations and also within many nations (Cf. Schor, 1991).

Given current trends, the global economic system can be expected to become more pervasive, drawing individuals and countries more thoroughly into it, including those at present only tangentially dependent on it. This is likely to mean greater emphasis on economic growth, markets, economic exchange and monetary systems, and this could pose increased environmental dangers. What should be the political reaction of conservationists to these trends?

One possibility is to oppose these economic trends and perhaps support the setting up of small self-sufficient, or almost self-sufficient communities (Schumacher, 1973). But such a system would not be without some economic cost because it would result in loss of scale economies and loss of some economic benefits from large-sized markets, such as productivity benefits of specialisation. But it is only an option and another would be to support centralised socialism in order to foster planned control. However, not only would this run against the tide of prevailing political sentiment but it is likely to entail economic and other costs. Furthermore, most centralised socialist systems have had a poor record in the past as far as environmental conservation is concerned. Yet another possibility is to accept the basic trend in the global economic system as described above, but to try to modify or transform it so as to harness its characteristics wherever possible to support conservation. This may, for example, involve the establishment of some private property-rights in natural resources, greater marketing of rights to use environmental resources, and application of fiscal policies such as taxes or subsidies in order to promote conservation. This approach of 'working with the trend' and supporting the use of economic instruments as a means to further conservation, has been adopted to a large extent in the update of the World Conservation Strategy (IUCN-UNEP-WWF, 1991).

INTERNATIONAL ECONOMIC INTERDEPENDENCE AND CONSERVATION

Because of growing international economic interdependence, individuals have been converted from being ecosystem people to being biosphere people, that is from being dependent upon local ecosystems to drawing upon the resources of the whole biosphere (Raymond Dasmann quoted in Klee, 1980). According to Dasmann, this has resulted in local communities showing less concern for sustaining local ecosystems because local people are no longer entirely dependent upon them. Furthermore, extension of the market system results in impersonal and often anonymous links. For instance, consumers know little or nothing about the geographical origins of ingredients used in products purchased by them, nor about the environmental consequences of producing these. In addition, company structures and competition between producers and economic agents results in the neglect of environmental spillovers by producers (Cf. Tisdell, 1990, Ch. 2). The whole socio-economic system tends to become de-personalised with possible adverse consequences for nature and, in some cases, for the mental health of individuals. Anxieties may develop because of worries about economic security or competition and because of the lack of a sense of belonging, due to the loss of community cohesion and impermanence of social and economic relationships (Cf. Toffler, 1970). On the other hand, the modern economic system generally results in less social pressure on individuals and allows them greater mobility, so in these respects it provides greater personal freedom than might have been typically the case amongst ecosphere people.

The main advantage of a global market economy is claimed by most economists to be a reduction in economic scarcity. This is because international trade allows specialisation in production according to comparative advantage, permits economies of scale in production to be reaped and allows (even in the absence of production advantages) welfare-enhancing exchanges, given differences in resource endowments or differences in the preference of individuals for commodities. Theoretically, the system permits greater economic production or human satisfaction to be achieved using the same amount of resources as would be utilised in its absence.

Alternatively, with such an economy operating, it is possible to produce the level of production of goods and services using fewer resources than in its absence. Potentially therefore, such a system provides greater scope for conservation or reduced resource-use than in its absence. Although theoretically this is true under the conditions specified in the relevant neo-classical economic theory, this potential is unlikely to be realised in practice. In reality, conservation is likely to suffer in countries brought most recently within the international system.

Western economists claim that human wants for economic goods are infinite. Business corporations energetically promote consumerism through advertising and other forms of product promotion; the potential of the system for greater conservation is likely to be forgone for greater production and consumption. Furthermore, contact with 'more developed' countries is likely to lead to greater emphasis on the acquisition of material possessions and expand the range of perceived needs (Yellen, 1990). Natural resource stocks such as forests and minerals can now be drawn on to provide income and funds for capital investment via international sales, and may provide a springboard to economic growth, as is reputed to have occurred in Sweden. Resources may now be utilised for the first time or utilised more intensively. Capital and new technology may flow in from abroad to speed up this process, if natural resource exploitation and the economic growth 'imperative' of centre-countries becomes globally pervasive. This seems to be the real situation.

Another possible adverse impact on conservation of natural living resources brought about by drawing less-developed economies into the international economic system, is that it may reduce limits to human population growth in the countries concerned. The potential, per capita, income-enhancing benefits of international trade and exchange may be frittered away because of Malthusian-like effects on the level of human population. In consequence, a country experiencing this difficulty ends up with a larger human population at subsistence level and less conservation of natural resources (Tisdell and Fairbairn, 1984). Bangladesh may be a case in point. There is also considerable argument amongst economists as to whether economic growth resulting from international economic contact, increases income inequality or even the incidence of poverty.

This is not to suggest that a return to economic autarky for nations and groups is desirable. In any case, there would be little social support for such a goal. On the other hand, we should not gloss over the difficulties posed for conservation by the international economic system, with its continuing emphasis on economic growth.

On the positive side, a fully developed market system provides new policy opportunities for environmental control. It enables use to be made of market mechanisms and fiscal policies (such as appropriate taxation policies) to achieve conservation objectives. For instance, it provides some (but not unlimited) scope for market-making in relation to environmental goods (for example, the creation of markets in rights for environmental use). But even in those advanced market economies where law and order is the norm, there are limits to these possibilities. In those less developed countries which are socially and politically unstable and not yet transformed into a complete market economy, there may be much less scope for such measures. Indeed, in some circumstances the conservation of an area may sometimes be best secured by minimising contact between it and the international economy; for example, by avoiding the construction of access roads to an area until such time as the socio-economic situation enables resource-use in that area to be controlled adequately by the government. Parts of Madagascar, for example, contain unique wildlife but at present difficulties of access to these areas means that they are not generally visited by foreign tourists. Better access, although it would encourage tourism, could lead to other economic developments in the area which might endanger conservation there. At least the government's continuing ability to control the development pattern it has started needs to be considered before an economic development project is launched.

TRADE POLICIES, BALANCE OF PAYMENTS DIFFICULTIES AND EXCHANGE RATES

International trade usually extends the size of markets for commodities and, as mentioned earlier, results in socio-economic benefits as well as disadvantages. Most economists are of the view that the net welfare benefits from international trade are positive and they usually support policies to reduce barriers to trade, such as initiatives taken through WTO or the type of 'structural adjustment policies' being pursued by the IMF and the World Bank. They are also sympathetic to the slogan which was common, at least in the 1970s, of 'trade not aid', that is of allowing the exports of developing countries access to the markets of developed countries on favourable terms, or at least allowing such goods to be imported free of trade discrimination.

Nevertheless, we should remind ourselves that the gains from international trade can be uneven. Some groups can lose from it. One can imagine conditions also in which international trade may not, on balance, be advantageous to a country, even though these conditions may be rare. Such conditions have been outlined by those proposing de-development theses based on the centre-periphery paradigm (Frank, 1971; Myrdal, 1956).

Even in those cases where international trade is judged to be economically advantageous, on balance it does not necessarily result in greater conservation of natural resources, even though theoretically it could provide scope for greater conservation. As mentioned earlier, international trade may stimulate greater consumption by residents of a trading nation. Second, it may provide markets or larger markets for natural resources which would be little used in the absence of access to the international market. Thus, international trade may provide an enlarged market for timber resources or for wildlife products. With international trade, countries with a 'comparative advantage' in supply of these commodities will exploit them more heavily. On the other hand, countries with a comparative disadvantage in supply of such natural products may indeed reduce their utilisation of them. For example, access to the natural resources of less developed countries to some extent reduced pressure on the natural resources of Europe but increased that in LDCs. Overall pressure on natural living resources appears to have increased as a result of the extension of the global economic system.

Again, restrictions on trade have possibly been unfavourable to conservation in some areas but may have assisted it elsewhere. The Common Agricultural Policy of Europe (CAP) actually has helped to maintain agricultural land use in Europe. In its absence, more land is likely to have reverted to woodland or forest. On the other hand, restrictions on agricultural imports from the rest of the world may have held back the expansion of agriculture elsewhere.

Lutz (1990) however suggests that the environmental effects of an agricultural trade liberalisation in industrial countries are expected to be positive, even though some adverse environmental effects, from increased price variability or uncertainty, might partially offset the positive conservation effects of lower agricultural production intensity and output, assuming normal supply curves. He suggests on the other hand, that agricultural trade liberalisation in industrial countries will result in higher prices for agricultural produce in LDCs and consequently greater intensification and extension of agricultural production, with adverse environmental impacts in LDCs. His view taking the world as a whole, is that the environmental effects of international agricultural trade liberalisation would be uncertain. Lutz indicates that no firm conclusion can be drawn without empirical work. I . would also add that one needs to decide conceptually on what is, and what is not, an environmental improvement before any firm conclusion can be drawn.

That free international trade does not necessarily result in optimal conservation outcomes is recognised by CITES (Convention on International Trade in Endangered Species) which restricts international trade in products obtained from listed endangered species. By reducing the market for such products, CITES aims to make poaching less attractive and thereby reduce this practice. But, of course, CITES does not address problems of preserving habitats (the disappearance of which is a principal cause of extinction of species) nor the difficulty of providing economic rewards for those who conserve species.

Georgescu-Roegen (1976) has recommended that consumption of commodities should be limited to those which can be sustained by the use of renewable resources alone. But this seems to be too restrictive a policy. It may result in the disappearance of a considerable amount of natural living resources, as their use is substituted for that of non-renewable resources. Furthermore, there seems to be no good reason why there should be total abstinence from non-renewable resource use. Up to a point, use of non-renewable resources can reduce pressure on living natural resources. The use of such resources could, for instance, be environmentally less destructive than widespread agriculture. Again, what is the point in never using non-renewable resources, that is, in leaving them until the end of the world? The appropriate policy seems to be to use them wisely, having regard to the needs of future generations. Nor do there seem to be sufficient grounds to ban all exports of non-renewable resources or, for that matter, all commodities which have some adverse environmental effect. In the longer term, such exports may produce a base for development of less environmentally destructive economic activities, for example, through the accumulation of man-made capital, growth of service industries, and growth in human capital such as knowledge. This is likely to have been the pattern of economic development of Sweden.

In practice, most LDCs experience balance of payment difficulties as a result of international trade. There are many reasons for this. There has been a long-term tendency for the terms of trade to move against exporters of primary products, and most LDCs tend to export primary products. Many LDCs, being short of capital, also have a tendency to live beyond their means, financing excess expenditure through foreign borrowing. External deficits are often covered by foreign loans because the international monetary reserves of most developing countries are meagre. In cases where the countries concerned also have substantial defence or war expenditure, additional pressure is placed on the balance of payments. Governments of LDCs often borrow from abroad to finance public consumption and capital works because their tax bases are weak and domestic financial markets are often limited. Furthermore, many residents of LDCs try to invest in developed countries rather than at home. All these factors have in recent years resulted in a mounting international debt for many LDCs, effects of which will be discussed later.

As a result of balance of payments difficulties, LDCs are likely to be forced to devalue their currency. The consequences of devaluation for conservation are unclear but provided a devaluation is sustained and not fully offset by inflation, it is likely to encourage the growth of export industries, reduce imports, and stimulate aggregate demand at home. It may result in less conservation at home but as discussed below its conservational impact is complex. Lutz and Young (1992) point out that 'Tracing the effects of changes in macroeconomic policies on the national resource base is difficult as interactions between the economic system and the environment are complex and our understanding of them limited. Also a policy change such as devaluation can have both positive and negative effects'.

In LDCs, international trade may encourage urbanisation, and it may be encouraged by urban elites because it often provides a base for taxation to support the public sector on which many urban groups depend for employment or economic support. It may also help to support a dual economy – a relatively advanced urban sector and a backward rural sector. In the urban sector of LDCs wages may be relatively rigid, and effective demand for labour, as well as government revenue for labour employment, can be heavily dependent on the extent to which the balance of payments is in deficit or surplus. Sudden reduction in exports, which could have unemployment and reduced government revenue flow-ons, may be countered by governments of LDCs drawing detrimentally on conserved natural resources. A discussion of recent International Monetary Fund (IMF) and World Bank policies on structural adjustment may help to place the above issues in wider perspective.

STRUCTURAL ADJUSTMENT AND THE INTERNATIONAL ECONOMIC SYSTEM – IMF AND WORLD BANK POLICIES

LDCs, especially in Latin America and sub-Saharan Africa, experienced economic difficulties during the 1980s involving balance of payments deficits, high interest rates, reduced availability of international finance and falling terms of trade. In many cases, these difficulties were compounded by inadequate domestic economic policies and left an unwelcome legacy for the 1990s. Major international donor agencies, principally the IMF and World Bank, have made it a condition of financial assistance to such countries that they adopt a package of policies aimed at macroeconomic stabilisation and structural adjustment of their economies. Sometimes, by way of shorthand, these are merely referred to as Structural Adjustment Policies (SAPs). Our interest in these policies is first that they are influential in the context of the global economic system and second, that there have been claims that on balance they are beneficial for conservation. Before discussing the latter contention, let me briefly outline the nature of these Structural Adjustment Policies.

SAPs basically involve a two-prong approach. The first entails:

(1) Reductions in domestic aggregate demand – that is expenditure reductions, especially by government with the aim of creating a smaller public sector.
(2) Measures to increase supplies, particularly by making greater use of free market forces.

The second prong involves:

(1) Expenditure switching within the government budget and within the economy of resources to more productive sectors, and between the home market and export markets via exchange rate devaluation.
(2) Liberalisation of controls on foreign trade.
(3) Liberalisation of the domestic price system, especially the prices received by farmers for their output and those paid by farmers for inputs such as fertilisers and pesticides.

Such measures are intended to ensure that the demands of LDCs conform more closely with their means of meeting them, and to increase their supply of commodities by improving the allocative efficiency of their resource use. The primary aim of such policies is not intended to be an environmental one. But claims have been made that a coincidental spin-off from such policies is greater conservation.

Sebastian and Alicbusan (1989), after reviewing the World Bank's structural adjustment lending operations, conclude that 'far from being a major source of environmental degradation in developing countries, adjustment policies appear, on balance, to have a bias in favour of the environment. With adequate complementary measures to make sure they are implemented correctly, the policies can be manipulated to achieve environmental as well as economic objectives' (Sebastian and Alicbusan, 1989, p. 28).

Hansen suggests that his studies also support this broad conclusion in relation to the Asian Development Bank (Hansen, 1990b, p. 8) and, with some qualifications, more generally (Hansen, 1990a, c).

On the other hand, Mearns (1991, p. 19) after reviewing structural adjustment in Malawi, concludes that such policies could well be environmentally detrimental. There are, in his view, no grounds for presuming them to be environmentally favourable; environmental effects can go either way. It seems that the view of Mearns is in fact correct.

But before discussing this matter, a particular conceptual problem should be noted. Discussants do not indicate their measure of environmental quality[1] nor the extent of conservation achieved. While one resource might show greater conservation with a change in economic policy, another may show reduced conservation. Sebastian and Alicbusan (1989) suggest that devaluation will result in a higher price being paid to farmers for export crops. This will encourage farmers to look upon their land as a valuable asset and pay more attention to soil conservation; although it may result in the extension of agriculture and the increased destruction of the habitat of native animals as it is transformed to agricultural use. Sebastian and Alicbusan ignore the latter and the effects of SAPs on natural areas. As pointed out by Mearns (1991), effects on the environment may also depend on the type of agriculture which is encouraged. If the growing of tree crops rather than field crops is encouraged this may be environmentally more advantageous than if the opposite pattern is instigated.

It is true that the elimination of subsidies on the use of pesticides and artificial fertiliser could have favourable environmental effects. It may also be, as Sebastian and Alicbusan suggest, that a reduction in the size of the government budget and expenditure could do the same. For example, such a reduction might result in less road building and thereby retard the 'development' of remote land areas with natural vegetation cover. On the other hand, a reduction in government expenditure could mean a pruning of governmental spending to protect the environment, for example, soil conservation services and a reduction in environmental education. Also, expenditure on national parks and wildlife services may be slashed and few, if any, areas may be acquired for state protection. Indeed, national parks and wildlife services seem as a rule to suffer when government budgets are cut.

Naturally LDCs must live within their means internationally in the long term if they are to remain economically viable. Therefore, they need to adopt appropriate adjustment policies. But the adjustment policies suggested by the IMF and the World Bank do not specifically address conservation goals. Their impact on conservation is likely to be mixed. In some circumstances, they could hasten the disappearance of natural areas and endangered species. We cannot rely on generalised policies which lack a definite conservation aim.   Policies must be targeted specifically to those conservational aims which are sought, and in certain cases this will require aid or income transfers to less developed countries from developed nations, for this specific purpose. International lending agencies, such as the World Bank, have started to recognise this. Some funds (for example, Global Environmental Facility) are now becoming available for projects on concessionary terms which have positive conservational benefits and which may provide favourable global spillovers (Anon, 1991).

Bauer (1989) has suggested that adjustment policies promoted by bodies such as IMF and World Bank (providing more aid to debtor countries agreeing not to repudiate their debts, or do so immediately), are rarely monitored or enforced. He says:

'Most [government] debtors, especially major debtors, rarely change their policies significantly under these arrangements. Policies such as the maintenance of a large state sector, extensive control over economic activity, state export monopolies and the like accord with their interests and may even be necessary for their political survival. They will abandon them only if continued pursuit would result in economic breakdown threatening their own position. If they are rescued they will persist in their policies though they may pay lip service to the market and effect some changes in their exchange rate policies' (Bauer, 1989, pp. 11,12). Clearly, if this is the case, the structural adjustment policies being praised by Sebastian, Alicbusan (1989) and others, are in reality not being put into effect.

In a more wide ranging criticism, Harris (1991) says that 'most of the global institutions presently in existence date from the period immediately following World War II – the IMF, the World Bank, the General Agreement on Tariffs and Trade (GATT), the United Nations and its various agencies are now obsolete, since they were developed to deal with problems of cyclical instability and mass unemployment and have been unable to adapt sufficiently to deal with the problems of population, development and environment that dominate the current global picture'. He suggests a set of new international institutions involving a combination of Keynesian and ecological perspectives, even though the connections which he makes between Malthus, Keynes, ecology and the environment appear rather tenuous. Nevertheless, such debate is healthy because it is possible that existing institutions are operating on outmoded perspectives. As mentioned later, outmoded perceptions of macroeconomic policy-maker – having either a Keynesian, monetarist, or neo-classical bent – are still strong because economic growth is seen as the main means to meet employment and welfare-enhancing objectives.

INTERNATIONAL CAPITAL FLOWS, MULTINATIONAL ENTERPRISES, LOANS AND AID

International capital flows, apart from enabling capital equipment to be purchased from abroad, help to transfer technology and provide a means for economic growth. But such transfers do not necessarily have friendly environmental effects. Such flows may result from direct private investment (for example, by multinational companies) through loans (private and public), through government aid, private aid and transfers (remittances).

Such international flows may enable incomes in recipient countries to rise and may promote urbanisation. In the long term this could prove favourable to conservation, even though it is not likely to be so in the shorter term. In the longer term for example, population growth might be reduced and a population with a higher per capita income may be more favourable to conservation. The Brundtland Report (World Commission on Environment and Development, 1987) was of the view that without a rise in per capita incomes in LDCs there is little chance of conservation occurring in LDCs on a significant scale.

Maybe a typical relationship exists between the pursuit of conservation objectives and the stage of economic 'development'. At low levels of per capita income and in the early stages of economic development, environmental conservation is not a high priority. Only after substantial economic development has been achieved does environmental conservation become a major goal. This seems to be because the demand for environmental goods is income-elastic and also education-elastic. This suggests that in the absence of substantial and effective foreign aid, pressure on the environments of LDCs is likely to intensify as they attempt to achieve economic growth. Many are still well below that stage of development where environmental conservation is a high priority. The only type of conservation which they are likely to favour at present is that adding demonstrably to production, income, or in certain cases, defensive conservation, that is conservation demonstrably necessary to prevent a substantial fall in their production or level of income.

On the whole, international capital flows seem to assist the economic growth of LDCs. However, some economists have argued that they may be a source of 'de-development'. In the initial stages of economic development, these flows are likely to add to pressures on natural resources. But apart from this, they may give rise to particular strains or environmental distortions.

Multinational enterprises, especially when they are part of a large public company, may not be sensitive to local environmental conditions and issues. Directors and shareholders of the overseas parent company of a multinational, being far away from the scene of operations of its subsidiary in a LDC, may have little knowledge of the environmental effects of its operation, and may escape the local criticism and social pressure which might be experienced by a local entrepreneur. Competition, both in the capital market and in commodities, may also help to make a company insensitive to its environmental effects. The main aim of commercial enterprises is to maximise their profit. As a rule they will only pay attention to those environmental effects which directly affect the profit of the firm (Tisdell, 1990, Ch. 2). Those environmental effects that are external to the firm will not be taken into account unless the host government adopts certain policies, such as taxing the company on its unfavourable environmental spillovers. But since many LDCs are eager to attract foreign investment, and investors have alternative investment possibilities, most governments in LDCs are reluctant to impose environmental controls.

Loans can be an alternative or a supplement to direct foreign investment in a country. They may be made by private lenders, in which case they are purely commercial loans, or they may be made by foreign governments or by international bodies such as the IMF or the World Bank. In the latter case, the terms of the loans may not be entirely commercial. Nevertheless, borrowers should be reasonably sure that the benefits expected from the loan exceed its costs, and that they have the capacity to repay the loan without undue economic difficulty, on the basis of the agreed terms.

The capacity of a government to repay a foreign loan for a particular project does not depend solely on returns and cash flows from that particular project, but also on the government's overall foreign commitments. For example, the financial capacity of governments of some LDCs to repay other foreign loans was reduced because of their large foreign debt incurred for purchases of armaments (Bauer, 1989). Armament purchases resulted in a drain on foreign reserves and, although there is some debate about this issue, were largely unproductive, did little to relieve poverty and possibly had adverse conservation consequences both directly and indirectly (consider the environmental impact of the Gulf War). The World Bank has been reported to be considering refusing to make loans to governments of LDCs who have large defence expenditures in relation to their GDP.

Soft loans may be made by lenders when they expect an indirect spillover benefit. The World Bank, for example, provides some loans to countries at concessionary rates of interest, for projects which have global environmental benefits. These are the kind of projects which assist in maintaining biodiversity of worldwide value, or projects which help to reduce global pollution. Nevertheless, the World Bank will still require the benefits received by the borrowing country from the project and the loan, to equal or exceed the concessionary rate of interest charged.

In foreign aid, environmental and sustainability factors are being increasingly taken into account by donors, for example in bilateral aid.

The Australian International Development Assistance Bureau (AIDAB) has indicated that in giving aid, it will in the future place greater 'emphasis on the reduction of population growth, alleviation of poverty, the use of renewable resources, the sustainable management of natural resources, energy efficiency and pollution control' (AIDAB, 1990, p. 8).

While this new emphasis seems desirable, it is not without some difficulties. For example:

(1) Some LDCs complain that the effective amount of aid (or loans) made available to them is reduced because of the environmental conditions and costs imposed upon them. Some complain that their available funds go less far, and that their benefits, as a proportion of global benefits, are reduced. This is a complex matter and will be discussed later when global spillovers are considered.

(2) There can be problems in measuring and valuing environmental spillovers. To some extent, valuation methods are cultural specific. Western value systems are not universally accepted. There may also be a clash between what is locally predicted to be the environmental consequences of a project and foreign predictions of these consequences. The 'truth' may reside with neither party and *a priori* it may be impossible to decide which party is likely to be closest to the truth. Even though some conservationists have argued that empowerment of local groups will result in improved environmental decisions, this result does not always follow (Tisdell, 1991a). Neither local experience nor foreign expertise ensures the correct environmental answer even if such an answer exists. Therefore, despite its psychological inconvenience, some agnosticism about all sources of knowledge seems appropriate.

NATIONAL DEBT AND DEBT FOR NATURE SWAPS

While in recent years many LDCs have had a larger foreign debt than they have been able (or willing) to service, foreign debt can provide a net economic benefit to a borrowing country. This will be so if the economic yields from the foreign loan exceed its costs. The loan may, for example, enable capital equipment and technology unavailable at home, to be imported. As a result, it can help to speed up economic growth. After 1979, China began to rely increasingly on foreign loans to provide foreign imports to help in its modernisation.

In the short run, such economic growth may be unfavourable to the natural environment both because it accelerates natural resource utilisation and increases pollution, as a result of industrialisation and urbanisation. In the longer run, if such growth raises per capita incomes and reduces population growth it could be favourable to the environment and conservation. With rising incomes, the demand for improved environmental quality rises and the real cost of supplying it is likely to decline. Meanwhile, however, the environmental situation could well deteriorate. The question remains unanswered whether the globe can environmentally sustain the existing world population at the standard of living of the more developed countries. For example, the industrialisation of China and India can be expected to add substantially to carbon dioxide emissions and may accelerate greenhouse effects (Myers, et al., 1990).

The optimistic view is that LDCs can follow a similar path of development to the present developed countries, and that eventually this will be beneficial to the environment. The pessimistic view is that this policy is environmentally impossible or unsustainable. Therefore, from a global perspective, LDCs should be less ambitious in their economic growth objectives, and developed countries should to some extent reduce their pressures on natural resources in order to provide greater environmental scope for economic growth by LDCs. In addition, it is argued that environmentally defensive policies should be supported by such initiatives as family planning, re-afforestation, research into increased energy-use efficiency, and alternatives to carbon fuels. According to this view, the previous economic growth path pursued by developed countries is not available to the bulk of remaining LDCs for environmental reasons. Late starters are subject to negative externalities from early starters and that raises the question of whether these late starters should be compensated by the early ones.

The position of the Brundtland Report (World Commission on Environment and Development, 1987) on the issue of economic growth in LDCs being compatible with environmental sustainability, seems equivocal, although it claims that economic growth in LDCs is a precondition for successfully dealing with environmental concerns. Basically, its remedy is more economic growth but with an increase globally in environmentally defensive expenditure. As interpreted by the World Institute for Development Economics Research of the United Nations University, Helsinki, this seems to require greater economic growth both in developed and less developed countries, with defensive environmental expenditure being largely financed by the 'peace dividend'; the reduction in global defence expenditure made possible by new international relationships between countries belonging to the former Soviet Union, Eastern Europe and the rest of the world (Jayawardena, 1990).

The Brundtland position seems to be consistent with the broad view of the People's Republic of China which is probably typical of that for many LDCs. For example, leading members of the Institute of Economics, Chinese Academy of Social Sciences, Liu Guoguang, Liang Wensen and others (1987, p. 420) say: 'We advocate a line of action which requires that economic growth and environmental protection go hand in hand. There are two aspects to the relationship between economic growth and environmental protection: While they are mutually contradictory, they are also mutually complementary. Economic growth does bring along environmental problems, but it can also strengthen man's hand in tackling these very problems whose successful solution will, in turn, create more favourable conditions for economic growth. This fact has been fully borne out by the experiences a number of developed countries have gained in improving the environment.'

China's environmental protection policies are still evolving and the above-mentioned authors outline several measures which China could adopt to improve environmental protection. In relation to wild animals and plants they state: 'China abounds in wild animals and plants. It is estimated that the country has over 400 species of animals, 1,100 species of birds and nearly 30,000 species of higher plants. Many among them are of rare varieties. It is necessary to enact laws and regulations to give rare animals really effective protection. We anticipate that in the near future, the number of nature preserves will increase from the present 85 to over 300 so that rare animals and plants, already endangered or liable to harm by man, can be taken better care of', (Liu Guoguang, *et al.*, 1987, p. 433).

China has taken the step of drawing up a strategy for unsustainable development (State Council, 1994). In the future, greater attention is likely to be given to the economic benefits of better management of the environment in China. For example, with the extension of the market system in China, polluters may more frequently be required to pay for the environmental cost of their pollution (Hong et al., 1991). And with China's opening up to the outside world, scope exists for the country to attract more ecotourists interested in its rare animals and plants, and earn extra income from its conservation of natural areas. There is a need however to follow up such possibilities effectively.

To return however to the foreign debt issue, the foreign debt may involve:

(1) private lending to private borrowers in the borrowing country;
(2) private lending to the government in the borrowing country;
(3) non-private lending to the government in the borrowing country.

While in the first case only private risks are involved, failure to repay loans can influence foreign perceptions about the general credit-worthiness of a country. Increased foreign debt held by governments can have wider community effects, even though all such loans could speed up economic growth and/or in some circumstances add to inflationary pressures. If a government has difficulty in repaying a loan because of shortage of foreign exchange, it may ration other users of the nation's foreign exchange, or allow natural assets to be exploited at a faster rate than desirable in order to sell such products abroad and obtain the much needed foreign currency. For example, after the *coup d'état* in Fiji in the 1980s, foreign exchange became short and exports of clam meat from the already depleted natural stocks were allowed for a time in order to generate foreign money.

Especially when foreign loans are obtained for military purposes, those in power may be prepared to run down the capital and natural assets of a country for their own short-term goals, particularly if actual war is occurring or imminent, or if the army is important domestically in maintaining the ruling group in power. Thus, the effect of a foreign debt on resource conservation in a country depends upon several factors which must be considered simultaneously.

P.T. Bauer (1989) has argued that the foreign debt crisis is a misnomer, that in effect it is politically contrived and that servicing it would not have affected living standards substantially. He rejects as fantasies views that debt service is a major cause of Third World misery. He suggests that 'the crisis' has been used selectively to enhance the power of Western governments, the IMF and the World Bank. His trenchant comments should be noted but have yet to be empirically tested.

The fact is that several governments in LDCs, especially in Africa and South America, have been unable (or unwilling) to meet foreign debt commitments in recent years. This has provided opportunities for debt-for-nature swaps. An article in *The Wall Street Journal* (January 20, 1988) entitled 'What Do Monkeys in Bolivia have to Do with the Debt Crisis?' provides some details about a debt-for-nature swap involving the Bolivian Government, a Swiss bank and Conservation International, a Washington-based non-profit group. This conservation group purchased $650,000 of Bolivia's foreign debt from a Swiss bank for $100,000. It then swapped the $650,000 debt with the Bolivian government for an extension of 4 million acres to the El Porvenir conservation reserve, and the Bolivian government agreed to provide $250,000 in local currency for administration of the reserve and to retain Conservation International as an adviser. Apart from Bolivia, Costa Rica, Madagascar and Mexico have been involved in debt-for-nature swaps (*Financial Times*, 21 March, 1991, p. 6). On a global scale their impact on nature conservation appears to have been very small.

While debt-for-nature swaps do provide a means for greater conservation, first, it should not be overlooked that they are likely to impose some costs on the borrowing country, especially if the benefits perceived from the conservation go mainly to foreigners. Land used for conservation is likely to have some opportunity costs locally, although it is possible that both local and foreign interests could gain by such conservation projects. But we cannot assume that mutual benefit is always the case. Second, the areas or species targeted for conservation under debt-for-nature swaps are unlikely to be determined systematically but are more likely to be chosen piecemeal, as a result of social and political processes. Swaps will depend upon the existence, particular focus and relative drive of conservation groups.

MACROECONOMIC POLICIES – INFLATION, FULL EMPLOYMENT AND ECONOMIC GROWTH

For more than 50 years, macroeconomic issues have dominated economic policies. The main policy issues in economics have been perceived as those of controlling inflation, of achieving full employment of labour (or of, at least, avoiding unacceptably high levels of unemployment), attaining a high rate of economic growth, and maintaining a satisfactory balance of payments or external account situation.

Policies have been directed towards:

(1) increasing effective aggregate demand without fostering an unacceptably high rate of inflation;
(2) to expanding aggregate supplies of goods and services so as to dampen inflation, achieve greater economic growth and increase international competitiveness. The main interest of macroeconomists in microeconomic reform has been as a vehicle to expand aggregate supplies and increase international competitiveness, thereby raising exports.

Many economists in government departments traditionally concerned with macroeconomic policy, such as the Treasury in Australia, often appear unsympathetic to conservation and environmental goals, or believe that they could be removed from their arena by sufficient 'market-making' for environmental goods and services. In fact this may be because conservation groups frequently ignore:

(1) the budgetary costs of their proposals;
(2) the opportunity costs of implementing them. Traditionally, neither Keynesians nor monetarists (nor for that matter most neoclassical economists) saw environmental issues as being of major economic significance and they usually have little sympathy with the views of neo-Malthusians.

This lack of sympathy seems to have two bases:

(1) doubt about the factual basis of the neo-Malthusian position;
(2) support of diametrically opposite policies, that is of pro-growth versus zero- or low-economic-growth policies. These economists may show even greater hostility to non-anthropocentric considerations in economic policy because economics, as it has evolved, is fundamentally anthropocentric in focus.

Harris' (1991) view, mentioned earlier, should also be noted here; that international organisations such as the IMF and World Bank (International Bank for Reconstruction and Development) are basically oriented towards economic growth because of their historical macroeconomic background. Despite Harris' view, there is little doubt that the World Bank has been paying greater attention to environmental issues in the last few years, even though some observers might still suggest that this attention is peripheral. But I do not intend to make a judgment at this point.

The political reality seems to be that few individuals are prepared to follow the prescriptions suggested, for example, by Daly (1980). Few individuals are prepared to limit or reduce their level of consumption – most still want to increase it. In modern economies and in the modern sectors of LDCs, wages tend to be inflexible downwards and to creep upwards over time. This creates difficulties for maintaining employment levels unless economic growth is always forthcoming. The structure of modern economies gives rise to this fundamental employment problem – a problem which requires continuing economic growth to avoid increasing unemployment.

Many LDCs are developing the same structure. In most a dual economy exists and so this problem is already present in urban or modernised areas. Western economists are encouraging the further development of this system, encouraging the remaining subsistence sectors and socialist countries to join the cash-market economy.

How to maintain full or near full employment and satisfy income aspirations, without creating environmental problems and ecological disaster, still remains the major policy issue to be solved. It may be that all these goals cannot be satisfied simultaneously. Still too many people want to have their income-employment aspirations met and hope to satisfy, as if by a miracle, all their conservation-environmental goals without any trade-off. We must give more attention to this fundamental issue. Should there be more job-sharing in developed countries to reduce unemployment and not raise production? Should service industries which make few demands on natural resources, be encouraged? Should individuals give more attention to the 'profitable' use of their leisure-time and should educational systems compared to current practice, provide more training for leisure relative to that for work?

GLOBAL ENVIRONMENTAL SPILLOVERS AND THE ECONOMIC SYSTEM

It has been said that the world has become a global village from an environmental point of view. Economic activities in a single country often have direct environmental impacts upon or consequences for other countries. Consider for example, acid rains, nuclear pollution, greenhouse gases, loss of biodiversity and loss of existence, option and bequest values as a result of the loss of natural environments and species of worldwide significance. Environmental spillovers may not only be of consequence for the country in which they arise but are often of much wider import (Tisdell, 1990, Ch. 4; 1991b, Ch. 4).

In relation to aid and soft loans, donors are paying much more attention to the environmental consequences of projects which they support. While broadly this is desirable from an economic viewpoint, leaders in some LDCs have expressed dissatisfaction with aspects of this emphasis. They have claimed that the net benefits to an aid recipient may be reduced by such considerations, given that a fixed aid allocation is available. It is suggested that an increased amount of aid is necessary, to compensate for the 'extra costs' imposed on LDCs or aid recipients for having to take environmental factors into account; for example, land which now must be kept undeveloped, and extra environmental protection controls on factories. But this assumes that the aid recipient loses when such allowance is made for the environmental effects, in allocating funds for economic projects. While this is possible, it is by no means the only possible outcome. A range of possible global welfare consequences as summarised in Table 6.1, exists for systems which take environmental factors into account in distributing aid funds. The welfare changes are evaluated in relation to aid policies which do not pay particular attention to environmental considerations. In Table 6.1, the second column lists the sign of the possible welfare change in the country given aid (LDC) and the third column, that in the rest of the world as a result of environmentally sensitive aid. The fourth column indicates the change in global welfare when the Paretian criterion is used, (namely, welfare increases in this context provided one country at least is made better off without another being made worse off).

Table 6.1   Distribution of possible net gains from environmentally sensitive aid policies and global welfare consequences using the Paretian criterion

Possibility	Net Benefit to Aid Recipient (LDC)	Net Benefit to Rest of World	Global Welfare Change*
1	+	+	+
2	+	0	+
3	+	−	?
4	−	+	?
5	−	0	−
6	−	−	−
7	0	+	+
8	0	0	0
9	0	−	−

* Using the Paretian Criterion

Leaders in some LDCs are concerned that possibility (4) will prevail. This involves a redistribution of welfare in favour of the rest of the (developed) world if environmentally sensitive aid programmes are followed. In this case, the net welfare benefits received by LDCs from aid will decline unless greater aid is supplied. However, as can be seen, cases (1)–(3) are also possibilities. In these cases, environmentally sensitive aid policies increase the welfare of recipients of aid. We cannot *a priori* rule out any of the sets of possibilities in Table 6.1, not even possibility (6). Possibility (6) may arise, for example, if the environmental consequences of projects are inaccurately or falsely predicted.

Of course, Table 6.1 glosses over many problems of evaluation and it should be observed that the Paretian criterion is essentially anthropocentric as are most existing economic evaluation criteria. Nevertheless, it does highlight some of the international distribution issues raised by environmentally sensitive aid policies.

CONCLUSIONS

Relationships between the global economic system, conservation and the provision and safeguarding of protected areas are complex. In its early stages, economic growth and the extension of the market system seem to be detrimental to the conservation of natural living resources, even though, in the medium term, such changes may result in an improvement of environmental quality judged from a human perspective. In the longer run, such developments may be increasingly beneficial for environmental protection. Thus to recapitulate, economic development in its early stages, may be. unfavourable to the state of the environment whereas development in its later stages may be favourable. Unfortunately a number of environmental changes which occur during the earlier stages, such as extinction of particular species, are irreversible at the later stages.

But if it were true that economic development eventually results in a more favourable attitude to the environment, it does not follow that economic growth is feasible for all nations. The global environment may not be able to support the level of economic production which would be required to raise the per capita income of populations in LDCs to the same level as that in developed countries. Indeed, environmental limits to economic growth may be reached well before this required level of global economic production is attained (Cf. Culbertson, 1971). We still have to come to terms with this possibility.

This is not to say that the early stages of economic growth and extension of the market system need to be as destructive of the environment as in the past. We are now more aware of the types of adverse environmental consequences that may occur, and have a clearer picture of circumstances in which state intervention in the development process and extension of the market system is justified. Incidentally, in this regard we should not discount the possibility that state intervention to achieve environmental goals is likely to be easier or more effective in a market system than in a relatively centralised socialist system.

This all suggests that we need economic policies specifically targeted to conservation of living natural resources. In particular, we realise that we cannot rely solely on broadbrush macroeconomic or even microeconomic policies, such as those recently supported by the IMF and the World Bank. Furthermore, we are still far from resolving the basic conflict between objectives of traditional macroeconomic policy and those objectives espoused by conservationists favouring steady-state economies or reduced rates of economic growth. Greater employment and rising incomes still remain high on political agendas, and those in employment do not seem to be very ready to share their jobs and their incomes with the unemployed, or to accept lower incomes for conservationist ends. This may be for several reasons:

(1) individuals may not believe that rising incomes have environmental consequences;
(2) they may take the view that only humanity should count and although other species may suffer, rising incomes may on balance have positive consequences for humanity;
(3) it may be universally accepted that rising incomes will have collective adverse consequences for humanity but individual selfishness may lead individuals to follow the income-raising path.

This is an example of a prisoner's dilemma problem – a case in which rational pursuit of individual self-interest conflicts with the collective self-interest. One example is the felling of the Amazon's rainforests.

Finally, observe that there is considerable discussion in the literature about improvement and deterioration in the conservation of natural resources without very much attention to the concept itself. How do we decide, for instance, whether conservation has increased if that of some resources, such as soil, improves but that of others declines. For example, if increased agricultural prices lead to greater conservation of soils used for agriculture, but result in extension of agriculture at the expense of survival of species or preservation of natural areas, does this constitute greater conservation? Biological diversity itself has not been a major focus in the structural adjustment debate. This matter does not appear to have been effectively addressed either in Sebastian and Alicbusan's (1989) review of the World Bank's adjustment lending operations or a similar review of the Asian Development Bank by Hansen (1990b). However, it is now more widely recognised that economic and environmental interconnections are rather more complex than were initially recognised.

NOTES

1. This suggests the need to develop or apply a suitable environmental quality, conservation or biodiversity index. The possibility of adapting Daly and Cobb's sustainability index to measure environmental change might be considered (Daly and Cobb, 1989, pp. 401–55) as well as the scope for using natural resource accounting methods. But it may be that a new index is needed which gives greater importance to the maintenance of biodiversity as a goal. I have suggested in Alauddin and Tisdell (1997, Ch. 2) that the human development index might be modified to create a new index which takes account of biodiversity as well as indicators of human conditions.

REFERENCES

Alauddin, M. and C.A. Tisdell (1997), *The Environment and Economic Development in South Asia*, London: MacMillan.

Anon (1991), 'The global environmental facility', *Finance and Development*, March 1991, p. 24, Washington: IMF and World Bank.

Australian International Development Assistance Bureau (1990), 'Ecologically sustainable development in international development cooperation', *AIDAB Discussion Paper*, November.

Bauer, P.T. (1989), 'The third world debt crisis: can't pay or won't pay?', Seminar Paper delivered to Department of Economics, University of Melbourne, 11 November, 1989. Mimeo.

Culbertson, J.M. (1971), *Economic Development – An Ecological Approach*, New York: Knopf.

Daly, H. (1980), *Economics, Ecology, Ethics*, San Francisco: Freeman.

Frank, A.G. (1971), *Capitalism and Underdevelopment in Latin America*, Hammondsworth: Pelican.

Georgescu-Roegen, N. (1976), *Energy and Economic Myths: Institutional and Analytical Economic Essays*, New York: Pergamon Press.

Hansen, S. (1990a), 'Macroeconomic policies: incidence on the environment.', paper presented at the Overseas Development Institute Conference on *The Environment, Development and Economic Research* at Regent's College, London, March 27–28, 1990.

Hansen, S. (1990b), *Environmental Considerations in Program Lending*, Environment Division, Manila, Philippines: Asian Development Bank.

Hansen, S. (1990c), 'Macroeconomic Policies and Sustainable Development in the Third World', *Journal of International Development*, 2(4), 533–57.

Harris, J.M. (1991), 'Global institutions and ecological crisis', *World Development*, 9(1), 111–22.

Hong Zhiyong, Bao Keguang and C. Tisdell (1991), 'Cadmium exposure in Daye County, China: environmental assessment and management, health and economic effects' *Environmental Management and Health*, 2(2), 20–5.

IUCN-UNEP-WWF (1991), *Caring for the Earth: a study for sustainability*, IUCN, Gland, Switzerland.

Jayawardena, L. (1990), 'The mission of the university in economic development and environmental preservation: management of local and regional resources in an interdependent world system', paper presented to the *Ninth General Conference of the International Association of Universities*, Helsinki, August, 1990. Mimeo, World Institute for Development Economics Research, United Nations University Helsinki.

Klee, G.A. (1980), *World Systems of Traditional Resource Management*, London: Edward Arnold.

Leopold, A. (1996), *A Sand Country Almanac*, New York: Oxford University Press.

Liu Guoguang, Liang Wensen and others (1987), *China's Economy in 2000*, Beijing: New World Press.

Lutz, E. (1990), 'Agricultural trade liberalisation, price changes and environmental effects', *Environmental Policy and Research Division,* Working Paper No. 1990–16, Washington: The World Bank.

Lutz, E. and Young, M. (1992), 'Integration of environmental concerns into agricultural policies of industrial and developing countries', *World Development*, **20**(2), 241–53.

Mearns, R. (1991), 'Environmental implications of structural adjustment: reflections on scientific method', *Institute of Development Studies Discussion Paper No. 284*, Brighton: Institute of Development Studies, University of Sussex.

Myrdal, G. (1956), *On International Economy: Problems and Prospects*, London: Routledge and Kegan Paul.

Myers, N., Ehrlich, P.R. and A. Ehrlich (1993), 'The Population Problem: as Explosive as Ever?', in Nicholas Polunin and John Burnett (eds), *Surviving With The Biosphere: Proceedings of the Fourth International Conference on Environmental Future (4th ICEF)*, held in Budapest, Hungary, during 22-27 April 1990, UK: Edinburgh University Press.

Schor, J.B. (1991), 'Global equity and environmental crisis: an argument for reducing working loans in the north', *World Development*, **19**(1), 73–84.

Schumacher, E.F. (1973), *Small is Beautiful: A Study of Economics as if People Mattered*, London: Blond and Briggs.

Sebastian, I. and A. Alicbusan (1989), 'Sustainable development: issues in adjustment lending policies', *Environment Department Divisional Working Papers 1989–6*, Washington, DC: The World Bank.

State Council (1994), *China's Agenda 21 – White Paper on China's Population, Environment and Development in the 21st Century*, Beijing: China Environmental Science Press.

Tisdell, C.A. (1990), *Natural Resources, Growth and Development*, New York: Praeger.

Tisdell, C.A. (1991a), 'Project appraisal, the environment and sustainability for small islands', a paper presented at an *International Conference on Islands and Small States*, Foundation for International Studies, University of Malta, 23–25 May, 1991.

Tisdell, C.A. (1991b), *Economics of Environmental Conservation*, Amsterdam: Elsevier Science Publishers.

Tisdell, C.A. and T.I. Fairbairn (1984), 'Sustainable economics and unsustainable development and trade: some simple theory', *Journal of Development Studies*, **20**, 227–41.

Toffler, A. (1970), *Future Shock*, London: The Bodley Head.

World Commission on Environment and Development (1987), *Our Common Future*, Oxford: Oxford University Press.

Yellen, J.E. (1990), 'The transformation of the Kalahari King!', *Scientific American*, 72–9, April.

7. Ranking Requests for Financial Support for Protected Areas

INTRODUCTION

The previous chapter argues that non-market methods are needed to support the provision of protected areas, in order to preserve biodiversity. Funds must be supplied by governments or by private donations for this purpose. International agencies of a quasi-public nature, as well as associations of private individuals and groups have grown up for the purpose of gathering funds for conservation and distributing these internationally. Such agencies and applicants for these funds are faced with a number of economic issues which are discussed in this chapter.

International aid and funding agencies usually receive more requests to support conservation proposals than can be met by their available funds, and therefore have to rank their applications. A checklist of questions or factors, which may be taken into account by funding agencies in prioritising inter-country and inter-regional requests, is given in this chapter. The mechanics of allocation of funds on the basis of net economic benefits are discussed and limitations of the cost-benefit approach are noted. A list of factors likely to favour the selection of particular projects is presented. Communicators should take those into account in framing proposals and approaching funding agencies. The possibility of non-economic and strategic factors influencing the distribution of funds for support of protected areas is discussed here.

International aid and funding agencies supporting conservation projects financially are often faced with the need to rank conservation proposals received from different countries and regions. To assign priorities to these is no easy task. In part, the way in which competing proposals are ranked will depend on the charter or aim of the funding organization. Some bodies or associations, such as societies for the preservation of birds, may have a relatively narrow focus in terms of the conservation projects to which they will give financial support. For example, they may only provide support for projects aimed at conserving particular species of birds. They are likely to give particular weight to this aspect rather than to more general types of benefits from conservation of protected areas. On the other hand, organizations such as the World Bank, in distributing loans from its available funds from the Global Environmental Facility (GEF), may have primarily economic criteria in mind in allocating their funds. Clearly, those seeking funds would be well advised in framing and communicating their proposals to potential providers of funds to take into account the guidelines or criteria of funders. Not only should such considerations influence the way in which proposals are presented, but they should also influence the bodies that are worth approaching about particular proposals. A number of basic economic and managerial questions are likely to be asked or considered by most funding agencies before providing funds for a project.

BASIC QUESTIONS LIKELY TO BE CONSIDERED BY FUNDING AGENCIES

Before providing funds for conservation projects, funding agencies may consider the following questions:

(1) Have the costs of the project for which funding is sought been realistically determined?
(2) Have the objectives of the conservation proposal been clearly specified and the reasons given for seeking the funds?
(3) Is the success of the project dependent upon funds being available from other funding sources apart from the funding agency being approached? What is the likelihood of these complementary funds being raised?
(4) Are there sources of funds within the country which could yet be tapped?
(5) Will funding by the agency lead to a significant reduction in financial support from local sources, or will it add to such support?
(6) What ability do those managing the conservation project have to carry it out successfully?
(7) Are there good prospects for sufficient financial support for the completed project to maintain or manage it on completion?

If funds are not likely to be available for maintenance of the project after its implementation, then it will not be sustainable. An article in *Ecologica* by Brian Houseal (1992) highlights this problem. He claims that there is a typical financial cycle for the establishment of protected areas and this involves three phases:

(1) planning;
(2) implementation;
(3) management or maintenance.

In his view, the planning stage usually takes 3–4 years with the implementation stage commencing around the fifth year and lasting 3–5 years beyond that. After this, from approximately the tenth year onwards, the long-term management plan begins and this basically involves maintenance of the project. He claims that it is only during the implementation phase that international funding is likely to be available as a major source of finance. The planning and management phases must, as a rule, depend mainly on local finance. The typical outlay-pattern suggested by Houseal for a conservation project is indicated in Figure 7.1.

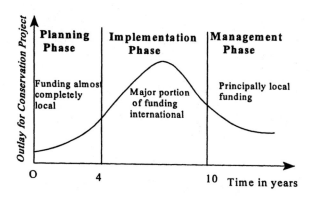

Figure 7.1 Typical cycle of outlays and funding for conservation projects as suggested by Houseal (1992)

As Houseal points out, the length of the stages of a project may vary from project to project. However, the variation could be even greater than he has indicated. If the project, for example, involves the development of a new national park in a remote area and this requires access roads, buildings and exclusion fencing to be constructed, the implementation phase may take much longer than 3–5 years. Furthermore, much depends upon how narrowly or widely one defines a conservation project. For example, the Project Tiger in India involves many sub-projects but even the sub-projects are often major ones. For instance, the implementation phase for Project Tiger in the Sundarbans of West Bengal, could have taken more than five years for all associated works to be completed. At the Sudhanyakhali Watch Tower Complex in the Sundarbans, not only had the watchtower to be built but a dam closer to the tower had to be constructed to attract wildlife; lodges and other accommodation were also built and 'clearways' (wide pathways in which vegetation has been removed) radiating from the watchtower had to be completed.

In some cases, the management or maintenance phase of the project is of vital importance and should be seriously considered for international financial support. For example, the Forest Department of West Bengal operates a captive breeding programme for saltwater crocodiles *Crocodylus porosus*, and olive Ridley turtles *Lepidochelys olivacea*, at Bhagabatpur in the Sundarbans. The purpose is to build up captive populations by breeding and to release progeny to the wild in the Sundarbans, for restocking of depleted natural populations. While considerable capital cost has been involved in establishing hatchery, nursery areas and enclosures for the breeding of captive stocks, a high level of costs and management expertise are needed in operating the complex successfully. Therefore, there is a case for international financial assistance for the management phase. The complex has obtained some international assistance from the World Wide Fund for Nature in its implementation and management phases. This assistance was first made available in 1982.

OBSERVATIONS ON ECONOMICS AND ALLOCATION OF FUNDS

If the benefits of all competing conservation projects could be quantified in terms of monetary values, then the process of allocating available funds in order to maximize global benefit would be relatively straightforward. Projects with the highest benefit-cost ratio would be preferred.

However, actual quantification is difficult. For one thing, it may not be possible to quantify all benefits and express these in monetary terms. In such cases, economists traditionally proceed by identifying (in conjunction with scientists or specialists) the favourable and unfavourable effects of a project;, quantifying those that they can and expressing the benefits and costs of these in monetary values. Using these monetary values gives a first ranking. On the basis of the economic analysis, projects which have the highest benefit-to-cost ratios based on estimated monetary values, are preferred. Ranking of projects is in direct line with these ratios. This ranking may then subsequently be altered to take account of values which are not captured by the economic analysis. This could however introduce considerable subjectivity. Nevertheless, in some cases the 'preference' ordering of alternatives, based on economic valuations, will be the same or similar to that based on more general considerations. In these cases, the economic evaluation reinforces the general valuation.

In practice, estimates of costs and benefits are likely to be uncertain. One should ask how accurate are the assessments? Furthermore, how sensitive are they to variations in any of the parameters, or the most important assumptions. For example, the economic benefit of a project might be predicted to be an increase in the net receipts from visitors to the protected area. But how sensitive is the predicted increase in net receipts to variation in the predicted increase in visitors to the area? In general, estimates should be subjected to sensitivity analysis.

After such probing, some projects may still have a very high benefit-to-cost ratio and therefore be given a high priority. They may be doubly acceptable on economic and other grounds.

While it would not be appropriate to discuss the matter in depth here, the question arises of what data, economic and otherwise, should be collected, analysed and presented. There is a need for an appropriate balance in the type of data collected and analysed. Economic assessments are frequently reliant on inputs of biological and non-economic data for the valuation process. Therefore, an appropriate balance needs to be struck in collecting economic and non-economic data and analysing it (Tisdell, 1983; 1993, Ch. 9).

Furthermore, different types of economic data can be collected and analysed. Some benefits may be tangible, for example, increased net revenue from visitors to a protected area, and other benefits intangible, for example, existence and bequest value (McNeely, 1988; McNeely *et al.*, 1990, Ch. 2; Tisdell, 1991; DeGroot, 1992). Alternatively, benefits may be classified according to whether they are obtained on-site by visiting the protected area or are off-site benefits.

For some purposes, it may also be important to specify the level of economic benefits appropriated by the authority managing the protected area, by the locality in which the protected area exists, or by the nation in which it exists. If benefits on a global scale are considerable but the protected area, or the host region is unable to appropriate these to any great extent, then there is a strong case for an international subsidy or grant for the area or for adopting special economic measures to ensure greater appropriation of benefits by the host region; for example, by ensuring the employment of a high proportion of local people in the management of the conservation area.

Usually, available funding for international conservation projects is limited in relation to the demand and qualifying projects. But it is possible, due to special circumstances, for funding in relation to a particular country or conservation objective to exceed absorptive capacity. In the case of GEF (the Global Environmental Facility) funds from the World Bank, it has been suggested that size of these funds and their rapid availability made it difficult for countries such as Brazil and Bhutan to absorb them most effectively for conservation ends; particularly since the funds were only available for a comparatively short term, that is around three years. From the viewpoint of the countries concerned, a smaller sum per year over a longer time period would probably have been more effective. GEF funding seemed initially to be donor-driven and may have been inspired by the political motive of appealing to the electorate in more developed countries. A trust-type fund or more even funding over a longer period is likely to be more productive from a conservation viewpoint. Donors should take this into account in their funding arrangements.

In calculating benefits, economists have traditionally put questions of income distribution to one side. Benefits are usually estimated given the existing distribution of income and by supposing initially that a unit of money is of the same value to everyone. At a later stage, weights may be introduced to take account of changes in income distribution. For example, a dollar increase in income for a poor person may be counted as $1.50 (given a weight of 1.5) compared with an increase of a dollar in income for a rich person. This weighting, however, involves value judgements.

In some cases, it might even be supposed that the only benefits that count for this exercise are those appropriated by the citizens of the country in which the conservation project is implemented. But this is an extreme assumption. A case can be made out for an international funding agency taking into account benefits not only to residents of a recipient country but also to citizens in other countries, even if a lower weight is put on benefits to citizens from other countries than on gains to local residents. Within the country, benefits appropriated by the poor might be given a higher weight than those received by the rich. Benefits to those in the protected area or its vicinity may also be given an extra weighting. There can be a good deal of argument about the appropriate weightings to assign. However, projects which favour the poor and those located in or near parks or protected areas possibly should be preferred, given prevailing sentiments.

Benefits to the poor, or those located in or near protected areas, from investment in parks are not always immediately obvious. Park facilities and complexes can provide infrastructure which can be used by locals, for example, a convenient place for holding meetings, or a useful facility for more rapid communication with the outside world. The park complex at Sudhanyakhali in the Indian Sundarbans, comprising buildings, cleared areas, pathways, electricity generation units, wharves and so on, is used by Hindus in the area to stage their annual festival in the honour of the Goddess-of-the-Forest. Locals come long distances to participate in this festival, which caters to local culture not tourists.

This is not to say that local residents do not constitute serious problems for conservation management in many parks and protected areas. Black kid goats *Capris hircus,* observed by the author, looked innocent enough but they belonged to 'squatters' in a protected part of the Indian Sundarbans, and were a part of a larger herd which is out grazing in the protected area. To provide economic benefits to such squatters may attract others to share them. The problem of squatting in, and immigration to, protected areas is a serious and politically sensitive one in many developing countries. It is especially troublesome given the need for local support for protected areas (Cf. Dahuri, 1992).

From what has been said so far, conservation projects likely to be favoured with international financial support are which those have the following features:

(1) are well presented;
(2) have capable managers;
(3) provide benefits for local people, especially the poor and those in protected areas or their vicinity;
(4) are expected to attract continuing financial support;
(5) provide positive net economic benefits;
(6) are incapable of being financed without international aid.

A NOTE ON COMMUNICATING REQUESTS FOR FINANCE

The importance of sound communication by managers of protected areas in their efforts to obtain finance, has been stressed by Ralph Cobham (1992). Economic factors should be borne in mind, and in communicating requests for finance for a conservation project, account should be taken of the following:

(1) the values of the targeted audience;
(2) the time available to them to consider proposals;
(3) the concepts which they do and do not understand.

Proposals appealing to values not shared by the targeted audience, presented in great detail, requiring much time to grasp, and if introducing concepts not understood by the audience, are unlikely to be successful.

Often there are variations in the ability of the audience to understand material or spend time on it. This can be overcome by the use of a summary general proposal, with more detailed material on the proposal being available to those who want to delve further into it. To some extent, the detail in a proposal should also be tailored to the circumstance. In relation to some funds, only broad information is required initially; detailed information is called for once the proposal is being seriously considered.

But no matter what the values of the audience are, most like to see value for money. Most donors giving funds, or financiers providing funds at concessional rates, like to believe that they will see a good return on their money. Whether or not they feel this is the case, is going to depend upon the nature of the presentation of the proposal and other factors.

In relation to value for money, there are basically two ways in which one can proceed from an economics point of view:

(1) To show that the objectives for which the funds are sought will be achieved at minimum cost, that is, without waste. For example, that biological diversity will be maintained at a low cost, or that the method proposed is a low-cost method of saving an endangered species.
(2) To show that there are positive economic benefits from the project(s) proposed, at least some of which can be quantified. It may

be possible to show that these will exceed costs or, if not, that they are substantial, and that together with the non-economic advantages of the proposal, make the proposal attractive.

However, some funders – for example those making loans to a conservation body – will be most interested in the extra net income which the protected area can generate and which may be appropriated by the protection body. In such cases, attention needs to be given to specifying the pososible economic benefits for the protection body.

For some purposes, it may be sufficient to state the projects intended for support, and their basic purpose, and to give a realistic estimate of cost. This approach has been taken by The Bahamas National Trust (1992) in presenting its prospectus for financial support by establishing a heritage fund.

DISCUSSION AND CONCLUDING COMMENTS

As noted earlier, not all funding agencies are likely to take an economic point of view or even an entirely anthropocentric one in allocating funds. Some may have as their aim the presentation of particular life forms. Their aim is to save those life forms which they find most valuable in relation to the cost involved. In essence, they are philanthropists who impose their values on others by sacrificing their own resources. But even they are affected by economics. For example, a conservation organization may want to save two species, X and Y, but its resources may be insufficient to save both, given the proposals available to it. It will then have to make a decision about which of the species to save. But if more cost effective management or methods of conservation of the species could be adopted, the agency might be able to save both. So the economics of management of protected areas, and the efficiency of conservation techniques adopted, will be of interest even to an agency which has ecocentric rather than anthropocentric goals.

Strategic factors can also influence funding by international agencies. For example, the imminence of loss may be a consideration. Areas which are under greatest immediate threat from economic development may be targeted for conservation support. A number of conservation agencies in the USA have adopted this approach. They have concentrated on applying political pressure for the establishment of marine national parks in areas where the granting of leases for seabed oil mining have either been imminent or have constituted an immediate threat. At first sight this may not seem to be an economic approach, but a realistic political one given the irreversibility factor. However, it can also be regarded as an economic approach if the aim of the protection body is to obtain maximum gains from using its available funds or resources for promoting conservation. In pursuing their objectives, conservation bodies should take into account the plans, actions and behaviour of other decision-makers in society and design their strategies with these in mind. While timely intervention by conservationists may not stop imminent development, it may enable a compromise solution to be reached.

Although the decisions by international funding and aid agencies about whether to support conservation projects financially should be influenced by economic factors, these are unlikely to be the only considerations. To some extent, donors like to impose their own value judgements, (for example in favour of biodiversity *per se* or maintenance of particular species), and are willing to fund projects which they believe have value in that regard. Many funders consider conservation generally, or the conservation of particular living things, as merit goods and this must be recognised. Such funders are often described in the literature as ecocentric. Where an individual or group believes that a particular 'commodity' is a merit good, they regard its supply as meritorious and attempt to influence social choice in favour of provision of more of the good in question.

Even those funders with an apparent non-economic bent, (for example, espousing ecocentric ethics), cannot, as pointed out above, afford to ignore economics if they want value for money. Ideally, they would like to see their objectives pursued at minimum cost and this requires efficient management of projects. Nevertheless, some conservation projects may be funded even when the projects are not efficiently managed. Of course, one would like management to be efficient in the sense of achieving desired results at minimum cost, or almost so. But the level of expertise and social structure in some countries may not allow this in the time required for the conservation action. Provided a positive net conservation benefit is achieved from this funding, this may be sufficient to justify the project. Up to a point we have to live with the world as it is, 'warts and all', and sometimes fund conservation projects which are executed rather less efficiently than is technically possible.

To conclude: there is little doubt that factors involving environmental economics are becoming increasingly important in the allocation of finance for the support of nature conservation projects, especially between countries and regions. The increasing involvement of bodies like the World Bank and a number of government international aid agencies, in providing financial support for such projects, is reinforcing this process because, given the limited availability of funds, priorities have to be established as objectively as possible, particularly since public accountability is required of such bodies. Furthermore, the Convention on Biological Diversity, agreed upon at the Rio Conference (5 June, 1992), has now come into effect and involves the provision of additional financial resources by developed countries for biodiversity conservation by developing countries (Article 20). The distribution of these funds is likely to be influenced, at least partially, by economic and social criteria. This is not to suggest that environmental economic guidelines can be mechanically applied to ranking financial proposals, nor that they should be the final arbiter in relation to nature conservation projects. Nevertheless, they have become an important factor in project evaluation and financial decision-making in relation to projects for protected areas. Managers of such areas are increasingly being forced to consider these factors. While the use of such guidelines does not mean that economists displace park managers and natural scientists in the evaluation of projects, park managers need to increase their awareness of such guidelines.

REFERENCES

Cobham, R. (1992), 'Communication with funders: developing an investment portfolio'. A contribution to Workshop 1.14, IVth World Congress on National Parks and Protected Areas, Venezuela, 10–21 February, 1992.

Dahuri, R. (1992), 'Dynamic Interactions Between Regional Development and Kutai National Park, East Kalimantan, Indonesia', J.M. Willison, S. Bondrup–Nielsen, C. Drysdale, T.B. Herman, N.W.P. Munro and T.L. Pollock, (eds), *Science and the Management of Protected Areas*, 55–62, Amsterdam: Elsevier.

De Groot, Rudolf (1992), 'Functions and values of protected areas: a comprehensive framework for assessing the benefits of protected areas to human society'. A contribution to Workshop 1.2 IVth World Congress on National Parks and Protected Areas, Caracas, Venezuela, 10–21 February, 1992.

Houseal, B. (1992), 'The cost of conserving', *Ecologica,* January/February 9: 6–9.

McNeely, J.A. (1988), *Economics and Biological Diversity: Developing and Using Economic Incentives to Conserve Biological Resources*, Gland, Switzerland: IUCN,.

McNeely, J.A.; J.N. Miller, W.V. Reid, R.A. Mittermier and R.B. Werner (1990), *Conserving the World's Biological Diversity*, Gland, Switzerland: IUCN, WRI, CI, WWF–US and Washington, DC: The World Bank.

The Bahamas National Trust (1992), *The Heritage Fund*, Nassau, Bahamas.

Tisdell, C.A. (1983), 'Cost-benefit Analysis with Particular Reference to Biological Resources', *Economic and Environment Policy: the Role of Cost-benefit Analysis*, 65–70, Canberra, Australia: Department of Home Affairs and Environment Australian Government Publishing Service.

Tisdell, C.A. (1991), *Economics of Environmental Conservation*, Amsterdam: Elsevier Science Publishers.

Tisdell, C.A. (1993), *Environmental Economics*, Aldershot, UK: Edward Elgar.

8. Ecotourism, Economics and the Environment

INTRODUCTION

There are generally few opportunities to earn income from protected areas. Therefore, as pointed out in the previous chapter, constant problems arise in financing their establishment and management. Ecotourism provides one of the few opportunities to earn income from them and its potential is considered in this chapter.

With growing interest in nature conservation, interest in the economic possibilities of ecotourism has increased. The appeal of ecotourism is that it may allow nature conservation and economic gain to be combined, thereby providing an economic incentive for nature conservation. The original World Conservation Strategy (IUCN, 1980) pointed out that nature-based tourism may provide a means by which developing countries may at least recoup some of the costs of conservation of biodiversity. Now that the Convention for Biological Diversity has come into effect, the questions of how to finance conservation of biodiversity, and to compensate local communities for reduced access to nature resources, have assumed increasing importance. These are important issues for China, which was one of the first signatories to the Convention.

Their importance is recognised in China: Biodiversity Conservation Action Plan (Xie Zhenhua et al., 1994). Prospects are explored for using nature-based tourism to provide income and employment to local communities located near or in protected areas, such as those in Xishuangbanna (Cf. Zhenhua et al., 1994, p. 84).

Tourism is one of the largest industries in the world and continues to grow strongly. It has in fact been growing at the fastest rate in the Asia-Pacific region (Tisdell, 1994). Nature tourism, also known as ecotourism, is an expanding segment of the tourism market. Lindberg (1991) estimated that developing countries earned US$12 billion from nature tourism in 1988. McNeely *et al.* (1992, p. 6) point out that 'Tourism to natural areas is economically important in many developing countries. In virtually all tropical areas, the attractions of nature are used in tourism promotion irrespective of whether national parks are appropriately developed for tourism. In the countries with particularly outstanding natural attractions, tourism is often used as the primary justification for the creation of national parks'.

One of the problems in determining the economic value of ecotourism is to know exactly what is meant by the term. As Valentine (1992) points out, many writers have used the term in different ways. McNeely *et al.* (1992) use the terms 'nature-tourism' and 'ecotourism' interchangeably and say that 'it is defined as tourism that involves travelling to relatively undisturbed natural areas with the specific object of studying, admiring and enjoying the scenery and its wild plants and animals as well as any existing cultural aspects (both of the past and present) found in those areas' (p. 2). Given this definition, many parts of Yunnan, especially Xishuangbanna Nature Reserve, have considerable potential for development for ecotourism purposes, both because of the extent of biodiversity present and because of varied cultural aspects. However, some definitions of ecotourism limit it to tourism based primarily on living natural things. A third definition is based upon the view that any type of tourism that is careful of its impact on the natural environment is ecotourism. This is, in effect, what one may call 'environmentally sensitive' tourism whereas the first set of definitions relate to environmentally dependent tourism. Tourism which is both dependent on the natural living environment and which takes particular care of it would satisfy both definitions. Some individuals restrict ecotourism to this set of circumstances.

The conceptual relationship can be seen from the Venn diagram shown in Figure 8.1. Set A represents tourism which is dependent on natural environments and set B covers tourism (including non-nature based tourism) which is sensitive to environmental considerations. The overlapping set or intersection of the sets (C = A ∩ B) shown as a hatched area, represents tourism that both depends on natural environments and which involves environmental care. It should be noted that environmentally-based tourism which fails to take care of its environment is doomed in the long-run. When such tourism destroys its prime attraction, it becomes unsustainable.

One may also consider whether there is a difference between ecotourism and nature-based tourism. It can be argued that ecotourism is tourism which depends mainly on living things in natural systems. If so, it would exclude tourism that is primarily geologically based or based on natural geographical physical features; for example, visits to volcanoes and some types of adventure tourism which primarily use natural physical features, such as mountaineering and rafting. In practice, it is difficult to draw a hard-and-fast line because many natural areas can be used for multiple purposes and often an individual visitor will do so.

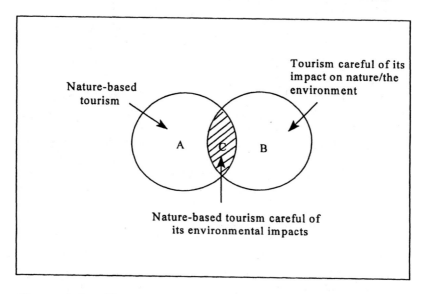

Figure 8.1 Illustration of some different approaches to the delineation of ecotourism

Some writers on ecotourism suggest that environmental education is an essential part of it. However, this seems to be too prescriptive. On the other hand, it is true that environmental education can enhance ecotourism experiences and can be important in convincing tourists that they should act in a more favourably environmental way. In general, environmental education would appear to be a desirable adjunct to ecotourism.

ECOTOURISM AND ECONOMICS

One of the appeals of ecotourism is its potential to provide economic gains in terms of incomes and employment while conserving nature. In order to provide specific evidence about the economic value of nature tourism, several writers have produced monetary estimates of its value. For example, Lindberg (1991) estimated the gross earnings from nature tourism in developing countries in 1988 to be US$12 billion with potential earnings not yet nearly reached. It was estimated that over 1 million US citizens went abroad primarily for nature-based tourism in 1985, and this group remained more than 8 million days abroad spending about US$800 million (McNeely *et al.*, 1992, pp. 7–8). In Kenya, tourism is the largest earner of foreign exchange and Kenya's tourism is primarily based on its national parks and its beaches. In an interesting study of Kenya's Amboseli National Park, Western (1982) showed that 'total park net returns (due mainly to tourism) amount to $40 per hectare a year compared to 80 cents per hectare under the most optimistic agricultural returns' (McNeely, *et al.*, 1992). Thus in some circumstances, nature-based tourism is by far the most profitable use of the land. McNeely *et al.* (1992) provide several examples to illustrate the economic importance of nature-based tourism, which covers not only living features but also physical features. Frequently, conservation of physical features of nature and the conservation of natural biota go hand in hand.

Clearly, estimates of the economic value and the potential economic value of ecotourism will depend upon how it is defined. Furthermore, when a tour is partially nature-based and partially non-nature based, one has to decide how to allocate it between the categories. So a considerable amount of subjectivity or discretion may be involved in determining the economic value of ecotourism.

Those who favour ecotourism tend to emphasise its socio-economic value. Some of the possible socio-economic benefits include:

(1) Employment generation directly in tourism and in the management of ecotourist assets. Both on-site and off-site employment may be generated by a protected area used for tourism.
(2) It can lead to the economic growth locally of profitable tourism-related activities, for example, hotels, restaurants, souvenirs, travel services, supporting this tourist industry.
(3) It can help to earn foreign exchange which may be in short supply in a developing country.
(4) 'It diversifies the local economy particularly in such areas where agricultural employment may be sporadic or insufficient' (McNeely *et al.*, 1992, p. 8). Such a situation may be found in Xishuangbanna Prefecture, in China.
(5) It may result in improved transport and communication systems,

and improved transport infrastructure such as airports, which assist local people.

(6) It may result in increased demand for local produce, for example, agricultural produce, to service the local tourist trade.

(7) 'It encourages productive use of lands which are marginal for agriculture enabling large tracts of land to remain covered in natural vegetation', (McNeely *et al.*, 1992, p. 8).

(8) 'If adequately conducted, it can provide a self-financing mechanism for the park authorities and consequently serve as a tool for conservation of the natural heritage', (McNeely *et al.*, 1992 p. 9).

(9) Ecotourism may also become a vehicle for providing economic support for the preservation of local culture, through sale by the local community of their culturally-inspired handicrafts, performing arts and so on.

(10) Such tourism can also do much to improve intercultural understanding and global communication, (McNeely *et al.*, 1992, p. 8).

This list of possible socio-economic benefits gives a favourable impression of ecotourism. The reality, however, from a socio-economic point of view is that every case must be assessed on its merits. Ecotourism can have all the benefits listed above, but in some cases it may bring little or no socio-economic gain to local communities.

In each particular case, questions or issues such as the following need to be considered.

(1) Is there sufficient demand for the tourist services to be provided (such as hotels or guest houses) to make the investment profitable? If not, there will be an economic drain.

(2) To what extent will ecotourism development generate local find jobs (and employment within the nation) either directly or indirectly? In some cases, for example, few local people find jobs in the local tourism industry because they lack the necessary skills.

(3) Even though significant expenditure occurs in the local region as a result of ecotourism, the regional leakage from these expenditures can be high because many of the goods and services required by tourists have to be supplied from outside the region. For example, many of the requirements of hotels or guest houses may be sourced from outside the region, especially when they are catering for foreign visitors. Consequently, the secondary impact of tourism on local employment generation may be low, because much of the

local expenditure by tourists leaks away to other regions to pay for 'imports' of commodities demanded by tourists in the local region. Some of the relevant issues are discussed in Tisdell (1993, Ch. 11).

(4) One of the supposed advantages of ecotourism is that it could enable protected areas to become self-financing. While this is so, one must be careful in pursuing this as an advantage for the following reasons (see also Tisdell, 1995):

(a) It is not always socially optimal to charge fees which maximise income or profit from protected areas (Tisdell, 1972).

(b) When the costs and difficulties of collecting fees are taken into account, it may not be economically worthwhile to impose charges for the use of a protected area.

(c) The economic value of a protected area cannot be judged solely from the income which it can earn from fees and sales of economic concessions. Income can usually only be earned from on-site uses but many protected areas also have off-site benefits. So income earned from on-site visits is liable to underestimate the economic value of the protected area.

(d) The fact that a protected area can earn little income now may not be very important if, in the future, it is expected to be a big income earner. The area must be protected now, so as to keep open the possibility of earning high levels of income from the protected area in the future. The upshot of this point is that if too much emphasis is placed on the achievement of self-financing of protected areas, the incorrect conclusion may be drawn, that a protected area which cannot finance itself should not be protected, from an economic point of view.

Despite the above comments, it is clear that there is considerable pressure at the moment for governments to apply the 'user-pays' principle, that is to make sure that those who benefit from a commodity pay for its use. Partly, this is an outcome of pressures from such bodies as the International Monetary Fund (IMF) and the World Bank, for countries to adopt structural adjustment policies. These policies favour maximum use of market mechanisms and a small government or state sector.

An additional risk, if strong requirements for self-financing of protected areas applies, is that those administering protected areas may sacrifice conservation for economic gain; for example, provide economic concessions for activities in protected area that are environmentally destructive, and so seriously compromise the conservation function of the area.

In determining the economic benefits obtained by local communities from tourism, account must be taken of the amount spent locally by tourists, and the extent of leakages from this. Although tourism is Kenya's largest foreign exchange earner, the foreign exchange leakages from it are very high. Sinclair (1991) estimates leakages of 62–78 per cent on beach-only package holidays and 34–45 per cent on safari/beach holidays. Leakages are highest for package tourism, and higher in Kenya for beach-type international tourism than for that which relies mainly on protected areas (Sinclair, 1991, p. 200). Sinclair (1991, p. 200) explains that 'the greater expenditure' on ground transport and national park and reserve entry fees are an important cause of the high Kenyan share for holidays including a safari component, and the mean expenditure for such holidays is considerably higher than for beach holidays. In addition to considering national economic leakages, ways need to be found of ensuring that not too high a share of tourist expenditure in a local area is lost to that area, and consideration needs to be given to encouraging tourists to spend in or near an ecotourism area.

One economic aspect of ecotourism which usually commands little attention, is the economics of operating ecotourism enterprises, such as tours and guide businesses, and accommodation facilities catering for particular ecotourist attractions. Economic problems encountered in operating such enterprises may include the following:

(1) Seasonality of demand can result in tourist facilities being underutilised for a significant part of the year, thereby raising average cost per user.
(2) Such variability may also lead to fluctuations in employment in the enterprise, making it difficult to retain staff and build up their skills.
(3) If the ecotourism is relatively remote, this will make it difficult to attract well qualified staff.
(4) Remoteness may also add to costs and problems of management. Transport costs may be high and the range of products available low. Furthermore, spare parts for equipment may be difficult to obtain and available skills for repairing equipment used in the tourist industry, for example air conditioning, may be inadequate compared to the situation in or near large cities.
(5) Communication costs and problems in remote ecotourism areas may add to management problems, and medical and other facilities for treating foreign tourists when ill, may be inadequate.

For the above reasons, ecotourism often faces greater economic difficulties than city-based tourism. That is not to say it cannot be profitable but to point out that it is not a sure means of making money. There are significant hurdles to overcome in order to make an ecotourism enterprise viable.

ECOTOURISM AND ENVIRONMENTAL ISSUES

While ecotourism has the potential to encourage conservation of the natural environment, it is also true that tourism which utilises the natural environment can result in its deterioration. Expansion of man-made facilities to cater for tourists is normally, to some extent, at the expense of the natural environment; for example the construction of buildings to accommodate tourists and catering staff, access roads and tracks, buildings for businesses selling curios, souvenirs and provisions for tourists. Tourism and tourists generate waste, so waste and rubbish disposal can become a problem. Furthermore, in some situations movement of tourists leads to physical damage to natural landscapes and plants and can have adverse impacts on the breeding and activities of wild animals. Some of the environmental problems which may arise from tourism in protected areas are listed in Table 8.1.

The fact that there can be some negative environmental impacts from tourism in natural areas does not mean that they should not be used for that purpose. However, it does mean that if tourism and conservation are to be combined effectively then tourism in natural areas must be managed or planned. By appropriate management and planning, adverse impacts on the natural environment can be minimized.

Approaches which can help to achieve this in relation to a protected area are:

(1) Zoning of the permitted uses of the protected area.
(2) Ensuring that constructions to cater for tourism are of a type which have minimal adverse impacts on the natural environment. Often a choice of constructions is available. Privately, the external environmental impacts of these will not be taken into account, but those responsible for the management of protected areas must see that businesses granted concessions do take these impacts into account.
(3) In some cases, it may be necessary to limit tourist visits to a protected area for environmental reasons. This may be done in a

number of different ways, for example by varying charges for entry, by the limiting the issue of permits, by making permits available on a lottery basis, by not reducing the travel costs and time needed to obtain access. The advantages and disadvantages of the various alternatives can be considered.

(4) Appropriate education on-site may reduce environmental damage by tourists.

(5) It must be realised that not all ecotourists are alike and searching for the same experiences. It may be that a facility located near, or concentrated in, a very small portion of a protected area may cater for the needs of a large proportion of ecotourists. These facilities may involve museums, captive animal displays, aquaria and so on, with short walks or excursions into natural settings also being available. The need, from a tourist point of view, for such substitutes for the 'real thing' is likely to be greater in areas where it is more difficult to come into contact with wildlife in natural settings. This is often the case in tropical rainforests, and in countries such as Australia, where much of the wildlife is nocturnal. When such substitute facilities are located in or near protected areas, they appear to result in greater 'authenticity', can serve a useful educational role, help mitigate disappointment of tourists at not experiencing in a natural situation many of the features which attracted them to the area, provide revenue from entry fees to the facility and serve as an outlet for sales of tourist items. Two examples of this type in Australia are the aquarium at Green Island near Cairns and the Great Barrier Reef aquarium at Townsville.

While ecotourism itself can create problems for the natural environment, in some circumstances ecotourism is threatened by the development of other industries, population growth and economic growth generally. Population growth and economic pressures in developing countries often result in human encroachment on protected areas. The water, energy and mineral requirements to sustain growing economies, often put protected areas under pressure as they become targeted for the construction of dams and reservoirs, and for mining. Furthermore, pollution from industrial, mining and agricultural expansion can have adverse impacts on natural areas. Their waterways may become polluted to the detriment of wildlife, acid rain may develop thereby altering the composition of flora and subsequently fauna populations, and pesticides may, directly or indirectly, harm wildlife such as birds. Many other adverse impacts on wildlife from economic growth

*Table 8.1 Potential environmental effects of tourism in protected areas:
negative visitor impacts that must be controlled*

Factor Involved	Impact on Natural Quality	Comment
Overcrowding	Environmental stress, animals show changes in behaviour	Irritation, reduction in quality, need for carrying-capacity limits or better regulation
Overdevelopment	Development of rural slums, excessive man-made structures	Unsightly urban-like development
Recreation:		
Powerboats	Disturbance of wildlife	Vulnerability during nesting seasons, noise pollution
Fishing	None	Competition with natural predators
Foot safaris	Disturbance of wildlife	Overuse and trail erosion
Pollution:		
Noise (radios, etc.)	Disturbance of natural sounds	Irritation of wildlife and other visitors
Litter	Impairment of natural scene, habituation of wildlife to garbage	Aesthetic and health hazard
Vandalism destruction	Mutilation and facility damage	Removal of natural features
Feeding of wildlife	Behavioural changes danger to tourists	Removal of habituated animals
Vehicles:		
Speeding	Wildlife mortality	Ecological changes, dust
Off-road driving	Soil and vegetation damage	Disturbance to wildlife
Miscellaneous:		
Souvenir collection	Removal of natural attractions, disruptions of natural processes	Shells, coral, horns, trophies, rare plants
Firewood	Small wildlife mortality habitat destruction	Interference with natural energy flow
Roads and excavations	Habitat loss, drainage	Aesthetic scars
Power lines	Destruction of vegetation	Aesthetic impacts
Artificial water holes and salt provision	Unnatural wildlife concentrations, vegetation damage	Replacement of soil required
Introduction of exotic plants and animals	Competition with wild species	Public confusion

McNeely *et al.* (1992, p. 14).

are possible, for example, from loss of wetlands, dams which reduce variability of waterflows and so on. This does not mean that economic growth should be halted, but points out the importance of taking account of any environmental costs and adjusting development projects accordingly.

It is clear that most conservationists are ambivalent about ecotourism in protected areas. This is apparent from the report on availability of training for local guides and managers; lack of international institutional support when compared to other assistance programmes; and lack of standardized, widely-applied evaluation procedures. On the other hand, the potential benefits that tourism can produce, if handled correctly, were also reviewed: contribution to conservation goals; stimulating employment and socio-economic development; and promoting training, research and education in environmental matters.' (IUCN, 1992, p. 101).

ASPECTS OF PLANNING FOR TOURISM IN NATIONAL PARKS AND OTHER PROTECTED AREAS

McNeely *et al.*, (1992, Ch. 4) provide useful advice about how to plan the development of tourism in national parks. They suggest seven steps:

1 collect and analyse data
2 identify resource conflicts
3 determine objectives
4 set tourism into the regional context
5 prepare management plan
6 guide construction procedures
7 monitor progress

In relation to step 1, McNeely *et al.*, (1992, p. 21) say: 'Tourism means managing people and it is thus necessary to be familiar with the human side of the equation. It is important to gather information on an area's visitors, just as it is important to monitor natural resources. Visitor information is required for

(a) budgeting and setting fees,
(b) allocating personnel,
(c) scheduling maintenance,

(d) understanding the users,
(e) detecting trends in use, and
(f) planning.'

As for step 2, McNeely *et al.*, (1992, p. 22) recommend that: 'On the basis of resource inventories and other data collected under Guideline 1, the management authority should identify resource conflicts and define options for solving such conflicts (including costs and benefits of each option)'.

For the objectives of tourism development in a national park, McNeely *et al.*, (1992) believe that it is important to consider

(1) who should be the beneficiaries? Should local people have the highest priority?
(2) to what extent should the local community become dependent on tourism for its livelihood?
(3) what scale of tourism should be aimed for?
(4) where should tourists be attracted from?

They point out (p. 24) that:
'International tourism, by definition, draws persons from diverse cultures. Regional resource inventories and evaluations for the development of tourism should therefore attempt to take into account diverse recreational preferences. The travel preferences of tourists from different cultures (or groups within cultures) should also be considered in the layout and design of tourist facilities. For large tourist zones, a wide range of varying interest can be met by different sorts of lodging and other facilities. For long-term security, the bottom line is the development of local support and therefore benefits to the immediate region of all tourism projects should be maximized'.

Appropriate zoning of park use should be a part of the plan, as should marketing. Marketing of course means advertising and providing information. The extent to which park authorities can engage in this will depend on their funding, and this will depend in part on what income they can earn from ecotourism, for example through rental of concessions, sale of permits, and so on. Although FAO (1988) and McNeely *et al.*, (1992) recommend that where possible, hotels, restaurants and other facilities should be located outside park boundaries to reduce human impact on protected areas, this will reduce the ability of the park to earn income from tourism, for example by rental of rights to cater for tourists, and the park authorities will have no control over development outside its boundaries. Ideally, of course, those businesses (located outside the park) which benefit commercially or economically from a park should contribute towards the financing of that park. Otherwise, they receive a rent or bonus from the presence of an amenity without payment for its existence.

From a marketing point of view, even the name of the protected area may be important, especially if the area is to attract foreign tourists. As mentioned in the UNDP-WTO (1990) review of tourist development in Uganda, native names of gorilla reserves there do not appeal to foreign tourists since they do not easily understand or relate to them. It is probably true in the case of Xishuangbanna protected area in Yunnan that the name would not come easily to most foreigners.

It is also important in planning ecotourism to make predictions about future demand for such tourism and to consider how best to cater for different segments of the ecotourism market. While a national park may cater for different segments, a particular park may not cater for all, either by intent or because of its natural features. As McNeely *et al.*, (1992, pp. 27–28) point out: 'For national parks, the travel market may be segmented along a scale from those seeking back-to-nature trekking to those satisfied with short, even vicarious, contact with a national park. Today, even though the former segment is growing, the great majority of travellers are satisfied with short-term contact and a well-interpreted description of the park features. Therefore, there is merit in concentration of tourists where they can be managed'.

At least one segment of the ecotourism market can be concentrated and this may make use of the display-type facilities, including museums and captive animals mentioned earlier.

CONCLUDING COMMENTS

From the above, it can be seen that there are many issues to consider as far as the development of ecotourism is concerned, particularly in relation to national parks and other protected areas. The economic value of such tourism can be high and many protected areas may be suitable for ecotourism management. That is not to say that all parts of all protected areas should be available for tourism. Some areas may need to be protected strictly for scientific purposes and others may be ecologically too fragile to allow any significant tourism. Furthermore, not all protected areas have a high potential for tourism or for economic gain from it. This is apparent from Table 8.2. Those protected areas for which the following are the case, would have little tourism potential: remote, reached by a long arduous or dangerous journey, little distinctive wildlife and unlikely to be seen, few cultural attractions, similar to other visitor reserves, limited recreation opportunities, and so on.

While some of the disadvantages indicated in Table 8.2 could be overcome with effort, (for example, accessibility could be improved by airport construction in some cases), others are a part of the natural characteristics and are not amenable to change – scenic beauty may be quite ordinary. Standards of food and accommodation can be improved if sufficient demand exists. Methods may also be available for enhancing the chances of tourists to see wildlife but some areas still may not be favourable for the viewing of wild animals.

Table 8.2 Checklist for deciding on tourism potential of protected areas

Is the protected area: – close to an international airport or major? – moderately close? – remote?	Does the area have additional: – high cultural interest? – some cultural attractions? – few cultural attractions?
Is the journey to the area: – easy and comfortable – a bit of an effort? – arduous or dangerous?	Is the area: – unique in its appeal? – a little bit different? – similar to other visitor reserves?
Does the area offer the following: – 'star' species attractions? – other interesting wildlife? – representative wildlife? – distinctive wildlife viewing, for example, on foot, by boat, from hides?	Does the area have: – a beach or lakeside recreation facilities? – river, falls or swimming pool? – no other recreation?
Is successful wildlife viewing: – guaranteed? – usual? – with luck or highly seasonal?	Is the area close enough to other sites of tourist interest to be part of a tourist circuit? – yes, other attractive sites – moderate potential – low or no such potential
What standards of food and accommodation are offered? – high standards – adequate standards – rough standards	

Source: McNeely *et al.* (1992, p. 17).

Pressures to use protected areas for ecotourism are likely to increase. Tourism is one of the world's major industries and is still growing. The growth of international tourism in the Asia-Pacific Region has been by far the fastest of all the major regions of the world. This growth is primarily a function of rising incomes in the region. Furthermore, educational levels are rising throughout the region, and the demand for nature-based tourism is positively correlated both with levels of education and income. In addition, many natural areas in Asia are becoming more easily accessible. For example, as China has developed, its communication and transport systems have improved. It is now much easier for international visitors to visit Xishuangbanna Prefecture in Yunnan than it used to be, because of improved air links. So demand to visit protected areas in China is likely to increase. On the other hand, as the protected area of China increases, there will also be financial pressure there to make economic use of these areas in ways compatible with the preservation of biodiversity and conservation of natural features, a matter discussed in some depth in the next part of this book. This pressure will provide a further impetus for the expansion of tourism in protected areas in China.

REFERENCES

FAO (1988), *National Parks Planning: A Manual with Annotated Examples*, Rome: Food and Agriculture Organization of the United Nations.

IUCN (1992), *Parks for Life: Report of the IVth World Congress on National Parks and Protected Areas*, Gland, Switzerland: International Union for the Conservation of Nature and Natural Resources.

IUCN (1980), *World Conservation Strategy*, Gland, Switzerland: International Union for the Conservation of Nature and Natural Resources.

Lindberg, K. (1991), *Policies for Maximizing Nature Tourism's Ecological and Economic Benefits*, Washington, DC: World Resources Institute.

McNeely, J.A., J.W. Thorsell and H. Ceballos-Lascurain (1992), *Guidelines: Development of Natural Parks and Protected Areas for Tourism*, Paris: World Tourism Organization, Madrid and United Nations Environment Programme.

Sinclair, M.T. (1991), 'The Tourism Industry and Foreign Exchange Leakages in a Developing Country: the Distribution of Earnings from Safari and Beach Tourism in Kenya' in M.T. Sinclair and M. J. Stabler, *The Tourism Industry an International Analysis*, pp. 185 – 204, Oxon, UK: C.A.B. International.

Tisdell, C.A. (1972), 'Provision of parks and the preservation of nature – some economic factors', *Australian Economic Papers*, 11, 154 – 164.

Tisdell, C.A. (1993), *Economic Development in the Context of China*, London: Macmillan.

Tisdell, C.A. (1994), 'Tourism in the APEC region and its promotion in an ecologically sound way through regional co-operation', *Discussion Paper* No. 160, Department of Economics, The University of Queensland, Brisbane.

Tisdell, C.A. (1995), 'Investment in ecotourism: assessing its economics', *Tourism Economics*, 1(4), 375–87.

UNDP-WTO (1990), *Uganda Tourism Development Projects Report*, UNDP-WTO.

Valentine, P.S. (1992), 'Ecotourism and Nature Conservation: A Definition with some Recent Developments in Micronesia' in B. Weiler (ed.), *Ecotourism Incorporating the Global Classroom*, Canberra: Bureau of Tourism Research, pp. 4–9.

Western, D. (1982), 'Human Values and the Conservation of a Savanna Ecosystem' in J. McNeely and Miller, *National Parks, Conservation and Development*, Washington: Smithsonian Press.

Zhenhua, Xie and others (1994), *China: Biodiversity Conservation Action Plan*, Beijing: National Environmental Protection Agency.

PART III

Experiences and Cases from Asia

9. The Environment and Asian Economic Development

INTRODUCTION

While economic growth in the Asian region is a potential means for low-income countries to improve their lot, it raises concerns about the natural environment. Political bias exists in favour of Asian economic growth both in Asia and abroad, even at considerable expense to the environment. The theoretical underpinnings of the bias are discussed in this chapter, which helps to place the individual case studies in their broader setting. The main emphasis is on East Asia, particularly China. A number of the environmental issues in Asia are considered involving water, air and soils, and particularly, the global greenhouse problem arising from China's use of fossil fuels. Conservation of living resources and biodiversity is difficult, given East Asia's rapid economic growth, and is made more difficult by the fact that many areas designated for nature protection are inhabited by villagers, or are subject to encroachment by migrating groups. Furthermore, in low income countries, nature protection is often considered to be a luxury and/or there is a perception that more distant frontiers are more suitable for nature conservation. It is difficult to provide those inhabiting protected areas with alternative means of livelihood to their utilisation of the natural area. Tourism development is a possibility but it has limitations. In fact, tourism development in Asia is a source of several environmental problems. Increased urbanisation is another environmental feature of Asia and may have positive long-term environmental impact by reducing the rate of population growth. With economic growth, interregional and transboundary conflicts will intensify in Asia. It seems possible that both market mechanisms and political ones will be inadequate to deal with Asia's growing environmental problems. This chapter is critical of the view that economic growth to the neglect of the environment is acceptable, even in low income countries, and suggests that given the public good/bad dimensions of Asia's development, that more assistance from high-income countries in relation to environmental conservation in Asia's less developed countries, is justified.

Asia, particularly East Asia, has experienced very rapid growth in recent decades. China, for example, experienced double-digit rates of annual GDP growth from 1978 to 1998. While rates of growth in East Asia are expected to be lower in the late 1990s, due to the Asian financial crisis (beginning September 1997), in the long-term, Asia's economic growth can be expected to continue.

The rapid economic growth of north-east Asian countries, which diffused to the south-east, provided new economic opportunities for Asian-Pacific countries as well as Europe. The Asia-Pacific Economic Co-operation (APEC) forum was formed to enable all APEC countries to share in East Asia's economic momentum and to promote freer trade. Such new opportunities are facilitated by peace in Asia and increasing accommodation between its nations; for example, between China and Vietnam, and between mainland China and Taiwan.

While APEC nations emphasize increased materialistic opportunities to be obtained from Asian economic growth, they are less vocal about the environmental impacts of this growth and its sustainability. Naturally, more developed countries in Asia would like to enjoy the economic advantages of Asian economic development without its environmental disadvantages. An important question is whether this is possible. To what extent are economic growth in Asia and environmental conservation compatible and likely to be achieved? Since the advantages of economic growth are expected to show up in the relative short-term, whereas many of the easily observable adverse impacts of environmental destruction are delayed, politicians are likely to be biased in favour of economic growth, even when it involves considerable environmental cost. Such myopia is fairly certain to be politically advantageous.

Economic growth can be a two-edged sword as far as the environment is concerned. It has both the potential to improve environmental conditions and to cause their deterioration. With rising incomes, demand for environmental improvement and protection usually increases, and the economic capacity to undertake such improvements and protection expands. The relationship in a country between the intensity of environmental pollution and income per capita appears to be a reversed U-shape, the so-called Kuznets' pollution curve (Cf. Tisdell, 1997a). Therefore, it also seems to be the case that the relationship between environmental quality and income per head is of a U-shape.

While empirical evidence supports such relationship, some caution is required in interpreting the Kuznets' environmental hypothesis. The following should be noted:

(1) Even if pollution intensity in relation to GDP falls, total levels of pollution may continue to rise (Tisdell, 1997a) both nationally and globally.
(2) Use of raw materials or natural resources per capita appears to continue to rise with economic growth.
(3) The Kuznets' environmental curve (or its reverse) gives the impression that environmental quality changes can be reversed. This is not always so. For example, biodiversity loss cannot be reversed, and some types of pollution are cumulative or only reversed in the long term.

So caution is called for in drawing policy conclusions on the basis of the Kuznets' environmental quality curve. Some Asian countries have yet to reach the top of their pollution intensity curve; some may be nearing its top, for example China; and others, like Japan, are beyond its maximum.

Political bias in favour of economic growth without corresponding concern for the environment is supported in international fora by two viewpoints:

(1) Greater use of market forces and the adoption of the type of structural adjustment policies recommended by the IMF and the World Bank, will provide positive economic forces for counterbalancing possible adverse environmental impacts of economic growth. In other words, thorough-going market systems are environmentally friendly (Sebastian and Alicbusan, 1989).
(2) In less developed countries, economic growth should be encouraged, even if it is initially environmentally destructive, because while their incomes remain low, individuals have no incentive to conserve their natural environment. Poor people look upon natural resource conservation as a luxury. Furthermore, for economic reasons, they are inclined to have large families so rates of population increase tend to be high among the poor, thereby placing even greater pressure on the natural environment (Todaro, 1981).

The policy implication of the above is that only by economic growth and modernisation, which raise per capita incomes sufficiently and alter the structure of society suitably (for example, encourage urbanisation), can low-income countries escape from their low-level equilibrium trap involving poverty, large families and environmental degradation. This is a variant of the Malthusian low-level equilibrium theory (Todaro, 1981) to which an environmental destruction component is added. This thesis was endorsed by the World Commission on Environment and Development (1987) and the World Bank (1992) has now become a part of the conventional wisdom.

Concerning the first hypothesis, market distortions do have adverse environmental consequences in Asia. Prices, for example, often do not reflect user costs or externalities in Asia, especially when state enterprises are involved in the use or control of natural resources. Considerable room exists for improvement in pricing of natural resource-use in Asian countries. However, it does not follow that market systems lead to an ideal result as far as environmental conservation is concerned (Tisdell, 1992; 1993d). Market failures do occur and the market system does not necessarily ensure sustainability (Hartwick, 1977). Furthermore, the very dynamic success of market capitalism (Schumpeter, 1942) may be a source of considerable environmental destruction. Market capitalism is a strong force for expanding the scale of economic activity (Tisdell, 1992) and expansion in aggregate economic activity is usually at the expense of the natural environment (Cf. Swanson, 1994).

The second hypothesis needs to be qualified. Extremely poor people with primitive techniques may be unable to damage the natural environmental greatly, even though poor people with more advanced techniques could well do so. This is not to deny that some people with relatively primitive techniques have managed to engage in activity that has undermined economic sustainability. For example, early Easter Islanders are reputed to have destroyed the tree cover on their island with catastrophic impacts on its economy (Ponting, 1991, Ch. 1). Secondly, economic growth utilising natural resources to fuel economic take-off does not guarantee successful escape from a low-level equilibrium trap. A 'premature' attempt to escape may result in irreversible natural resource-depletion, making it more difficult to escape subsequently. Possibly, this has already happened in the Philippines. So even if one believes in this modified Malthusian theory, there is a difficult decision to make (in theory) about when to attempt economic growth in order to escape from the trap (Tisdell, 1994). However, politically, governments may have little choice but always to try for economic growth, even when it is bound to be abortive in the medium term.

The World Bank (1992) in general identifies improved environmental quality with higher incomes, and uses both cross-sectional and time-series data to convey this view. Nevertheless, some negative environmental consequences are noted by the Bank, such as reduced biodiversity and increased global environmental risks as a result of rising incomes. This underlines the point that environmental quality must be judged in relation to a set or vector of variables and so, at the very minimum, involves an index question. For the individual, it involves a preference or utility function, with elements or variables of such attributes as air quality, water quality, soil quality, biological diversity and so on, and may involve attributes of the natural environment as well as of the man-made environment. Consider trends in a number of these attributes for Asia.

SOME ASIAN ENVIRONMENTAL RESOURCES – AIR, WATER, SOIL

Only some elements of environmental quality and availability can be discussed here, for Asia. We shall consider water, air and soil.

Water

Water is becoming increasingly scarce in Asia. In 1990, the per capita consumption of water in China and India was 520 cubic metres, less than half of that of high-income countries, which in 1990, had a per capita consumption of water of 1 217 cubic metres, on average. However, the intensity of water use in China and India was higher than in high-income countries because 18 per cent of total available renewable water resources was withdrawn for use in China and India, compared to 11 per cent for high-income countries (World Bank, 1992, p. 197). The combined population of China and India in 1990 was estimated to be 1 984 million and is predicted by the World Bank to rise to 2 945 million by 2025, and eventually to stabilise at about 3 752 million. This means that per capita renewable water resources available for consumption in China and India will fall from 2 345 cubic metres (in 1990) to 1 579 cubic metres in 2 025, and to 1 239 cubic metres eventually. Given the same level of water consumption per head in China and India as in 1990, their utilisation of theoretically available water resources will rise sharply by 2025. Both countries can be expected to face serious water problems, especially in drought years. The World Bank (1992, p. 192) suggests that countries having less than 1 000 cubic metres of per capita annual availability of water, face chronic water problems, and those with less than 2 000 cubic metres will have serious problems, especially in drought years. So China and India will have a serious water problem in the 21st century.

If per capita consumption of water rises in China and India, as it is likely to do, as per capita incomes increase and industrialisation occurs (industry is the major user of water in high-income countries), this will place an even greater demand on their available water resources. If, for example, their per capita water consumption was to reach the level of high-income countries then at the predicted (World Bank, 1992) stable population levels for China and India, their total annual consumption of renewable water would be approximately 100 per cent of that theoretically available to them. While it is possible for use of available water resources to exceed 100 per cent, due to re-use of water, the economic costs are likely to be high.

The available water resources of China and India could support their projected population increases, but water will become scarcer and involve major economic and environmental issues, as well as international political conflict when water bodies are shared in the Asian region. High rates of utilisation of available water create many problems. They increase the risk of pollution of water; in the case of underground water use, they may lead to land subsidence; infrastructures for water supply, such as dams, result in flooding of lands and their loss from traditional uses, and often involve significant ecological losses and losses to tribal people, such as occurred with the building of the Kapatar Dam in the Chittagong Hill Tracts of Bangladesh. Moreover, altered or regulated streamflows have significant ecological impacts, for example, on the functioning of wetlands. Wetlands in the Yangtze River are likely to be adversely affected by the Three Gorges Dam. Furthermore, such changes tend to reduce natural fish stocks, lower streamflows, restrict navigation in internal waterways, increase risks of eutrophication, algae and weeds in water bodies, and in many cases raise the salinity of rivers with adverse economic consequences. Examples of all these problems are available for countries of mainland Asia such as Bangladesh (Tisdell, *et al.,* forthcoming).

Another problem is that water resources are not evenly distributed in Asia, including China and India. In China, for example, the north has a severe water deficit, whereas in south China water resources are more abundant. A critical water problem already exists in north-east China. One must not only take into account the aggregate availability of water in a country but the cost of making use of it at the points where it is demanded.

The World Bank (1992) provides a substantial amount of data on water quality in Asia. In the less developed countries of Asia, water quality, using most indicators, is much poorer than in high-income countries.

Air

According to World Bank (1992) data, air quality is worse, on the whole, in major Asian cities of less developed countries than it is in those of high-income countries. Unfortunately, air quality in Asian low-income but developing countries can be expected to deteriorate further as their total energy use rises, even though in the longer run this trend may reverse itself.

Amongst other things, acid rains will become more common in Asia as China increases use of its high-sulphur coal. Acid rains are a significant problem in China. Already international effects from such rains are present. For example, some believe that the death of pine trees in Hiroshima Prefecture, Japan, is due to acid rains transported from China. In south-west Yunnan, there are fears that industrial development could threaten tropical forests containing considerable biological diversity by generating acid rain. However, let us consider briefly the global dimension of greenhouse gas emissions in Asia, particularly China.

China, because of its extremely large reserves of coal and rapid economic growth, has the potential in the near future to become the world's major emitter of carbon dioxide. Currently the United States occupies this position (World Bank, 1992, p. 204). By world comparisons, the USA is an extravagant user of energy resources and emits about 10 times the carbon equivalent of China (See Table 10.1). If China were to achieve the same type and nature of energy use as the United States per capita, then China's annual emissions of carbon dioxide in carbon equivalents, given its present population, would exceed the aggregate level of current global emissions of carbon dioxide. While such a situation may be unlikely in the very near future, it raises the question of whether the globe has the environmental capacity to withstand a situation in which all low-income countries, or a large number of them, attempt to achieve and maintain levels of per capita income approaching those of high-income countries.

Even though China is unlikely to achieve per capita levels of economic activity comparable to the USA by 2025, substantial expansion in

Chinese income levels and economic activity can be expected. Possibly, China's carbon emissions per person will be in the range of 1–1.5 tons by 2025. This would still be well below the per capita level for high-income countries. China's population is predicted by the World Bank to be 1 597 million by then and it may have overtaken the US as the world's major carbon dioxide emitter, or have roughly an equivalent level of emissions. China's emissions, following the above predictions, would be 1 597 – 2 395 million tons of carbon annually in 2025. Given that the United States level of emissions stabilises at its 1989 per capita level, and given a predicted population for the United States in 2025 of 307 million, the emissions of the United States would be 1 639 million tons of carbon annually in 2025. From a world perspective, the USA would still be a very large carbon polluter (perhaps the major one) and comparatively a much greater polluter than Europe. If carbon dioxide emissions do really constitute a serious global problem (a public 'bad'), then the equity of some countries maintaining very high levels of per capita energy use and greenhouse gas emissions, can be expected to become a major international political issue. While the issue of tradeable global carbon emission permits has been suggested as a way to deal with this problem, one international stumbling block is likely to be political concerns about the initial country by country allocation of such permits. Nevertheless, some progress in limiting CO_2 emissions was made at the Kyoto Summit held in late 1997.

Soils

Both in China and India, agricultural production has increased substantially since 1965 and annual crop yields have risen significantly. To a large extent, this can be attributed to the use of green-revolution input packages, involving high-yielding seed, chemical fertilisers, pesticides, and irrigation water. An extremely important factor influencing increased crop yields has been the increased incidence of annual multiple cropping, particularly cropping in the dry season under irrigation (Alauddin and Tisdell, 1991). However, increasing scarcity of water in Asia can be expected to limit the expansion of the use of green-revolution technologies. Furthermore, the sustainability of yields from this type of intensification of agriculture must be considered. For example, multiple cropping can result in falling levels of humus in the soil and in deteriorating soil structure, and the use of common chemical fertilisers can be expected to lead to acidification of soil. So falling soil fertility as a result of new agricultural technologies is a danger in Asia.

While falling soil fertility can be counteracted up to a point by increasing artificial fertiliser applications, this may eventually become uneconomical and falling yields will then become apparent. In order to obtain greater sustainability of yields, it is wise to place greater emphasis on organic agriculture with limited use of fertilisers and pesticides, and special emphasis on return of crop residues to the soil to enhance their humus content, improve their structural properties and increase their resistance to erosion. The rapid increase in use of chemical fertilisers in Asia, with its side-effect of nitrification of water bodies and their nutrient enrichment, may be more a source for environmental concern than an indicator of sustainable development (Cf. Tisdell, 1991, Ch. 9; 1993a, Ch. 11). Fertiliser consumption per hectare of agriculture land in China is already very high. It is greater than in the United States but not as high as in many Western European countries.

The natural fertility of soils in much of Asia is being depleted. Furthermore, the quantity of land suitable for agriculture may be slowly declining due to urban encroachment, soil erosion and deterioration. It is estimated that the total area of agricultural land has fallen by 0.3 per cent per annum in China since 1965 (World Bank, 1992). This may partly reflect ecological impacts on soils, urban encroachment and less emphasis in Chinese policy on agricultural production compared to production from forests and grazing.

The Hong Kong press has expressed concern about the high levels of pesticides used on vegetables in Shenzhen, China because 50 per cent of Hong Kong's fresh vegetables is imported from China (*The Standard*, January, 15, 1994). Residues of pesticides on these vegetables have caused food poisoning.

GENERAL PERCEPTIONS OF ENVIRONMENTAL ISSUES IN THAILAND

There is a widespread belief in Thailand that Thais face a severe water shortage. While some believe that the disappearance of much of Thailand's forested area is to blame, the *Bangkok Post*, September 14, 1993, p. 25 reports: 'It is not that there is less rain this year: according to the Meteorological Department, rainfall is normal. But it appears no longer enough to meet our ever-increasing demand and wastage'. Presumably this situation is being worsened by inadequate water pricing policies.

The King of Thailand has, in the last year, expressed concern about controversial dams in Thailand, regional foreign policy, the unbearable traffic problem in Bangkok, the proposed road construction linking China and Thailand, and the use of the water in the Mekong (*Bangkok Post*, September 5, 1993, p. 23). Currently there is a scheme co-operative sharing the water of the Mekong River involving Thailand, Laos, Burma, Cambodia and Vietnam. But it does intend to include China. The headwaters of the Mekong are in China, where it is called Lancang Jiang. China could construct a dam on the Mekong headwaters and divert much of its water for its own use. The flow and level of the Mekong would then be at the mercy of China. The King of Thailand is reported as saying: 'To ensure the success of the Mekong project, we [the Thais] should get China involved as a big brother' (*Bangkok Post*, September 5, 1993, p. 23). In fact, China is proceeding with the construction of dams on the Mekong River and has come to an agreement to sell some of the hydroelectricity from the project to Thailand.

This is a relevant illustration of the international dimension of water problems throughout much of Asia.

LIVING NATURAL RESOURCES AND BIODIVERSITY

Since 1965, in the world as a whole, the proportion of land area allocated to agriculture has grown, that used for permanent pasture has remained stationary, whereas the area used for forest and woodland has declined (World Bank, 1992, Table A6). The percentage of land allocated for other purposes such as urban use, has increased. However, since these estimates are crude, it is difficult to be precise about the trends. The decline in forest and woodland is probably even greater than indicated because the crown cover of much of these areas has been severely reduced.

The estimates for forest and woodland also include forest plantations. Sometimes these monocultures have adverse environmental impacts. Introduced eucalyptus forests in India have been criticised because of their environmental impacts, such as lack of compatibility with native flora and fauna, and high water demands (Tisdell, *et al.*, 1996).

In the period 1965–89, the area of forest and woodland in China fell by an estimated 0.8 per cent per annum (World Bank, 1992) and the country's forests continued to be harvested unsustainably. However,

China is planning to reverse the trend. Her Eight Five-Year Plan states that: 'The negative situation symbolised by the constant decline in the standing volume of forests should be ended, and the deficit of [use of] forest resources should be eliminated so as to reach the objective of increasing forest area and standing volume. To this end the first step is to achieve balance between the overall increment and consumption of forest resources, the second step is to make the increment dominate the overall consumption.' (Ministry of Forestry, 1992, p. 20).

On average, the proportion of a country officially afforded nature protection rises with per capita income levels. In 1990, this proportion in low-income countries was 3.8 per cent, in middle-income countries, 4.6 per cent and in high-income countries, 10.2 per cent (World Bank, 1992). The effectiveness with which natural areas are protected also usually rises with the per capita income level of a nation. In 1990, the nationally protected also area of China was 3 per cent of its land area. This is below the average proportion for all low-income countries and contrasts with 4.3 per cent for India which is above the average for low-income countries and almost equal to that for middle-income economies. Some comparative indicators of biodiversity conservation in Asia are outlined in Alauddin and Tisdell, Ch. 2 (1997).

Many countries on the Asian mainland have to deal with the difficult problem of people resident in protected areas and their encroachment on such areas. Nature protection often leads to conflict with the local population because it interferes with their traditional way of life and may reduce their incomes. Furthermore, they may not know that their economic use of the forests or natural areas is unsustainable.

In remote or resource-poor areas (often occupied by tribal people) where protected areas are frequently located, it is usually difficult to provide local people with alternative means of livelihood to their use of the natural area. Their forced relocation away from a protected area, is a drastic option which still requires viable economic opportunities for them at their point of relocation if their life is not to be a misery. Employment in tourism related to the protected area, or in protected area management, may provide some possibilities for employment of locals. Very often, however, such positions are not filled by them because they lack adequate skills and training. This is a problem in China, India and many other countries in Asia. It is a problem being faced in the Xishuangbanna Nature Reserve in Yunnan, Southwest China, where it has been noted that: 'The location of 90 villages in and around [this] reserve places direct pressure on the protected area's forests which are still being degraded as a result of tree cutting, fires and hunting in many areas' (Ministry of Forestry, 1993, p. 44). Xishuangbanna Nature Reserve is being given a high priority for conservation by China because it is considered internationally to be an area with great biodiversity.

TOURISM AND THE ENVIRONMENT

Tourism provides one way in which local people can gain from conservation of local natural areas. However, in remote areas the economic leakages from such tourism can be large and local people frequently do not get a chance to participate in the local tourism industry on a large scale, if at all (Cf. Hohl and Tisdell, 1995). Furthermore, tourism itself can be destructive of the environment and difficult to manage in relation to its environmental impacts.

In addition, unfortunately, there is a tendency for tourism to expand for private benefit at the expense of social benefit. In China, for example, hotel accommodation (a private good), has expanded greatly but without a concomitant increase in funding for conservation of public or semi-public tourist attractions (Tisdell and Wen, 1991).

International tourist developers are active throughout the Asian-Pacific Region. As incomes rise in this region, demand for tourism, including the nature-based type can be expected to rise. International tourism from Japan is already considerable in the Asian-Pacific area. (Japan is now the chief foreign investor in the tourist industry in Australia, and its main source of foreign tourists). Tourism from other high income countries in Asia, such as Taiwan and South Korea, has increased. However, there is always a chance that tourism development will destroy the natural attractions which are a drawcard for many visitors. In Okinawa, for example, the run-off of water containing fertiliser and sediment from golf courses constructed for tourists has been a factor in the destruction of coral reefs. While there are still relatively pristine coral reefs further afield, many of these are fast disappearing, as in Thailand and the Philippines.

A further danger is that international developers may effectively promote their private interests at the expense of the public interest. They may, for example, competitively play one country or region off against another to obtain the use of prime natural sites for their tourism developments, and/or in some cases they may make suitable side-payments (bribes) to local politicians for this purpose. Conservationists, because of the free-rider problem involving large groups or because they are gagged politically, may find it difficult to offset the special interests of private tourist developers in appropriating natural sites to their own use. The final result could be the socially unsatisfactory use of natural tourism assets in the Asian-Pacific area; a development which would be unfavourable in the long run for the tourism industry itself. The problem is akin to that of the prisoner's dilemma.

It is interesting to note that deterioration in Thailand's environment is given as one of the major reasons for declining Japanese tourist visits to the country. *The Bangkok Post*, September 15, 1993, reported: 'The decline has set in due to several problems, especially the security image of Thailand, the AIDS crisis, and the ongoing environmental situation'.

URBANISATION

Asia is undergoing substantial urbanisation and its degree of urbanisation will increase in the years ahead. This has both positive and negative environmental implications. On the positive side, it is likely to lead to falling family sizes, since the net cost of having children is usually higher in urban society than in a rural one. On the other hand, it will pose increasing problems for disposal of wastes, and continuing difficulties in controlling urban air and water pollution. Furthermore, in many large urban areas in Asia, transportation within cities has become a major problem (almost chaotic) for example in Bangkok, Jakarta, and Manila, and is causing major social problems and affecting economic efficiency.

INTERREGIONAL AND TRANSBOUNDARY ENVIRONMENTAL PROBLEMS

Some international environmental problems involving Asia have already been mentioned. These include air pollution problems and water use, and pollution problems in relation to water bodies shared internationally. Collective solutions are necessary, for example, concerning the use of water in the Mekong River.

Even within countries, provincial authorities often fail to take account of their environmental impact on neighbouring provinces. Local authorities in Beijing have in the past failed to take account of the effects of their additions of pollutants to water on nearby Hebei Province, and of the extra treatment costs this imposed on water users downstream (Tisdell, 1993b, Ch. 12). However, Chinese authorities are becoming more aware of the costs of adverse externalities and are increasingly expecting polluters to pay (Zhiyong Hong, *et al.*, 1991; Tisdell, 1997b).

Some countries in East Asia still have considerable stocks of natural resources which have been little exploited thanks to their relative isolation from the global economic system. These include Laos, Myanmar and, to some extent, Cambodia. Large portions of these countries are still covered in tropical forests.

With peace in Indo-China, these economies are likely to be drawn increasingly into the world economy and the international community. Consequently, their natural resources may be rapidly 'exploited' by the economic demands of their more advanced neighbours, such as Thailand and China, or even slightly more distant ones, such as Japan. Improved communications in the Asian region will facilitate this process; for example, the Australian-built bridge across the Mekong linking Thailand and Laos, and the proposed Yunnan-to-Thailand highway via northern Myanmar.

Surprisingly, there appears still to be a 'frontier mentality' in parts of Asia. The point has been raised in China as to why is it important to conserve biodiversity in Xishuangbanna Nature Reserve in Southwest China. A Chinese feasibility study for a GEF loan from the World Bank points out: 'It must also be realised that the great richness of Xishuangbanna is mostly due to the tropical affect. Even richer forests exist further south in Laos and Vietnam' (Ministry of Forestry, 1993, p. 43).

The implication may be that tropical biodiversity could be conserved further south with greater ease and therefore conservation of Xishuangbanna should not be over-rated. But will conservation further south happen?

Frontiers everywhere, as far as nature conservation is concerned, are rapidly disappearing. Once much of Thailand was a natural forest frontier but this frontier has now moved to its neighbouring states. It is not at all clear that the exploitation of the natural resources of Myanmar, Laos, Vietnam and similar Indo-China countries will set them on the path to sustainable development at this time in their history. Nor is there any guarantee that their rich biodiversity will be conserved.

Conservation of nature and biodiversity is a high priority for many high-income countries. To some extent, it is an international public good. This raises the question of the extent to which high-income countries should pay for conservation in LDCs. The Global Environmental Facility (GEF) of the World Bank provides a subsidy for nature conservation (in terms of reduced interest) to developing countries, but large-scale official aid for nature conservation from high income countries may be required (with appropriate delivery mechanisms), if high income countries are to achieve their demands for sustaining biodiversity globally.

GENERAL POLICY MATTERS

Market-making policies will not be enough to solve all the environmental problems likely to arise from Asian economic growth. Communal and international co-operation (outside market mechanisms) will be necessary.

Traditional policy instruments proposed by environmental economists, for example, pollution taxes, Co-asian property rights and tradeable environmental-use permits, are unlikely to be sufficient to address all of Asia's environmental problems effectively. In many cases, geographical zoning of economic activities and, in some cases, prohibition will be needed on environmental economics grounds (Tisdell, 1993c).

At the macro-level, will the optimistic development scenario be fulfilled in East Asia, involving sustainable development and eventually population stabilisation? Or are we to expect severe environmental degradation and global pollution (when combined with the impact of high-income countries) resulting in serious global environmental consequences via either the greenhouse effect or biodiversity loss? Market systems do not seem capable of ruling out the latter possibility and, as observed earlier, political mechanisms are likely to be biased in favour of economic growth at the expense of the natural environment.

CONSERVATION OF BIODIVERSITY IN CHINA

China was one of the first nations to sign the United Nations Biodiversity Convention, and is a country with valuable biodiversity. It has been claimed that, 'China's biodiversity ranks eighth in the world and first in the Northern Hemisphere' (Chen Jinghun, 1994, p. 171). China has many diverse ecosystems, a great variety of plants and animals and 'has been very successful at cultivating hybrid plants from a wide range of wild species, making China one of the world's three largest centres of origin for cultivated plants' (Chen Jinghun, 1994, p. 171). Nevertheless, there are major threats to the conservation of its biodiversity.

China has experienced a substantial reduction in its natural forest, woodland and grassland so that the proportion of its area under natural vegetation cover is now substantially smaller than that of India (World Resources Institute, 1994). Furthermore, at least in the recent past, China's forests have been harvested at an unsustainable rate. Its forest cover diminishes annually by about 5 000 square kilometres and grassland and water catchment areas are subject to considerable degradation (Chen Jinghun, 1994, p. 173). These effects are primarily results of increased population and pressures of economic growth; for example, encroachment of agriculture on naturally vegetated areas and the intensification of agriculture, and the need for fuel and timber supplies. Consequently, the proportion of threatened and endangered species in China is up to twice the world's average (15–20 per cent compared to 10–15 per cent) and so globally, conservation action in China needs to be a high priority. Apart from this, the introduction of exotic species and the use of high-yield varieties of agriculture has been a factor in the disappearance of genetic material in China.

A number of measures are proposed in *China's Agenda 21* to deal with these problems. These include the establishment of an Office for the Conservation of Biodiversity, extension of the systems of nature reserves, conservation of habitats other than those within the nature reserve systems, establishment of a national network for off-site conservation of genetic materials, increased efforts to domesticate rare and endangered species and work towards the restoration of degraded ecosystems. Various measures are outlined to strengthen the management of the protection of biodiversity, improve information systems for monitoring biodiversity, for encouraging international and regional co-operation in the protection of biodiversity and for expanding scientific research on the protection of biodiversity and its sustainable use.

Three models are mentioned (Executive of the State Council, 1994, pp. 177–178) as demonstration projects for combining the conservation of biodiversity and its utilisation. These are:

(1) an ecotourism development model;
(2) a domestication and artificial breeding model of species in nature reserves. Steps will be taken to conserve the habitats and natural species by means of artificial reproduction;
(3) multiple use of biological resources on a sustainable basis.

Specific areas are mentioned where these demonstration models can be trialled.

The document *China: Biodiversity Conservation Plan* (National Environmental Protection Agency, 1994) provides further details on China's strategies for biodiversity conservation and expands on Chapter 15 of *China's Agenda 21* (Executive of the State Council, 1994). This document identifies a number of reserves in Yunnan Province as having a high priority for protection of their tropical and sub-tropical forest ecosystems. All the tropical reserves mentioned for Yunnan are located in Xishuangbanna Prefecture, and the sub-tropical forests occur in the south of the Hengduan Mountains. One of the important projects mentioned in *China: Biodiversity Conservation Plan* is the 'investigation of the feasibility of integrating conservation of biodiversity with efforts for economic development by people living in areas surrounding nature reserves' (p. 83). The reason for this project, which will involve test cases at four selected nature reserves, has been explained as follows:

Most of China's nature reserves are located in poor rural areas with limited opportunities for economic development. People depend heavily on natural resources for subsistence and cash generating activities. They continue to utilize resources from high biodiversity ecosystems set aside for protection, and increasing population and economic growth lead to over-exploitation of the land and degradation of the resource base on which the people depend. Pressures then increase to use resources inside nature reserves, and ecological damage of surrounding areas threaten the function of protected ecosystems. As a result many nature reserves have been severely degraded since they were established, and some have entirely lost the biodiversity values they were intended to protect.

The future viability of the nature reserve system depends on developing successful programs to address the economic needs of local people while still fulfilling the conservation goals. Instead of simply discouraging unwise development, nature reserve managers need to cooperate with local communities to encourage the search for types of development sustainable over the long term and compatible with reserve management goals. The issue is whether the natural resources outside reserves can support the human population in the long term.

The chief obstacles to sustainable development are:

– lack of coordination among the various agencies;
– lack of information among the local people about the values of
   biodiversity and of methods of development that protect

biodiversity;
- lack of opportunities developed to allow local people to benefit from biodiversity while not destroying the biological resources;
- lack of funds necessary for the short-term investments that will generate long-term benefits;
- too much focus on immediate financial gain (this can ruin the most carefully planned sustainable development projects, because a few people may not be satisfied with the benefits provided by the 'sustainable activities' and may decide to over-exploit the natural resources as before, for extra personal or community gain), (Environmental Protection Agency, 1994, p. 83).

These are all important issues in Xishuangbanna Prefecture, where population pressures and desires for higher levels of cash incomes continue to place pressure on nature protection and on the nature reserves located there. Ways are being considered by the Ministry of Forestry and the Nature Reserve Protection Bureau of Xishuangbanna to reduce these pressures. Methods considered, or being trialled, include ecotourism, economic assistance with community (village) development projects such as agroforestry, and regulated multiple economic use of reserves by local people. These will be subjects for attention in later chapters of this book.

CONCLUDING COMMENTS

Economic growth in Asia has already done much to reduce poverty there and promises rising incomes in China and throughout most of East Asia. This economic growth has been welcomed by many high-income countries, for example Australia and the United States, as providing them with new market opportunities, including growing export markets. However, the environmental consequences of Asian economic growth have had less public attention in high-income countries and 'official' documents (such as those of the World Bank) paint a favourable long-term picture environmentally.

Nevertheless, we need to be more cautious about the environmental consequences of this economic growth. How confident can we be that the environmental results of this economic growth in Asia will be favourable, especially on a global scale? Furthermore, are special measures needed to protect the natural living resources of those southeast Asian countries such as Laos which have not yet felt the brunt of economic growth?

In addition, we should be more critical of the view that it is acceptable for a country to deplete or degrade its environmental or natural resource stock to obtain economic growth if its per capita income is low. Depletion would only seem defensible if it enabled escape from a low-equilibrium trap and, possibly, should only be attempted at an 'appropriate' time.

Nevertheless, in the early stages of the economic growth process, selective conservation of natural resources (as well as man-made ones) is likely to be justified, taking into account the probable value of such conservation to future, as well as current, generations. It is probably never optimal to throw all concern for environmental conservation to the wind, even in low-income economies, including the remaining low-income economies in Asia. However, low-income countries are likely to require economic assistance for environmental conservation (including conservation of biodiversity) from high-income ones, if the conservation objective is to be afforded a high priority. Such assistance should be considered sympathetically both from global equity point of view and from a global economic efficiency viewpoint, namely the optimal provision of conservation-type public goods of global value (Tisdell, 1990, Ch. 4). In addition, high-income countries may have to shoulder a greater part of the cost of preserving the globe's environment by reducing their own levels of emissions of 'pollutants', such as greenhouse gases. Asian economic growth can be expected to accelerate international political concerns about these issues.

The remainder of this book will focus on case studies of living natural resource conservation in Asia, particularly in nature reserves or national parks, concentrating on Xishuangbanna State Nature Reserve, located in southern Yunnan (China), to provide most of the case material. In the penultimate chapter, conservation in north-east India is given particular attention. Both Yunnan and north-east India contain a rich variety of living resources and cultural diversity, which are threatened by economic change and development. The biodiversity present in these regions and its preservation, are of worldwide interest, and the world may also be poorer if these regions are lost. Furthermore, such loss is irreversible.

Measures to conserve biodiversity, such as the establishment of nature reserves, can have positive and negative effects on local communities. In relation to Xishuangbanna the following are considered: the costs and benefits of biodiversity conservation through the province of

Xishuangbanna State Nature Reserve; strategies for reconciling economic development, nature conservation and local communities; tourism (especially ecotourism) and the conservation of nature and cultures; the economic costs of agricultural pests protected by nature and reserves and associated compensation policies for agriculturalists; and the political economy of financing nature reserves in China. Although this part of the study focuses on Xishuangbanna, the case material is of wider relevance, both for China and for developing countries in Asia and elsewhere. The penultimate chapter introduces problems involved in achieving sustainable development and conserving biodiversity in northeast India. It illustrates the complexities of co-evolution; the interaction between cultural and institutional factors, socio-economic change and the conservation of nature and its life-support systems, as well as problems involved in sustaining and expanding agricultural production. Similar problems are experienced in other parts of Asia, especially in those hilly areas where shifting agriculture is still practised.

REFERENCES

Alauddin, M. and C.A. Tisdell (1991), *The 'Green Revolution' and Economic Development*, London: Macmillan.

Alauddin, M. and C.A. Tisdell (1997), *The Environment and Economic Development in South Asia*, London: Macmillan.

Chen, Jinghun (Executive Editor)(1994), *Environmental Action Plan of China 1991–2000*, Beijing: China Environmental Science Press.

Executive of the State Council (1994), *China's Agenda 21 – White Paper on China's Population, Environment and Development in the 21st Century*, Beijing: China Environmental Science Press.

Hartwick, J.M. (1977), 'Intergenerational equity and the investing of rents from exhaustible resources', *American Economic Review*, **67**, 972–974.

Hohl, A. and C.A. Tisdell (1995), 'Peripheral tourism: development and management', *Annals of Tourism Research*, **22**(37), 517–34.

Ministry of Forestry (1992), 'Feasibility study – GEF-B project', World Bank Loan Project, mimeo, Beijing: Ministry of Forestry.

National Environmental Protection Agency (1994), *China: Biodiversity Conservation Action Plan*, Beijing: National Environmental Protection Agency.

Ponting, C. (1991), *A Green History of the World*, London: Sinclair–Stevenson.

Schumpeter, J.A. (1942), *Capitalism, Socialism and Democracy*, 2nd ed., New York: Harper Brothers.

Sebastian, I. and A. Alicbusan (1989), 'Sustainable development: issues in adjustment lending policies', *Environment Department Divisional Working Papers 1989–6*, Washington, D.C.: The World Bank.

Swanson, T. (1994), *The International Regulation of Extinction*, New York: New York University Press.

Tisdell, C.A. (1990), *Natural Resources, Growth and Development*, New York: Praeger.

Tisdell, C.A. (1991), *Economics of Environmental Conservation*, Amsterdam: Elsevier Science Publishers.

Tisdell, C.A. (1992), 'Conservation, Protected Areas and the Global Economic System: How Debt, Trade, Exchange Rates, Inflation and Macroeconomic Policy Affect Biological Diversity'. Pp. 35–55 in *Parks for Life: Enhancing the Role of Protected Areas in Sustaining Society*, Plenary Session and Symposium Papers, IVth World Congress of National Parks and Protected Areas, Caracas, Venezuela, February, 1992, Gland, Switzerland: IUCN.

Tisdell, C.A. (1993a), *Environmental Economics*, Aldershot, UK: Edward Elgar.

Tisdell, C.A. (1993b), *Economic Development in the Context of China*, London: Macmillan,

Tisdell, C.A. (1993c), Aquaculture and environmental economics'. A paper presented to International Symposium on the Socio-economics of Aquaculture, Keelung, Taiwan, 14–17 December, 1993.

Tisdell, C.A. (1993d), 'Combining biological conservation, sustainability and economic growth: can we overcome potential conflict?', *Discussion Paper No. 130*, Brisbane: Department of Economics, University of Queensland

Tisdell, C.A. (1994), 'Population Economics, Development and Global Security', in N. Polunin and M. Nazim (eds), *Environmental Challenges, Population and Global Security*, Geneva: Foundation for Environmental Conservation.

Tisdell, C.A. (1997), 'China's Environmental Problems and its Economic Growth', in C.A. Tisdell and J.C.H. Chai (eds), *China's Economic Growth and Transition*, Brisbane: Department of Economics, The University of Queensland, pp. 1–14.

Tisdell, C.A. (1997a), 'Protection of the environment in transitional economies', *Regional Development Dialogue*, **18**(1), 32–49.

Tisdell, C.A. (1997b), 'China's environmental problems with particular attention to its energy supply and air quality', *Economics, Ecology and the Environment*, Working Paper No. 10, Department of Economics, The University of Queensland, Brisbane, Australia.

Tisdell, C.A. and Jie Wen (1991), 'Investment in China's tourism industry: its scale, nature and policy issues', *China Economic Review*, **2**(2), 175–193.

Tisdell, C.A., K. Roy and J. Gannon (1996), 'Sustainability of Tribal Villages in West Bengal: The Impact of Technological and Environmental Change at Village Level', in R.N. Ghosh, Y.M. Melotte and M.A.B. Siddique (eds), *Economic Development and Change: South Asia and the third World*, Calcutta: International Institute for Development Studies and Perth: Centre for Migration and Development Studies, The University of Western Australia, pp. 54–67.

Tisdell, C.A., M. Alauddin and M. Mujeri (forthcoming), 'Water Resource Availability, Management and Environmental Spillovers in Bangladesh', in P. Thakur (ed.), *Perspectives in Resource Management in Developing Countries*, New Dehli: Concept Publishing.

Todaro, M.P. (1981), *Economic Development in the Third World*, 2nd edn, New York: Longman.

World Commission on Environment and Development (1987), *Our Common Future*, New York: Oxford University Press.

World Bank (1992), *World Development Report: Development and the Environment*, New York: Oxford University Press.

World Resources Institute (1993), *World Resources 1994–95*, New York, Oxford University Press.

Zhiyong, H., B. Keguang and C.A. Tisdell (1991), 'Cadmium exposure in Daye Country, China: environmental assessment and management, health and income effects'. *Environmental Management and Health*, **2**(2), 20–25.

10. Economics of *in situ* Biodiversity Conservation in China: Xishuangbanna Nature Reserve as an Example

BACKGROUND

Considerable loss of biodiversity has been occurring in China, as in most developing countries, and threats are increasing because of China's rapid rate of economic growth. China is therefore developing and considering plans and policies, with assistance from international organisations such as the World Bank, to improve its wildlife programmes systematically. However, being still a low-income country, China must carefully weigh up the economic benefits and costs of its biodiversity conservation programme and design it to generate as much economic benefit as possible, without compromising its conservation objectives. Such considerations are especially important at the local level, to gain support for conservation measures and maintain or increase local standards of living. This is illustrated by Xishuangbanna Nature Reserve in southwest China. Policy-makers recognise the importance of integrating conservation within this reserve with harmonious economic development in Xishuangbanna Prefecture, and reject the isolated 'island' concept of conservation planning. Such an approach calls for regional integration of economic development and conservation and will make for greater sustainability of conservation programmes. Prospects for sustaining biodiversity in China will be heavily influenced by socio-political factors which, in turn, can be expected to reflect economic considerations.

Biodiversity conservation has become a major international issue. This is underlined by the establishment of the international Convention on Biological Diversity, as a result of the United Nations Conference on Environment and Development held in Rio de Janeiro in 1992. It is, however, one thing to adopt conventions and another to put them into practice. Because the major part of the globe's remaining biodiversity exists in less developed countries, particularly in tropical and subtropical zones, success in maintaining biodiversity will depend significantly on the success of conservation programmes in these countries and areas. Unfortunately, from an economic viewpoint, less developed countries are not well placed for nature conservation. Reasons include the following:

(1) Because per capita incomes in less developed countries are low, economic growth is likely to be favoured even when it is at the expense of nature conservation. Individuals with low income usually regard conservation of nature and biodiversity as a luxury.

(2) Even though practices exploiting or mining nature may be unsustainable, local people may fail to appreciate this (Cf. Tisdell, 1986). They may therefore favour such practices.

(3) Even though local people may realise that their economic exploitation of nature is unsustainable, they may discount the future very heavily (Tisdell, 1991, sec. 4.7) or have no other viable economic alternatives to such exploitation.

(4) Techniques for excluding poachers and trespassers from nature reserves may be costly and the socio-economic incentive of rangers to enforce the rules may be weak. Being relatively poor themselves, they may be tempted by bribes or inclined to turn a blind eye to transgressors. Furthermore, because government budgets in LDCs are small, few rangers may be assigned to protected areas and they may be ill-equipped.

(5) In many cases, villagers are already resident in areas set aside for nature protection, and depend on the use of these areas for their livelihood. To remove them forcibly is a difficult decision to take, particularly if viable economic alternatives cannot be guaranteed elsewhere.

(6) With economic growth and social change, traditional communal mechanisms for nature conservation are liable to be undermined (Tisdell, 1991, Ch. 4). Natural areas may, therefore, increasingly become open-access areas, resulting in repetitions of the tragedy of the commons, or they may be put under the control of central authorities unable to exert much influence on local resource-use.

(7) There may be a widespread perception that a country receives little or no material benefit from nature conservation. Therefore, nature conservation may be given a low priority by most politicians in

LDCs.

The above points are significant constraints to conservation of biodiversity in less developed countries. For the most part, they are also problems facing biodiversity conservation in China.

BIODIVERSITY CONSERVATION IN CHINA

Considerable loss of biodiversity has occurred in China and the number of endangered species has increased (Fan and Song, 1993, p. 24). Threats are increasing because of the country's rapid rate of economic growth. Therefore, China is developing and considering plans and policies, with assistance from international organisations such as the World Bank, to make its programmes for wildlife conservation more effective. However, because China is still a low-income country, it must carefully weigh up the economic benefits and costs of its conservation programmes and design these to generate as much economic benefit as possible without compromising its conservation objectives. In particular, if its programmes are to obtain local support, they must deliver economic benefits at the local level.

The World Bank (1992) indicates that, in 1990, 3 per cent of the land area of China was afforded official national nature protection. This compares with 3.8 per cent, on average, for low-income countries, 4.6 per cent for middle-income countries and 10.2 per cent for high-income countries. By comparison, the percentage for India is 4.3 per cent. Thus, on the basis of these figures, the proportionate area afforded nature protection in China is low by international comparison[1]. The reason for this is not entirely clear because it is not explained solely by low incomes and high population densities, as is apparent from the Indian case. Fan and Song (1993, pp. 24, 25) suggest that 'a weak economic base and backward science and technology cannot satisfy the needs of social development. As China is a developing country with a large population, it cannot put enough money into nature conservation. This problem will remain for a long time.' Incidentally, they estimate a slightly higher proportion of China's territory to be in nature reserves than does the World Bank, namely 4 per cent. This is not surprising because the World Bank statistics only refer to nationally protected areas. However, this does not change the broad picture – by international comparison (particularly comparison with high-income countries) only a relatively small proportion of China has official nature protection.

Nevertheless, the area protected has increased considerably since 1979 and at the end of 1991 was estimated to have reached 4.5 per cent of its land area (Zhu, 1993).

The largest proportion of nature reserves and their land area have been under the control of the Ministry of Forestry. However, in 1998, the National People's Congress announced changes which could result in the National Environment Protection Agency (NEPA) assuming major responsibility for nature protection in China. The management of nature reserves in China is made difficult by several factors most of which have an economic basis. These include (see Yan Xun, 1993):

(1) Shortage of funds for capital works and management within the reserves.
(2) Lack of well trained personnel for nature management and for more general management tasks in reserves.
(3) Use and pressure to use (exploit) nature reserves for subsistence and commercial purposes by human populations from neighbouring reserves or resident within them. In some areas, population increases are intensifying these pressures.
(4) Lack of interest in nature conservation of the local people in some regions, which may sometimes arise from inadequate education about its value.
(5) In some cases, increased tourism is also considered to be a threat to nature conservation (Yan Xun, 1993, sec. 3.6).
(6) Absence of national scientific research which would be useful for nature management.

The management of protected areas in most countries suffers, as a rule, from shortage of funds. This is because protected areas can normally earn little income and so rely for their finance primarily on government handouts. However, there are exceptions – national parks in South Africa are largely self-financing. In the Chinese context, particularly in the past, economic self-reliance has been stressed as desirable (even at the local level) (Jia, 1993) but the scope for nature reserves to be self-reliant financially is likely to be limited, particularly when conservation goals are given a high priority. Lack of economic self-reliance has weakened the ability of managers of protected areas to obtain resources.

Lack of well trained managers and rangers for protected areas is a problem in many countries. In the case of China, many of its nature reserves occur in remote areas and it is difficult to recruit and retain suitable personnel in these places. This also seems to be the case in

Australia.

In many less developed countries, local populations threaten nature protection in reserves, this is because the people concerned are usually poor and have few viable economic alternatives to exploiting the resources within the reserve. One way to meet this problem is to develop alternative economic possibilities for local people, but unfortunately this is often too difficult, especially in remote regions. However, it is a strategy being explored in China. Lack of interest of local people in nature conservation, while it may sometimes arise from lack of education, may more often be traced to the idea that nature protection can threaten their livelihood or provides them with little or no economic benefit.

Tourism, particularly ecotourism, may be a means to give economic benefits from nature protection to local people. However, the benefits can vary considerably from case to case, and often only a small share of these benefits trickles through to locals. Local people will be especially interested in whether their economic gains from this source exceed the other economic opportunities forgone by them as a result of nature protection. Clearly the matter is complex. Some managers of nature conservation believe that tourism and nature conservation should not be mixed, or that the former should be kept at arm's length from the latter (Yan Xun, 1993, see 3.6), whereas others see it as a means to improve economic self-reliance and a force which will favour nature conservation in the long term.

XISHUANGBANNA NATURE RESERVE – ITS NATURE MANAGEMENT AND ECONOMIC ISSUES

Xishuangbanna State Nature Reserve is located in Xishuangbanna Prefecture in the southwest of Yunnan (see Fig. 10.1) in the tropical zone of China. Internationally, it is considered to be rich in biodiversity (Myers, 1988, 1990; Mittermaier and Werner, 1990). Although the whole reserve consists of 241 800 hectares, it is divided into five sub-reserves, (see Figure 12.1). This fragmentation may reduce its conservation value to some extent. Its core area is 132 500 hectares.

Unlike nature reserves in Australia and the United States, a sizeable local population is resident or adjacent to Xishuangbanna Nature Reserve and dependent on it for their livelihood. The residents engage in agriculture, forestry, animal production, fisheries, and small-scale retailing and commercial activities. Approximately 15 400 people reside in 90 villages in the reserve. About half of their gross economic production is obtained from livestock production – mainly pigs and cattle. Crops account for about 44 per cent of the value of gross output of the population resident in the reserve and, in declining economic importance, consist of rice and vegetables, sugar cane, cinnamon, tea, fruit and rubber. A small amount of gross output is derived from forestry in the reserve, rice-processing, brick-making and bamboo-processing. Slash-and-burn agriculture is the norm. While hunting and other activities detrimental to conservation in the reserve are prohibited, these laws are difficult to police in practice.

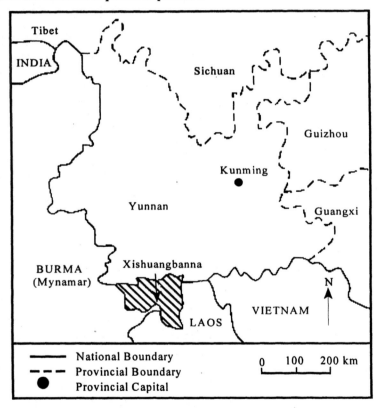

Figure 10.1   The location of Xishuangbanna Dai Autonomous Prefecture, Yunnan Province, South-west China

There are pressures on the reserve from the population within it as well as from those contiguous to it. In 1990, 354 000 people lived in the area adjoining the reserve, which has been classified as a buffer zone.

It is claimed that: 'Principle threats to the biodiversity riches of Xishuangbanna are continued shifting cultivation, the collection of firewood and construction timber, and hunting. All these factors are increased by the relentless build-up of human density which still increases by 3 per cent per year. The situation is complicated as a result of the diverse ethnic make-up of the population and the different ethnic rights and traditions that depend on forest utilisation', (Ministry of Forestry, 1993, p. 44).

Dai, Hani, Bulang, Lahu, Yao, Wa, Yi and Jinuo minorities are resident or near the reserve. This adds sociological complications to its management and can give rise to sensitive issues.

The Ministry of Forestry is concerned that more effort must be made to protect the reserve. It is believed that areas which remain in good condition are not so much due to good protection or stewardship but to the fact that population pressure has not yet reached them. It is, however, predicted that within the next few years, human population pressure will impinge on all areas of the reserve.

There is also a remote threat to nature in the reserve from climate change, this is due to global influences as well as local deforestation and acid rain from the increasing numbers of industrial pollution sites in Yunnan. Tourism, if it is not well managed, can also be damaging to the natural environment in the reserve.

Each of the sub-reserves (see Figure 12.1) has its own management division and all except Shangyong have a management station. Shangyong Sub-reserve is managed from the Mengla management station. A number of benefits have been identified for conservation of the reserve but these have not been quantified or estimated in economic terms. They include:

(1) Biodiversity conservation.
(2) Favourable regulation of water flows throughout the year, maintenance of water quality and reduction of siltation. Some of these benefits are obtained in Cambodia, Laos and Vietnam because this area is part of the catchment area for the Mekong.
(3) The forests of Xishuangbanna are believed to be important for regulating local climate. Change of climate as a result of forest loss would adversely affect tropical moist crops such as rubber and tea which are important in the region.
(4) An attraction for tourists (see Chapter 12). The forests of the region are already a significant attraction and could become even more

important. In 1994, three sites in the reserve received tourists on a
fee-paying basis. These were the Bubong tree-top walk site, Menglun
Limestone/Forest Cliff and San-Ca-He. Total annual fees of
approximately ¥30 000-40 000 (equivalent to US$4 000-5 000) were
raised through visitors to these sites. Development plans were under
way to increase the number of visitors to the San-Ca-He and
Menglun sites. Many visitors to Xishuangbanna travel along roads
which pass through or alongside the reserve and enjoy nature
without any payment for this privilege.

(5) The reserve provides a useful resource for scientific research.

(6) An educational resource for training and formal education in tropical
biology, environmental management, conservation and wildlife
management, as well as for general education of the public.

The following economic costs have to be offset against these benefits:

(1) The costs of management of the reserve. In the 1993 financial year,
the Chinese government contributed ¥1.74m for the running
expenses of the reserve; that is the equivalent of about US$230 000.
While the reserve received some income from other sources, such as
the sale of concessions to villagers for using some of the resources
and fees from visitors, government funds covered most of its
expenses.

(2) Losses in income from agriculture, forestry and so on within the
reserve due to restrictions on these activities. Limited use of the
reserve by villagers is permitted on a fee basis. They are, for
example, permitted to cultivate a special ginger in the forest. This
ginger is used for medicinal purposes. Firewood collection is
possible, and some concessions for cutting timber for village
construction are available. Concessions have also been given on
occasions for the growing of passionfruit and other fruits, and in one
sub-reserve (Shangyong), for rubber tree plantings. Doubts have
been raised about the compatibility of these latter projects with the
conservation goals of the reserve.

(3) Economic damage to agriculture, caused by animals or other
protected wildlife, as the result of their straying from the reserve (see
Chapter 13). Elephants *Elaphus maximus*, are the main source of
agricultural damage, accounting for about 90 per cent of the
economic damage caused by wildlife straying outside the reserve.
WWF has donated electric fence equipment to some villages near
the reserve, in an attempt to reduce the damage by elephants to

crops. Wildlife straying from the reserve is estimated to cause, on average, ¥1 million (about US$125 000) in agricultural damage annually (personal comment, Director, Bureau for the Protection of Xishuangbanna State Nature reserve, October 1994). While a compensation scheme is operated by the Bureau protecting the reserve, villagers receive only about 10 per cent compensation for the damages caused. Other wildlife which cause agricultural damage include monkeys, (for example, rhesus monkey *Macaca mulatto*), the black bear *Selenaratos thibetanus*, the gaur *Bos gaurus*, sambar deer *Cervus unicolor* and the wild pig *Sus scrofa*. It should be noted that agricultural damage by wildlife from a reserve can become a source of local political agitation against it, and thereby politically threaten its sustainability.

Although quantification of benefits and costs for protection of the reserve would be useful, insufficient data are available to do this accurately at present. However, some quantification is possible and there is scope for economic input in considering whether the conservation goals or standards for the reserve are being achieved most economically.

From the above, it can be seen that the annual economic costs of the reserve are equivalent to at least US$345 000 per year (consisting of expenses met by the Chinese government for its management, plus agricultural damages from its wildlife). The economic benefits appropriated by the administrators of the reserve are very small. These consist of the equivalent of about US$4 000-5 000 from ecotourism (fees from visitors) and about the same amount from concessions, mostly from villagers allowed to use the resources of the reserve. Thus, at present, positive economic net benefits (taking account of all benefits and costs) would largely rest on the size of offsite benefits (for example, the sizes of values for existence, options and bequests associated with preservation of the reserve, offsite environmental benefits in terms of favourable impacts of water flows and microclimates) and on potential future income from ecotourism. The benefit-cost ratio of the reserve, therefore, depends on a number of unknowns and intangibles. If, on the other hand, the reserve were to open for agricultural development, yields on the average could be expected to be low and unsustainable. Consideration of this alternative strengthens the case from a sustainability viewpoint for maintaining this protected area. Given the global significance of the reserve, China appears to have a case for financial assistance in achieving its conservation objective. Already, WWF (Europe) has given considerable help towards this and the Global

Environmental Facility (GEF) has provided further foreign assistance.

The Ministry of Forestry of China proposed a project to the World Bank for funding from the Global Environmental Facility (GEF) to improve the management of nature conservation in Xishuangbanna and elsewhere in China. Allocation of funds from the GEF is the responsibility of the United Nations Development Programme and the World Bank and is designed to provide financial support to less developed countries for environmental projects of global significance. Let us consider this project and the prospects for tourism development associated with the reserve.

CONSERVATION GOALS FOR XISHUANGBANNA AND TOURISM

As a primary objective, the Ministry of Forestry is to develop Xishuangbanna as a key example of nature conservation in China. It would like Xishuangbanna to act as a pilot for the integration of ethnic communities into conservation, to be a leader in the development of ecotourism and for co-ordinated research programmes to be developed there.

Specific goals mentioned in connection with the Ministry of Forestry draft request for GEF funding for Xishuangbanna State Nature Reserve include:

'– strengthen the reserve management and protection to safeguard the region's unique wealth of biodiversity;
– develop ecotourism facilities so as to help pay for and justify protection of the forest area, in ways that do not threaten the biodiversity resource base;
– develop processes for assisting villages in and around the reserve to reduce their dependence on forest resources, strengthen their involvement in forest protection and protect their ethnic rights and features;
– provide a favourable environment for conducting scientific research on tropical biodiversity resources and the relationship between such resources and human utilisation; and
– forge co-operative linkages with other institutions involved in agriculture, forestry, and tourism extension and in research.' (Ministry of Forestry, 1993, p. 45)

The new plan for the reserve focuses on a stronger programme for the patrolling and monitoring of the reserve, and involves plans for tourism development, village assistance and new research. Minority groups are expected to be more involved in the conservation programme. There will be, for instance, training and assistance to buffer zone villages to support conservation. This will build on the conservation of holy hills or longshans. In the past, the local Dai and other minority people have left some hills in their natural state because these have been considered holy places. Information will be gathered about traditional knowledge and used where relevant for resource management.

Tourism is a notable factor in the conservation plan. It is planned to develop tourism (including ecotourism) further to provide an economic basis for conservation of the reserve. It is possible that many people coming to Xishuangbanna Prefecture will not make heavy use of the reserve in the same way that many of the visitors to the Great Barrier Reef region in Australia do not make significant use of coral reefs. There is, however, a regional 'halo-effect' from such natural attractions and secondary tourist attractions, such as appropriate exhibitions and museums located in the region (but not necessarily in the primary attraction), may prosper. Supporting tourist attractions for the reserve, such as interpretative information centres about local ecology or culture, may be developed in Jinghong or Menglun.

Tourism is already a significant industry in Xishuangbanna Prefecture. The prefectural capital, Jinghong, received about 250 000 visitors a year and Menglun 100 000, in the mid-1990s. Between 1986 and 1990, 23 000 international tourists visited the prefecture.

A five-year tourism development plan for the prefecture was drawn up containing the following key elements:

'– Jinghong will be developed to handle increased levels of tourists with enhanced facilities, such as new international air routes and increasing number of hotel facilities. In addition, international marketing will be improved with the opening of new offices in Bangkok and Hong Kong;
– the Mekong [Lancang Jiang] will be improved as a tourist route through the building of lodges along the river and by increasing and improving tourism boat traffic; and
– improve [access to and facilities] at 22 scenic spots within the prefecture', (Ministry of Forestry, 1993, pp. 41 – 42).

Many of these developments will not be in the reserve.

In developing tourism, it will be necessary to keep an appropriate balance between the provision of private tourist facilities and supply and construction of public tourist amenities and assets. In the recent past in China, there has been a tendency to expand private tourist facilities without a concomitant increase in expenditure on public facilities such as public gardens and parks, museums, historical buildings and natural attractions, many of which cannot or do not earn revenue or sufficient funds for their upkeep (Tisdell and Wen, 1991). Nevertheless, they can be extremely important in attracting tourists to an area and indirectly contribute to the expenditure of tourists locally on hotel accommodation, food, souvenirs and other private goods.

It is necessary to plan tourism development carefully, including ecotourism, if it is to be of greatest economic value to Xishuangbanna Prefecture and to support rather than damage nature conservation in the reserve. While the development of ecotourism is one of the interests of the Reserve Bureau (a body located in Xishuangbanna which helps administer the reserve), other tourism agencies may compete with it in the future. It will be necessary to exert some control over the development of tourism in the reserve. If the Bureau has a commercial interest in the business, this could compromise its overall conservation management function, or it may use its power to restrict or prevent legitimate commercial competition with its own interests. There are, therefore, some difficult decisions to be made about the role of the Reserve Bureau.

Agroforestry has been suggested as an economic activity which could be encouraged to provide local people with an alternative to exploiting the reserve for their livelihood. The economic prospects for this would, however, need to be the subject of research and analysis. One cannot prejudge the matter in advance. There is a firewood problem in this area, for example, because a considerable amount of wood is burnt in processing latex from rubber trees grown in the region (Zhu and Santiapillai, 1992). There might therefore be a market for firewood but this does not necessarily mean that agroforestry will be profitable. The following has been observed: 'There is no guarantee that untested agroforestry models will meet the living requirements of local villages and no guarantee that raised living standards among the villages inside and around the reserve will in fact reduce their levels of exploitation of the forest resources. Indeed there are several reason why such progress could increase pressure on the forest.' (Ministry of Forestry, 1993, p. 47).

The reasons for increased pressure on the reserve are not stated in the

Forestry document, but the need to improve management and protection of the reserve is stressed and it is recommended that any development of agroforestry be considered in an integrated prefectural programme rather than in isolation by the Ministry.

The need to integrate the conservation of the reserve with the harmonious development of its prefecture is increasingly recognised by Chinese policy-makers (Cf. Zhu and Yang, 1992). The isolated 'island' concept of conservation planning is unrealistic. Regional integration of economic development and conservation programmes is likely to make for greater sustainability of both.

CONCLUDING COMMENTS

China, like most developing countries, faces serious problems in maintaining biodiversity and protecting nature due to its economic situation and its strong impulse to maintain economic growth. To these general factors are added socio-economic difficulties in protecting or managing particular nature reserves. Local people strongly desire to exploit such areas for their livelihood because of their past and continuing practice of doing so. Furthermore, rising regional populations add to pressure for increasing the exploitative use of such areas.

The problems are well illustrated by the management issues faced by Xishuangbanna Nature Reserve in Yunnan. The difficulty of conserving the rich biodiversity of the reserve is compounded by economic pressures from villages in the buffer zone as well as by minorities resident in villages within the reserve. Population levels in Xishuangbanna Prefecture are rising rapidly and economic opportunities independent of the reserve's resources are expanding at an insufficient rate to cater for the rate of population increase.

The prospects for conserving nature in the reserve have to be approached in terms of the economic needs of the Prefecture, and the ability of the reserve to help satisfy these needs. Thus, planning the management of the reserve must be done in a regional context.

It is necessary to determine more exactly the costs and benefits of conserving Xishuangbanna Nature Reserve and to consider economic mechanisms that will support nature conservation, particularly at the local level. Whether tourism will provide a valuable and useful means for such support will depend on how it is developed. Although conservation of biodiversity depends ultimately on the maintenance of appropriate ecological conditions for living things, the likelihood of these being sustained by managers of protected areas depends on socio-political support, which in turn, is often influenced by economic factors. Thus, in pursuing the long-term goal of sustaining biodiversity, consideration must be given to ecology, politics and socio-economics. This is well illustrated by the situation facing Xishuangbanna State Nature Reserve in China[2].

NOTES

1. Xing Zhu in a personal communication (March 1995) pointed out: 'China's protected areas have witnessed a great increase in both number and size since 1978, with a rocketing increase occurring after the end of the 80s. The figures 3 per cent, 4 per cent and 4.5 per cent all probably only reflect the status of protected areas in different years within the forestry sector, which manages about 75 per cent of nature reserves in China. Most of these are forest and wildlife type, in line with the responsibility division set by the State Council. *China Biodiversity Conservation Action Plan* (National Environmental Protection Agency, 1994) shows the change in number and size of protected areas in recent years. The figures provide a total profile of all relevant ministries. As for the situation within the forestry sector by the end of 1993, official figures were published indicating 501 reserves, covering 50.5 million ha or 5.26 per cent of China's land area. Anyway, they would not alter the general picture you drew'.

2. Note that this chapter is a revised version of C.A. Tisdell and Xing Zhu 'Economics, gains and costs of biodiversity conservation in China', pp. 110–116 in G.C. Grigg, P.T. Hale and D. Lunney (eds), *Conservation Through Sustainable Use of Wildlife*, Brisbane: Centre for Conservation Biology, The University of Queensland.

REFERENCES

Fan, Zhiyong and Song, Yangling (1993), 'On the importance of nature reserves in nature conservation in China and giant panda protection', *Tigerpaper*, **2** (2), 23–27.

Jia, Liqun (1993), 'Examination of the prerequisites for implementing an economic self-reliance policy in China', *Revista Internazionale di Scienze Economiche Commerciali*, **39** (3).

Ministry of Forestry (1993), 'Xishuangbanna National Nature Reserve, Yunnan Province – Feasibility Study: GEF-B project', World Bank Loan Project Management Centre, Ministry of Forestry: Beijing.

Mittermaier, R.A. and T.B. Werner (1990), 'Wealth of plants and animals units 'megadiversity' countries', *Tropicus*, **4** (1),1, 4–5.

Myers, N. (1988), 'Threatened biota: hotspots in tropical forests', *Environmentalist*, **8**(8), 1-20.

Myers, N. (1990), 'The biodiversity challenge: expanded hot-spot analysis', *Environmentalist*, **10** (4), 243–56.

Tisdell, C.A. (1986), 'Conflicts about living marine-resources in Southeast Asia and Australasian waters: turtles and dugongs as cases', *Marine Resource Economics*, **3**, 89–109.

Tisdell, C.A. (1991), *Economics of Environmental Conservation*, Amsterdam: Elsevier Science Publishers.

Tisdell, C.A. and J. Wen (1991), 'Investment in China's tourism industry: its scale, nature and policy issues', *China Economic Review*, 2 (2),175–93.

World Bank (1992), *World Development Report: Development and the Environment*, Oxford University Press: New York.

Xun, Yan (1993), 'The management of nature reserves in China', mimeo; Beijing: Ministry of Forestry.

Zhu, Xiang (1993), 'China's personnel training in biodiversity conservation – background information for GEF Proposals', mimeo; Ministry of Forestry: Beijing.

Zhu, Xiang and C. Santipillai (1992), 'The Dai approach to the problem of timber extraction in Xishuangbanna Nature Reserve, China', mimeo; WWF-Asia Programme, PO Box 133, Bogor, Indonesia.

Zhu, Xiang and Yang Yuanchang (1992), 'Current management of Xishuangbanna Reserve and approaches to the existing problems', mimeo; Kunming: Southwest Forestry University.

11. Reconciling Economic Development, Nature Conservation and Local Communities

INTRODUCTION

The State Council has adopted *Agenda 21* for China, and biodiversity conservation is one plank of this agenda for China's sustainable development. This chapter provides a brief discussion of China's White Paper on *Agenda 21* and examines, as a case study, the problem of sustaining biological diversity in Xishuangbanna Dai Autonomous Prefecture in Yunnan. This area is rated as one of 'megadiversity' and deserving of high priority for conservation purposes. After discussing the general socio-economic obstacles to biodiversity conservation in Xishuangbanna, the paper examines types of strategies for reducing pressures on biodiversity and nature conservation, adopted by local communities. The preferred strategy in China for easing such pressures is to try to improve economic opportunities outside the reserves and thereby raise the income levels of people living in the neighbourhood. This approach has been adopted in Xishuangbanna and there are plans to extend it. Community development projects such as agroforestry, joint ventures in tourism and so on, are being encouraged. Mechanisms for selecting suitable community development projects, for example, using Rapid Rural Appraisal (RRA), are also considered. Without economic development at the local level, plans for biodiversity conservation are unlikely to succeed in China, or for that matter elsewhere in the developing world.

China continues to show rapid economic growth and is well on its way to its target of becoming a middle-income country in the 21st century. However, the question has been raised whether China's economic growth is environmentally sustainable and whether or not the cost to its environment is higher than it ought to be. Internationally, there are concerns about the potential of China's economic growth to add to global pollution (See Chapter 9, Tisdell, 1993, Ch. 12; Hall *et al.*, 1994; Tisdell, 1995), loss of biodiversity and loss of natural environments through for example, greenhouse gas emissions. It is also believed that a number of China's development projects will show negative returns when they are evaluated by means of extended cost-benefit analysis, and that economic welfare in China could be increased by adopting improved policies governing the use of scarce environmental goods. To a large extent, China has exploited its environment by treating it virtually as a free good. The Chinese government has, however, signalled that it no longer intends to do this.

In 1994, the State Council adopted China's *Agenda 21 – White Paper on China's Population, Environment and Development in the 21st Century*. This lengthy document presents an initial framework for China to achieve sustainable development in the 21st century, and will provide a guide in drawing up its medium- and long-term plans on economic and social development. It will, for example, influence the Ninth Five-Year Plan (1996–2000) and the Plan for 2010. It is difficult to say at this stage how much of *Agenda 21* is window-dressing and how it will be put into effect. Furthermore, as is to be expected, the document provides a broad framework and guidelines rather than a definite prescription for policy. However, we are told in its preamble that: 'The Chinese Government is determined to implement China's *Agenda 21*. This is not only because Chinese highest leaders take it seriously, but also because it will help to create a sound environment for sustainable economic development, for deepening reforms and opening to the outside world and for establishing a socialist market economy.' (State Council, 1994, p. 3).

Agenda 21 arose from the United Nations Conference on Environment and Development (UNCED) held in Brazil in 1992, when it was resolved that all nations should draw up strategies to achieve sustainable development in the 21st century (Islam, 1994). China appears to be one of the first developing countries to do this. This helps to reinforce its aim of being a political leader among developing countries on environmental issues, and to allay some international fears about China as a possible global polluter. In any case, China's *Agenda 21* is a significant policy document which takes a holistic view of development and specifically rejects the development policy of polluting now and cleaning up later.

Agenda 21 consists of 20 chapters, one of which covers conservation of biodiversity. China is a country rich in biodiversity but much of this is under threat due to habitat change caused by economic growth and, in some cases, due to population and hunting pressures. This is clear from case studies such as the one for Xishuangbanna Dai Autonomous Prefecture, reported here. Xishuangbanna Prefecture, which is located in southern Yunnan, has been rated as an area of 'megadiversity' and worthy of a special conservation effort from a global point of view (Mittermaier and Werner, 1990; Myers, 1990). However, socio-economic changes in the Prefecture are a threat to biodiversity and are creating difficulties for sustainability of production. Let us consider this matter, paying particular attention to the role of the local community in environmental conservation.

SOCIO-ECONOMIC PRESSURES ON BIODIVERSITY CONSERVATION IN XISHUANGBANNA PREFECTURE

The sustainability of biodiversity conservation often depends on political support from local communities and their willingness to avoid taking actions which destroy biodiversity. When agricultural land and other resources are in short supply, and incomes are low or are below levels strongly aspired to by local communities, political pressure is likely to build up to permit 'the development' of areas set aside for biodiversity conservation, such as nature reserves. Furthermore, incursions into such areas by illegal settlement, poaching and use of their resources are liable to occur without these actions being stopped. This often occurs in developing countries and threatens the conservation of biodiversity in nature reserves and parks (Dixon and Sherman, 1990). At the same time as this pressure increases to utilize the land to raise production on protected areas, biodiversity and conservation of natural resources is often greatly reduced outside the protected nature areas. Pressures of this type are a source of concern for biodiversity conservation in Xishuangbanna Dai Autonomous Prefecture in Yunnan, China. (See Figure 10.1).

Satellite imagery indicates that, in recent years, natural vegetation cover on land outside such protected areas has been severely reduced. Furthermore, hunting pressures in Xishuangbanna Prefecture are considerable. It is a common sight to see members of minority groups carrying guns, not only outside the reserve but even on the roads leading through it. This was observed on many occasions during a field trip to the area in October 1994. It is said that some of these guns are homemade. Their use is so widespread and traditional amongst minority groups that it would be very difficult for Chinese authorities to ban effectively the carrying of firearms in this prefecture, especially in its more remote localities. For many people, hunting is a traditional means of supplementing their incomes and a form of recreation. As human populations have increased and wild animal populations have fallen (to a large extent due to habitat changes), hunting has become an increasing threat to the preservation of wild animal populations in the prefecture.

Population Pressures

The population of the prefecture continues to increase relatively rapidly because the majority of its population consists of minorities who are not subject to the one-child rule applied to Han Chinese. In the case of the Dai nationality, for example, a family size of three is acceptable. However, penalties begin to apply for the fourth and subsequent children, typically through reduced educational support. While the available land-to-population ratio in the prefecture is relatively high by Chinese standards, agricultural productivity is low and pockets of poverty occur. Many of the Han Chinese attribute the low agricultural productivity of the land in the prefecture to the 'inefficient' traditional techniques of the minorities. At the same time, because this prefecture is somewhat remote from major markets like Kunming, little manufacturing growth has occurred. Most manufacturing in the Prefecture involves the processing or semi-processing of local agricultural products like rubber and tea.

Rubber Production

In this respect, it is interesting to consider the local rubber industry. The prefecture is an important producer of rubber for China. During the period of China's relative international economic isolation and perceived belligerent threats to it (up to 1978), the area planted to rubber in the prefecture expanded considerably. At the present time, virtually all rubber plantations are a monoculture and the density of planting and shade cover results in there being virtually no understorey. So these plantations have an extremely adverse impact on biodiversity.

Xishuangbanna is on the northern edge of the tropical zone. Therefore, it is at the northern limit of the region ecologically available for the growing of rubber trees. Conditions for growing rubber are best (because of higher temperatures) to the south of the prefecture and the crop does best of all in the river valleys. Towards the north, the crop has low productivity on higher ground because cool weather in the winter induces leaf-drop and thereby reducing latex production. Hence, to achieve satisfactory levels of productivity in the north, rubber plantations need to be confined to lower elevations. However, their planting here is at the expense of other valuable crops and/or considerable loss of biodiversity, since natural biodiversity tends to be greater at lower elevations than at higher ones. In some areas of the Shangyong and Mengla sub-reserves of the Xishuangbanna State Nature Reserve, concessions have been granted for the planting of rubber trees, a development which would clearly have an adverse impact on biodiversity.

In the past, rubber processing has also had serious consequences for tree cover because timber was used to process the rubber latex. It was estimated that for every tonne of raw rubber produced, several tonnes of timber were used in its processing, thus adding to deforestation in the prefecture. Now greater use is made of electricity in processing, but electricity, according to the Deputy Administrator of Mengla County, is in short supply and a constraint on economic development.

Nevertheless, important changes are occurring which are more favourable from a conservation and sustainable development viewpoint. Farmers are being encouraged to remove older and lower-bearing rubber trees, progressively replacing these with cocoa trees and tea bushes so that intercropping develops. In addition, the area of land used for rubber plantations in Xishuangbanna is not increasing. This is mainly because of China's open-door policy and perceived reduction in military threats. Rubber is now being imported, and imports are actually cheaper than home production. Furthermore, China's production of synthetic rubber has risen, and by mixing natural rubber with synthetic rubber, a superior tyre to the all-natural rubber tyre can be produced.

Although China's total demand for rubber products has risen, there is a possibility that rubber production in Xishuangbanna Prefecture will decline as a result of imports of rubber and substitution. However, past Chinese polices may slow or prevent this decline. Costs are involved in removing rubber trees, and replacement crops such as cocoa and tea take time to mature, so adding an extra cost. In addition, local rubber factories rely on local supplies of rubber latex for processing. In the absence of such supplies, most or all of these factories might be forced to close down and this would reduce local factory employment. Politically, this is likely to be unacceptable in Xishuangbanna, so local government is liable to take action to prevent it. Whether the factories could operate economically using imported latex or rubber is uncertain, but it seems improbable. Nevertheless, in the longer term, structural adjustment in China as a result of its open-door policy, cannot be avoided and possibly should not be prevented. However, as Longworth and Williamson (1993, Ch. 19) point out in relation to wool, important political considerations are often involved, especially if employment of minorities is at stake.

Shifting Agriculture

While most of the Dai and many of the Han people in Xishuangbanna Prefecture are engaged in settled agriculture in the river valleys and basin areas, some minorities engage in agriculture on steeply sloping lands. Slash-and-burn agriculture still occurs. With increasing population densities, the length of the cycle of this type of swidden agriculture and the productivity of the soil is being reduced. The growing of corn (maize) on steeply sloping lands by minorities is common. Corn can be eaten directly and the grain can be sold in village markets for cash. However, this crop (and many other cereals) exposes the soil to severe erosion during the wet season, since no terracing or soil conservation measures of any kind are used. Severe soil erosion combined with a shorter length of cultivation cycle is reducing the productivity of the land, and so agricultural production using this system is gradually becoming unsustainable, resulting in increasing pressures to use land still covered by natural vegetation.

Other Forms of Cropping on Uplands

It is not only minorities who grow crops on uplands in Xishuangbanna, nor is cultivation always of a shifting type. Tea is sometimes grown on steeply sloping land but it is often terraced. A few large pineapple plantations also occur on sloping ground, for example near Gannanba. Because the soil is left bare between pineapple plants, considerable soil erosion occurs on these plantations.

Chinese authorities are concerned that agricultural productivity in

Xishuangbanna may not be sustainable, given many of the current practices being used. There is also concern that agricultural production will not suffice to feed the prefecture's rising population. This may lead to greater incursions into nature reserves and place increased pressure on the conservation of biodiversity.

STRATEGIES FOR REDUCING PRESSURES ON BIODIVERSITY AND NATURE CONSERVATION IN CHINA

The strategy preferred at present in China for easing pressures on biodiversity conservation in nature reserves, is to try to improve economic opportunities outside the reserves and raise the income levels of people living in the neighbourhood. China is therefore considering, and intends testing, models to promote economic development by people living in such areas. Development and conservation in Xishuangbanna involves such an approach.

This approach has been explained as follows: 'Most of China's nature reserves are located in poor natural areas with limited opportunities for economic development. People depend heavily on natural resources for subsistence and cash generating activities. They continue to utilize resources from high biodiversity ecosystems set aside for protection, and increasing population and economic growth lead to overexploitation of the land and degradation of the resource base on which the people depend. Pressures then increase to use resources in nature reserves, and ecological damage of surrounding areas threatens the function of protected ecosystems. As a result, many nature resources have been severely degraded since they were established and some have entirely lost the biodiversity values they were intended to protect' (National Environmental Protection Agency, *et al.*, 1994, p. 83).

Therefore, promotion of economic development outside the reserves is seen as important for conservation within nature reserves. It is believed that, 'The future viability of the nature reserve system depends on developing successful programs to address the economic needs of local people while still fulfilling the conservation goals. Instead of simply discouraging unwise development, nature reserve managers need to cooperate with local communities to encourage the search for types of development sustainable over the long-term and compatible with reserve management goals. The issue is whether the natural resources outside reserves can support the human population in the long-term' (National Environmental Protection Agency *et al.*, 1994, p. 83).

Although this approach is a promising one, it is not a water-tight solution to conserving biodiversity. Often measures to increase economic productivity outside nature reserves involve intensification of land use and a reduction on biodiversity in such areas. This intensification, particularly in the case of agriculture, normally involves the greater use of resources external to the land. This could add to pressure on the resources of a reserve itself, for example, the use of its timber for construction, or perhaps, its water (in it or passing through) for irrigation and electricity generation. Higher incomes could also lead to higher effective demands for speciality items (such as special foods) which can only be provided by a nature reserve. Again the economic damage caused by animals from reserves when they move outside may rise as higher valued and more productive agriculture is introduced. Thus, social hostility to the reserve may grow. Also, as economic productivity per hectare rises outside a reserve, the view may be increasingly accepted that the reserve involves an economic waste of natural resources, not because it really does, but because the apparent relative disparity in productivity inside and outside the reserve increases. In any case, it would be unwise to relax measures to protect reserves as economic development in their surrounding areas proceeds. In fact, a strengthening of these measures may be needed as discussed again later in this chapter.

AGROFORESTRY AND SOCIAL FORESTRY PROJECTS

A popular suggestion for community projects to ease pressures on nature reserves has been to encourage villagers to engage in agroforestry. This is one of the approaches being tested in Xishuangbanna. The Bureau for the Protection of State Nature Reserve is willing to supply tree/shrub seedlings free of charge to landholders bordering the nature reserve, if they wish to engage in agroforestry. Some financial support has been received by the Bureau from World Wide Fund for Nature for the purpose and trials have begun in Zhong Tian Ba village bordering Mengyang sub-reserve. Other villages in which trials are taking place include Ba Jia Zhai, Nan Gong Shan and Hui Meng.

In Zhong Tian Ba, a small stand of mixed trees has been planted on a sloping site (but not steep). This has been contoured and tea has been planted in the depressions of the contours with the trees being planted on the ridges. Some trees for timber and some for fruit have been planted. The trees being trialled are:

Caganus cagan
Cassia siamea
Fiemngia macrophylla
Gliricidia sepium
Sesbania bispinosa
Sesbania sesban
Ligustrum lucidum

Cassia siamea has traditionally been grown by the Dai people in their villages to provide fuel. It is a nitrogen-fixing species and enriches the soil. At Zhong Tian Ba, some Cassia trees have been planted at a second site, on relatively flat land where there are now some mature tea bushes and some vegetables. Agroforesty in this village is basically intended to meet subsistence needs. Whether it will be a success remains to be seen.

Inspection in October 1994 indicated that little or no attention was given to tending the young trees. Most were being crowded out by weeds. It has been suggested that because the village does not have a serious soil erosion problem, their perceived need for agroforestry is low. However, there are no trees suitable for firewood or timber left on the land of the village. The only possible source of supply nearby is the sub-reserve. The project appears to have been a top-down initiative rather than one wanted by the village, so this may reduce its chances of success.

It should be observed that supply of seedlings may be one of the minor costs involved in agroforestry. Planting and tending young trees can be costly, and once they become established they take space away from possible alternative crops, compete with them for sunlight and in many cases, for nutrients. Also, a considerable waiting period may be required before any fruit-bearing or harvesting is possible, and this involves an economic opportunity cost which economists usually allow for by means of discounting. However, there may be symbiotic relationships with some crops and the nitrogen-fixing properties of some tree/shrub species can be an advantage.

These relationships all need to be assessed on a holistic basis, using a farming system approach. Unfortunately, *in situ* tests involving agroforestry may require many years to perform and no long-term experiments have yet been completed in Xishuangbanna. Because of lack of information about the likely economic performance of agroforestry and social forestry in Xishuangbanna, some risks are involved in encouraging local villagers to engage in these trials. On the other hand, social forestry has been practised for some time in parts of India, so it may be possible to draw suitable inferences from results there, and elsewhere. Nevertheless, *in situ* uncertainty will remain.

The economics of agroforestry and social forestry are liable to vary with location and the economic returns from alternative forms of land use. On degraded land, such as steeply sloping ground, productivity may be low, and economic returns from annual crops may also be low. Therefore, the opportunity cost of agroforestry or social forestry on such land is low, whereas on agricultural land which continues to be very productive with current cropping systems, the opportunity cost may be high. So, other things being equal, degraded lands and those of low productivity might justify a higher priority for social forestry or agroforestry than agriculturally more productive land. Degraded areas may give rise to the greatest adverse external effects, for example, through higher rates of soil erosion under their present use. Hence, the case for adopting social forestry or agroforestry on such land is strengthened, if it reduces adverse external effects. Some of the general economic issues involved in adopting agroforestry or social forestry as a land use are discussed below.

One of the main purposes of agroforestry in Xishuangbanna is intended to improve the soil, especially in areas where slash-and-burn agriculture is being practised. The trees selected for agroforestry in Xishuangbanna are native species able to withstand poor soil conditions. They are mostly nitrogen-fixing species or fruit trees. The possibility of improved soil fertility should be taken into account in the economic analysis of agroforestry.

DIGRESSION ON FORMAL ECONOMIC ASPECTS OF AGROFORESTRY AND SOCIAL FORESTRY

In considering whether to recommend to villagers projects for agroforestry or social forestry, one needs to consider the flow of net benefits from these, relative either to the best alternative projects or those which would be otherwise adopted. Suppose that one is considering a planning interval of length $t = t_n$. Then as a first step, it is necessary to compare the flow of net benefits over this interval ($0 \leq t \leq t_n$) from the agroforestry or social forestry project under consideration with the alternative. The alternative may be cropping with annuals with no tree planting. Let

$$J = J(t) \qquad (11.1)$$

represent the net benefits to be had from the alternative land use, for example, continuation of current practice and let

$$F = F(t) \qquad (112)$$

represent the net benefit from the agroforestry or social forestry project being considered. Then

$$G(t) = J(t) - F(t) \qquad (11.3)$$

represents the opportunity cost of the agroforestry or the social forestry project.

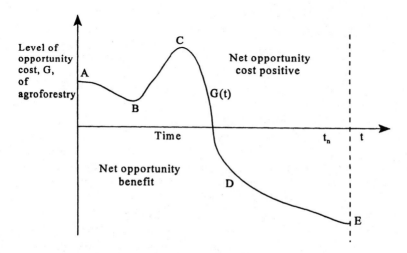

Figure 11.1 A possible opportunity cost curve for the introduction of agroforestry or social forestry

It is difficult to say *a priori* exactly what form function $G(t)$ will take. One possibility is, however, a form like that shown by Curve *ABCDE* in Figure 11.1. A net cost is incurred initially, for example planting and weeding costs for the young trees. Some loss of other crops to leave space for the newly planted trees can be expected, but intercropping may be carried on quite successfully. However, as the trees mature they may shade and compete with intercrops thus reducing their yields. Benefits from the trees may start to be realised only when they come to maturity. The discounted stream of net benefits will need to be positive if the villagers are to find agroforestry or social forestry an economic advantage.

The possibility considered in Figure 11.1 is however, just one of several. In some respects, the trees may have symbiotic relationships with intercrops, or provide windbreaks which add to productivity. Some high-value intercrops may also require shade in order to thrive; this would be so for cocoa. Much depends upon the exact type of agroforestry or social forestry being promoted; however, a major obstacle is likely to arise at the village level when a considerable period must elapse before net benefits are achieved and upfront investment is needed.

SOME ALTERNATIVE COMMUNITY DEVELOPMENT PROJECTS AND METHODS TO BENEFIT LOCAL COMMUNITIES

Agroforestry/social forestry is just one possible development to provide local economic opportunities and ease pressures for the unsustainable use of nature reserves. Other possibilities include:

(1) The adoption of improved agricultural techniques to increase yields or to enable the introduction of higher valued crops. In Xishuangbanna, many of the agricultural methods and techniques are traditional. Rice is harvested and threshed by hand. Buffalo are used for ploughing and other draft purposes. Productivity tends to be low.

(2) Although Xishuangbanna receives a heavy annual rainfall, this is concentrated in the monsoon season. For at least six months of the year Xishuangbanna is relatively dry. Irrigation of crops during this period would increase annual agricultural production. In the longer term, however, multiple cropping can have a negative effect on yields. Furthermore, a number of the suggestions for introducing irrigation would be at the expense of conservation of Xishuangbanna State Nature Reserve. This includes a proposal to dam the Lancang Jiang (Mekong River). The dam would submerge a portion of the Mengyang sub-reserve but would supply electricity and irrigation water. It has also been suggested that small dams or weirs might be constructed in the reserve itself, to allow local irrigation on the currently farmed 'river' flats located in or near the reserve. However, such development might conceivably have an adverse impact on ecosystems in the reserve.

(3) Opportunities for villagers to make greater multiple use of economic resources in the reserve may be considered if these uses are

compatible with conservation objectives. Currently, some multiple use by villagers is permitted in Xishuangbanna State Nature Reserve. For example, concessions have been granted for the cultivation of a local special ginger *Amomum villosum* which grows only on the shaded forest floor and which is used for medicinal purposes. Its culture does not appear to compromise conservation values. But this is not true of all multiple uses. Concessions to grow rubber trees or passionfruit would compromise conservation values in the reserve. Concessions for rubber plantations have been given in Shangyong Sub-reserve and for growing passionfruit in Menglun Sub-reserves. Ecotourism is another possible multiple use of a protected area. Ecotourism within the Nature Reserve has been used at one site to increase the economic opportunities of local villagers. A joint business venture has been started between a local farming co-operative and the management of Xishuangbanna State Reserve to utilise the site at the Forest/Limestone Cliffs site near Menglun. The capital for developing this site with bridge construction and walking tracks, has been provided by the local farming co-operative. At another site in the reserve, San-Ca-He, the Nature Protection Bureau has invested in tourism development without local participation or a joint venture. It seems likely that it will lose financially from this development.

(4) Another possibility is to employ local people in the management of the nature reserve. This is in fact done in Xishuangbanna and village people (mainly villager leaders) are paid a retainer to act as guards for the reserve.

(5) Yet another way to increase local economic opportunities is to expand employment opportunities in urban areas and encourage migration from the countryside to urban areas. Most towns in Xishuangbanna have economic development zones, and some are eligible for international trade concessions as a part of China's drive to increase cross-border trade with Laos, Myanmar and Vietnam. Considerable expansion is under way in service industries to cater for the expected expansion of the tourist trade. However, the capacity of Xishuangbanna to absorb a large proportion of the population in urban areas may be limited by the cost of transport of commodities to and from major markets. Such costs, combined with the small local market may make most local manufacturing uneconomic. If, on the other hand, outward migration becomes easier to larger cities in Yunnan such as Kunming, this would ease population pressures in Xishuangbanna Prefecture.

SEARCHING FOR SUITABLE PROJECTS FOR THE ECONOMIC DEVELOPMENT OF VILLAGES

Traditional cost-benefit analysis concentrates on choosing between projects the set of which is already known. However, often the more important and difficult issue is to discover and ensure that all promising projects are included in the set of decision possibilities. How does one go about this?

Sometimes projects are suggested from above by authorities living outside the village. This appears to have been so for the agroforestry and social forestry projects in Xishuangbanna. Suggestions have also come from the same source that villagers should grow rice on hilly areas using terracing, even though opinions differ about the desirability of this. For one thing, terracing is costly. Although those villagers practising slash-and-burn agriculture are being encouraged to abandon it, few viable economic alternatives seem to have been made available to them or yet discovered. It is important to find economically viable alternatives and all alternatives should at least be subjected to preliminary economic analysis before being recommended to villagers.

A way round the top-down approach is to involve villagers in the search for community development projects. This may be done using Rapid Rural Appraisal (RRA) techniques which involve direct interviews with villagers and on-the-spot appraisal of villages. Villagers have an opportunity to indicate the community projects or the type of projects that they most prefer. These are likely to be projects which, if funded, the villagers will be motivated to support. Furthermore, as a result of such direct interaction, authorities may discover promising new projects which would not otherwise be considered by them. These might have economic value not only in the villages where they are suggested, but in other villages as well.

It is sometimes claimed that projects suggested at the village level are likely to be more soundly based from an environmental and economic perspective, than those originating from the top. However, such a generalisation would appear to be dangerous. In reality, the knowledge sets of villagers and those of outside 'experts' are limited, and often different. By sensitively combining their knowledge, these two groups can usually improve their decisions relating to villages. This involves a side-by-side approach rather than either a top-down approach or a bottom-up approach. One further reason for not relying solely on the preferences of villagers for projects, is that they may assess projects solely on the benefit to their own village, ignoring any adverse external effects.

Conceptually, this knowledge situation may be illustrated as in Figure 11.2. The points in the rectangular set D might represent all the potential development projects available to a village. The set A may indicate those known to the villagers and the set B those known to authorities outside the village, with the overlapping set C representing those potential projects known both to the villagers and to the authorities.

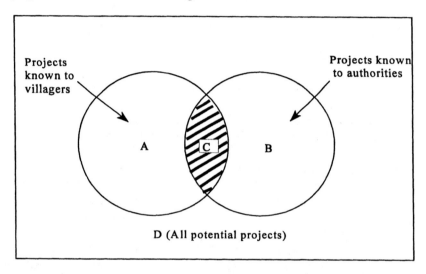

Figure 11.2   Knowledge sets relating to possible community development projects

Having discovered a set of economically viable development projects supported by the villagers, a government may wish to provide financial assistance for some or all of these. For villages in areas surrounding Xishuangbanna State Nature Reserve, it may be thought that economic benefits obtained by the villagers from pursuing such projects will ease their pressure to utilize the resources of the reserve. However, there can be no guarantee that this will be so. For this reason, it may be wise to enter into a formal agreement with village leaders to the effect that in return for governmental financial support for their community projects, they will assist in protecting the reserve in their area. Currently, the Ministry of Forestry is exploring this strategy and is considering a revised system to encourage the reporting of poachers.

CONCLUDING COMMENTS

In relation to the whole procedure for conserving Xishuangbanna State Nature Reserve, the likely question is: why conserve it at all? Possible answers include the following:

(1) the returns from agricultural use or logging may be low and not very sustainable;
(2) once the reserve has been fully utilized for commercial purposes, such as agriculture and logging, the problem of inadequate natural resources will occur again.

At best, the intensive utilization of the reserve would be a palliative or temporary solution to natural resource shortages. Furthermore, economic benefits from its conservation would be lost. The conserved area has some economic value for tourism, maintenance of waterflows and so on. It may have considerable existence value, both for China as a whole and individuals overseas who know about it. It is very rich in botanic specimens, some of which may have future use-values. The benefits from using the reserve for intensive 'development' purposes seem, in all probability, to be very low in relation to the likely alternatives foregone. To utilize the reserve in this way would be to pursue short-term gains at the expense of long-term benefits. Politics is unfortunately often heavily influenced by short-term perspectives. So nature reserves, particularly in less developed countries, are always subject to the risk of economic incursions by special interest groups searching for economic gains. This problem is present both in socialist and non-socialist countries.

Without economic development at the local level, plans for biodiversity conservation are unlikely to succeed in China or elsewhere in most of the developing world. However, economic development at the local level does not always assure conservation of biodiversity and natural living resources. As already pointed out, additional measures may be needed. Because a large portion of benefits from biodiversity and nature conservation spill over globally or internationally, total benefits are not captured by local communities (Pearce and Moran, 1994). Therefore, they are likely to engage in less conservation than is desirable from a global welfare point of view (Tisdell, 1990, Ch. 4; 1994) and international assistance to them for conservation purposes is likely to be justified. In particular, both on welfare efficiency and equity grounds, assistance from developed countries to communities involved in conservation in less developed countries seems justified. However, policy measures to affect these transfers are not straightforward. Some are being trialled, involving the Global Environmental Facility (GEF) and much research is being undertaken to devise additional measures.

Biodiversity conservation (and environmental conservation generally) involves interdependent processes, including socio-economic ones. The design of conservation policies must be completed within an interdependent framework if these policies are to succeed. *Agenda 21* is a useful first step in this process as far as China is concerned.

REFERENCES

Dixon, J.A. and P.B. Sherman (1990), *Economics of Protected Areas*, Washington D.C.: Island Press.

Hall, J.V., D.L. Chapman, W.F. Barron, and C.A. Tisdell, C.A. (1994), 'Environmental problems of Pacific rim development', *Contemporary Economic Policy*, 12: 1–22.

Islam, N. (1994), 'Rio conference on environment and development: an overview in retrospect', *Asia Pacific Journal on Environment and Development*, 1(1): 1–27.

Longworth, J.W. and G.J. Williamson (1993), *China's Pastoral Region: Sheep and Wool, Minority Nationalities, Rangeland Degradation and Sustainable Development*, Wallingford, Oxon; England: CAB International.

Mittermaier, R.A. and T.B. Werner, (1990), 'Wealth of plants and animals unites 'megadiversity' countries', *Tropicus*, 4(1): 1, 4–5.

Myers, N. (1990), 'The biodiversity challenge: expanded hot-spot analysis', *The Environmentalist*, 10(4): 243–56.

National Environmental Protection Agency *et al.* (1994), *China: Biodiversity Conservation Action Plan*, Beijing: National Environmental Protection Agency.

Pearce, D. and D. Moran (1994), *The Economic Value of Biodiversity*, London: Earthscan.

State Council of People's Republic of China (1994), *China's Agenda 21 – White Paper on China's Population, Environment and Development in the 21st Century*, Beijing: China Environmental Science Press.

Tisdell, C.A. (1990), *Natural Resources, Growth and Development*, New York: Praeger.

Tisdell, C.A. (1993), *Economic Development in the Context of China*, London: Macmillan.

Tisdell, C.A. (1994), 'Conservation, protected areas and the global economic system: how debt, trade, exchange rates, inflation and macroeconomic policy affect biological diversity', *Biodiversity and Conservation*, 3: 419–36.

Tisdell, C.A. (1995) 'Asian Development and Environmental Dilemmas', *Contemporary Economic Policy*, 13: 1–12.

12. Tourism Development and Conservation of Nature: the Case of Xishuangbanna, Yunnan

INTRODUCTION

With the opening up of China to the outside world commencing in 1978, tourism became an expanding industry (Tisdell, 1996). Furthermore, with economic reforms in China, this service industry, as with others, came to be looked upon more favourably as a legitimate form of economic activity. However, the development of tourism in China has been uneven, with the greatest growth, occurring in the major cities. Xishuangbanna Prefecture in southern Yunnan, for example, was not targeted for tourism development until 1985, and its southernmost county, Mengla county, was not opened to foreign tourists until 1993.

Tourism is growing rapidly in Xishuangbanna Dai Autonomous Prefecture, located in southern Yunnan. It is now regarded as a leading industry in the development of this prefecture, and it may provide a positive economic incentive for nature conservation. This chapter outlines the nature and pattern of the development of tourism in Xishuangbanna Prefecture. Features, such as average length of stay of tourists, their level of expenditure, its composition, type of tours available and taken, are all highlighted. Tasks being undertaken to improve facilities for tourism and its management are also discussed. Obstacles to the development of tourism in this prefecture are noted.

Tourism in Mengla County, the last county in Xishuangbanna Prefecture to be opened to tourism, is examined as a particular case, and special attention is paid to the role that Xishuangbanna State Nature Reserve is playing in the development of ecotourism, including the involvement of local communities. A master plan has been drawn up for

177

tourism development in Xishuangbanna State Nature Reserve and this is outlined and examined. Ecotourism development in this prefecture requires a sound financial basis, as well as to support the conservation of its rich biodiversity. Involvement of local communities, such as is occurring near Mengla, can assist in this regard. Let us consider the above mentioned aspects.

THE NATURE AND DEVELOPMENT OF TOURISM IN XISHUANGBANNA PREFECTURE

According to the Director of the Tourism Development Bureau of Xishuangbanna, the tourism industry caters for six activities:

(1) eating and dining;
(2) accommodation;
(3) travelling;
(4) purchases of souvenirs and commodities;
(5) entertainment;
(6) local sightseeing.

It is consequently an industry with wide economic implications, especially when one considers the indirect economic impacts of such activities.

As reported by the Director of Tourism Development Bureau of Xishuangbanna, the number of domestic tourists to Xishuangbanna in 1993 was estimated to be 1 million and foreign tourists were 15 300, including those from Hong Kong and Taiwan who constituted the bulk of such visitors. In terms of tourist numbers, Xishuangbanna is the fourth prefecture in Yunnan, but in terms of income generated, it is second only to Kunming (personal comment, Director of Tourism Development Bureau of Xishuangbanna, Oct. 1994). Numbers of tourists are increasing at the rate of about 20 per cent per year.

Tourism has been accepted by the Ministry of Economic Development as a pioneer or key industry for the economic development of Xishuangbanna. It is expected to become a major industry in that prefecture. The Ministry of Economic Development of Yunnan is providing special incentives to promote tourist and border industries supportive of tourism. Development zones have been established in a number of towns, and tourism-related industries encouraged to locate in these.

It is estimated that there were, in 1994, about 100 tourism-related enterprises in the prefecture. Before that, in 1993, tourism accounted for an estimated 20 per cent of the value of the gross product of Xishuangbanna, so it was already a significant industry in the prefecture.

The Director of the Xishuangbanna Tourism Development Bureau has outlined a number of tasks to be done and difficulties to be overcome in order to develop tourism further. These are (personal comment, October, 1994):

(1) To improve the 'software' of the local tourism industry, mainly to upgrade the quality of services and mechanisms for the management of tourist businesses and the industry.

(2) Major constraints on the growth of tourism in the prefecture are transport bottlenecks and difficulties. Although Jinghong, the capital of Xishuangbanna, is only 20–30 minutes from Kunming by air, the only airline permitted to fly there in 1994 was Yunnan Airlines. Demand for seats exceeds available places. The alternative is a rather arduous bus journey of about 2½ days from Kunming to Jinghong. To rectify this situation, authorities in Xishuangbanna Prefecture in 1994 were pressing for:
   (a) permission for airlines from any part of China to fly directly to Jinghong;
   (b) for Jinghong Airport to be upgraded to an international one, able to receive direct flights from other countries. Flights from Thailand, Singapore and Vietiane (Laos) are seen as possibilities.
   Since 1994, these requests have been fulfilled; Jinghong is now an international airport and more than one airline company uses it.

(3) Surveys, on a county basis, of the tourism resources of Xishuangbanna was completed. These surveys have helped to identify tourism assets which were previously not known, and have assisted the preparation of an overall plan for tourism development in the prefecture.

(4) The Tourism Bureau will focus on the training of tourist guides and managers. It will require guides to be registered and to wear an identification card.

(5) The Bureau plans to accelerate scenic site development and the manufacturing of tourist products, while at the same time, instituting quality control and measures to ensure conservation of tourism assets. The following is intended:
   (a) Scenic sites – using the catalogue of scenic sites for the

prefecture, a limited number have been selected for development; these are those which it is easiest to reach. In the selection, account has also been taken of the likely environmental impact of tourism on the sites and any difficulties in managing them. Expression of minority cultures are encouraged and steps are being taken to preserve minority-built environments.

(b)   The Tourism Development Bureau will control investment in tourism by the state, collectives, individuals, the Nature Reserve Bureau and the Forestry Department, under regulations which give the Tourism Development Bureau this power. Each authority involved in tourism, or having a substantial investment in it, will be required to draw up a tourism development plan for approval by the Xishuangbanna Tourism Development Bureau. Investment in tourism development will require the approval of the Bureau and must accord with the Prefectural Tourism Development Plan.

(c)   The Bureau will address the question of competition between development and conservation. It intends to support conservation actively not passively. In cases where a tourist site is to be opened, it will need to ensure that it can be protected. If insufficient resources are available to protect any site, the preference of the Tourism Bureau is to have these closed to tourism, therefore preserving them for future generations.

The average tourist to Xishuangbanna spends 3 nights there. This is also the average length of stay in Jinghong. Most tourists make Jinghong their base, only venturing out for day tours. These are often very long and may involve journeys to Laos and Myanmar (Burma). The length of stay of Chinese tourists in Xishuangbanna is quite short because the period which Chinese have for annual holidays is very short. Given the range of attractions available in Xishuangbanna, a stay of 5–7 days would appear to be more appropriate for a tourist to see the main attractions. The Director of the Xishuangbanna Tourism Development Bureau estimates the tourists to Xishuangbanna spend on average ¥1000 during their visit (personal comment, October, 1994). His suggested breakdown of this expenditure for a 3-night (4-day) stay is set out in Table 12.1.

He estimates that approximately 40 per cent of the goods purchased by tourists in Xishuangbanna Prefecture are bought in from outside the prefecture. However, leakages are bound to be much higher in some

cases than indicated by this figure, for example in relation to the air fare.
Six standard tours are available using Xishuangbanna as a base. These
are:

(1) Jinghong to Daluo at the border with Myanmar (Burma) crossing to
    Xiao Mengla on the Burmese side;
(2) Jinghong via Gannanba (Menglun and Mengla) to the Menghan
    crossing to Laos;
(3) down the Lancang (Mekong) River by ferry to the Golden Triangle
    in Thailand;
(4) tours within Jinghong County;
(5) tour from Jinghong to Mengyang village to San-Ca-He scenic site in
    Mengyang Sub-reserve.

*Table 12.1 Typical expenditure by a Chinese tourist to Xishuangbanna
Prefecture on a 3 night/4 day stay*

Item	%	¥	¥ per day (approx.)
Food and Drink	12	120	30–40
Accommodation	15	150	50
Local Transport	20	200	40
Air Fare	35	350	–
Other	18	180	45
Total	100	1 000	165 – 175

Source: Estimate of Director of Xishuangbanna Tourism Development Bureau

The Director of the Xishuangbanna Tourist Development Bureau said
that 90 per cent of tourists to Xishuangbanna participate in a cross-
border tour, with most travelling to Burma. Most Chinese visitors do not
participate in ecotourism, even though the Chinese government is
interested in developing this activity. He suggested as reasons that:

(a) Chinese adopt a passive rather than an active approach to recreation
    as a part of tourism;
(b) most Chinese have a very short time for their holidays;
(c) they generally regard the forest as a dangerous and hostile
    environment.

Despite this, the Director agreed that the Bureau for the Protection of Xishuangbanna Nature Reserve and the Ministry of Forestry have an important role to play in promoting tourism in Xishuangbanna. Xishuangbanna is regarded as the 'green gem' of China and its nature reserves and forests may be attractive to foreign visitors. It seems, in any case, that a 'halo effect' from the presence of the reserve and forests may help generally in attracting tourists to Xishuangbanna but no in-depth study has been done on this subject as yet.

DIGRESSION ON SOME SPATIAL ASPECTS OF TOURISM IN XISHUANGBANNA AND IN YUNNAN

Development of the tourism industry in China is seen as a means of helping to decentralise its economy, and as a possible way to reduce the disparity between income in coastal provinces compared with inland. Studies by J. Wen and myself (Wen and Tisdell, 1996), however, indicate that at least in recent times, tourism development in China has reinforced rather than reduced regional inequalities. The regional inequality of tourism indicators has been shown to be greater than that of socio-economic indicators, and these indicators also show greater bias in favour of coastal areas than other socio-economic indicators (Wen and Tisdell, 1996). Nevertheless, the interior provinces of China, such as Yunnan, have experienced positive economic impacts from growth in tourism in China. They have experienced growth despite the lopsided nature of tourism regionally in China. Furthermore, there is evidence that the contribution of tourism to regional inequality in China is declining (Wen and Tisdell, forthcoming) and that the comparative position of interior provinces in attracting tourists is improving.

The spatial distribution of tourism within Yunnan and within Xishuangbanna Prefecture is interesting. Although Kunming, the capital of Yunnan, received the major share of domestic expenditure on tourism, other areas, especially Dali, also fared well. While Xishuangbanna, the third most important tourist area in Yunnan, was well behind Dali in terms of tourism indicators, it was a significant area. It is only in recent years that Xishuangbanna's development of the tourist industry has taken off, so it has the potential to reduce the gap between it and Dali. Table 12.2 sets out tourist indicators for Yunnan Province and for its major tourist areas in 1994. Note that there appear to be some differences in these statistics and those for Xishuangbanna in Table 12.1. They may be estimated on a different basis.

A noteworthy feature of Yunnan is the relative spatial spread of tourism in the province. For many provinces in China, tourism is likely to show less spatial dispersion. In most cases, visitors seem to centre more strongly on the provincial capital city.

The spatial distribution of tourism within Xishuangbanna Prefecture is also worth mentioning. It is very much concentrated in Jinghong, the capital of this prefecture. Tourists generally use Jinghong as a base for day trips to other parts of the prefecture and into Myanmar. This may well mean that the economic benefits derived from tourists in Xishuangbanna are primarily obtained in Jinghong (Cf. Tisdell, 1997). Day-trippers usually spend relatively little money in localities which they visit, but these areas may benefit from income-multiplier links with the main tourism centre.

Table 12.2 Tourist indicators for Yunnan Province and its major tourist areas, 1994

	No. of Hotels	No. of Travel Agencies	No. of Overseas Tourists	Average Length of Stay (days)	(Overseas Tourists) Tourism Receipts (USD millions)	No. of Domestic Tourists (millions)	Domestic Tourism Income (million Yuan)
Total	171	258	522 059	1.59	124.397	14.58	3 077.98
Kunming	42	119	378 672	1.61	74.0961	4.83	1 019.66
Dali	19	14	34 579	1.91	8.034	2.49	525.66
Lijiang	5	3	16 885	2.29	4.705	0.2	42.22
Xishuang-banna	14	47	15 312	2.30	4.289	1.25	263.89

Source: Based on data from Travel and Tourism Bureau of Yunnan, 1995 and Wen (1997, Table 1).

Information about the distribution of number of tourists by major regional tourist centres in Yunnan are given in Table 12.3 which shows these items as a percentage of those for Kunming. This table, together with Figure 12.3, makes it clear that Chinese domestic tourists, compared to their overseas counterparts, are more likely to visit tourist centres other than Kunming, Lijiang being a slight exception. The figures indicate that expenditure by overseas tourists, in proportion to their visits, is slightly higher outside Kunming than in Kunming but is much the same for Chinese domestic tourists. The fact that the percentage distribution of domestic tourism income is the same as for the distribution of domestic tourists, may raise questions about how the estimate of the former was obtained.

Attempts to decentralize tourism in Xishuangbanna, away from Jinghong, have been relatively unsuccessful in the past. For example, a joint venture with a Hong Kong company providing accommodation in Menglun Botanic Gardens, proved to be a financial failure because of low occupancy rates for the accommodation provided. It remains to be seen whether tourism accommodation being provided within Xishuangbanna Nature Reserve will more successfully attract tourists and increase decentralization in Xishuangbanna. Nevertheless, the problem faced by tourism in such localities is usually a lack of varied attractions. Many tourists demand varied experiences during their vacation, and these cannot be so easily provided at remote places.

Table 12.3 Tourist visits and expenditure for major tourism centres in Yunnan as a percentage of those for Kunming, 1993

Tourist Centre	No. of overseas tourists as % of Kunming	Receipts from overseas tourists as a % of Kunming	No. of domestic tourists as % of Kunming	Expenditure by overseas tourists as % of Kunming
Kunming	100	100	100	100
Dali	9.1	10.8	51.6	51.6
Lijiang	4.5	5.5	4.1	4.1
Xishuangbanna	4.0	5.5	25.9	25.9

Source: Based on Table 12.2

TOURISM IN MENGLA COUNTY

Mengla is the southernmost county of Xishuangbanna Prefecture and has borders with Laos and Myanmar. Its principal international border is with Laos. It was only opened for foreign tourism in 1993 and its experience with tourism development has been rather recent. Being a county on an international border and given China's extension of its open-door policy, it has adopted policies to expand its cross-border trade with neighbours, especially Laos. Economic export zones have been developed in its main towns, Mengla and Menglun.

Mengla was the first county in Xishuangbanna Prefecture to complete a survey of its tourism assets. As mentioned earlier, all counties in Xishuangbanna completed such surveys in preparation for the compilation of a tourism development plan for the whole prefecture. In addition, the Tourism Development Bureau of Mengla County was to prepare a tourism plan for the county in conjunction with the county administration. The final plan should be consistent with the Prefectural tourism plan.

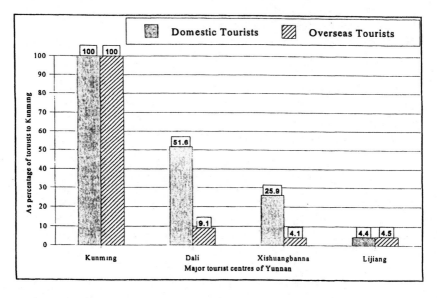

Figure 12.1   Percentage of tourists from overseas and from China visiting major tourism centres in Yunnan, as a percentage of those visiting Kunming, 1993

The survey of tourist resources of Mengla County was conducted by the Geographic Institute of the Chinese Academy of Sciences, and 15 specialists were engaged in this task. They concentrated on the physical tourism resources (man-made and natural) and, according to the Director of Mengla Tourism Development Bureau (personal comment October, 1994), identified 30 first-class scenic sites in Mengla County, and 36 categories out of 68 possible designated categories of tourism resources, as present in the county. Of these, 16 were regarded as particularly noteworthy. They were:

(1) mountains;
(2) exposed rock cliffs;
(3) unique shapes (such as animal-like shapes San-Ca-He of natural

features);
(4) caves;
(5) scenic views along rivers;
(6) reservoirs;
(7) waterfalls;
(8) springs (hot and cold);.
(9) the greenery created by forests;
(10) ancient and large trees;
(11) animal habitats;
(12) religious sites;
(13) Buddha statues;
(14) bridges;
(15) villages and townships;
(16) the botanic gardens at Menglun.

It might be observed that the survey is basically a top-down one with the importance of sites and assets being determined by the survey panel. No similar survey of tourists appears to have been undertaken. The Bureau suggested that Mengla County is very favourably placed for development thanks to the above tourism assets, the extent of its forest cover, its location on the border with Laos and its access to the Mekong River, which can provide transport for tourists. In addition, the county has three border markets, interesting minority cultures, food and festivals.

In order to develop tourism in the county, any legal form of business venture will be permitted, for example, independent businesses, co-operatives, and joint ventures. Selected tourist routes will be promoted (some involving journeys to Laos and Thailand), as well as attractions such as the botanic gardens at Menglun and the Forest/Limestone Cliffs site. The Deputy Director of the Mengla Tourism Development Bureau suggested that much more investment is needed in tourism development and in the training of their relatively inexperienced tourist personnel.

One of the main aims of the county is to link its economy to that of South-east Asian countries and to encourage cross border trade.

According to the Deputy Director of Mengla Tourism Development Bureau, 200 000 tourists visited the county in 1992. This would amount to about 20 per cent of tourists visiting the prefecture. Of these 200 000 tourists, 150 000 terminate their journey in the county at Menglun Botanic Reserve, so only 50 000 come as far as Mengla town. Of these, 20,000 travel across the international border, mainly to Laos.

The Deputy Administrator of Mengla County, in an interview in

October 1994, felt that the main constraints on tourism development and economic development in her county were:

(1) transportation difficulties;
(2) limited energy supply;
(3) deficiencies in telecommunications.

As for roads, these all needed to be improved; many become impassable during the wet season. However, the road between Kunming and Menghan on the Laotian border is being improved. Efforts are also being made to establish an airport at Mengla; if possible, with direct communications to South-east Asian countries. Telecommunications are inadequate and a bigger PABX system needs to be installed. A large supply line is going in to help overcome electricity supply problems.

The county is determined to encourage tourists to come from South-east Asian countries such as Thailand, Malaysia and Singapore, and will develop industries to service tourism. Factories will be set up in development areas to manufacture products for tourists, such as articles made from bamboo and the roots of trees. Clothing incorporating the fashions of minority people will be manufactured along with local artefacts. It is hoped that the border-crossing customs posts can be upgraded to receive foreign visitors directly from Laos.

The Deputy Administrator stressed the need for a 'reasonable' balance between conservation and development. Measures are being taken to protect local cultures. For example, the Dai people are being encouraged to maintain their building styles. However, in some townships which have recently experienced considerable growth, modern concrete buildings are starting to intrude on traditional Dai buildings. Strict zoning seems to be necessary to preserve the traditional character of some localities.

The administrators of the county also acknowledged that increased tourism training and improvements in hotel management are needed. Tourist guides in particular need more training. If more foreign tourists are to be catered for, greater knowledge of foreign languages and customs would be required.

XISHUANGBANNA STATE NATURE RESERVE AND ECOTOURISM

Xishuangbanna State Nature Reserve consists of five sub-reserves, identified in Figure 12.2, namely Mengyang, Menglun, Mengla, Shangyong and Mangoa (Menghai). This nature reserve is the major conservation system in Xishuangbanna Dai Autonomous Prefecture and plays an important role in the conservation of tropical forest ecosystems; it is essential to the conservation of the only remaining Asian elephant population in China. As one of its strategies for obtaining some economic return from biodiversity consideration, the Bureau for the Protection of Xishuangbanna State Nature Reserve is encouraging the use of the reserve for tourism, and is developing ecotourism.

The reserve helps to give Xishuangbanna its reputation as the 'green gem' of China. Several main roads pass through or by its sub-reserves and from these roads excellent views of the natural scenery of the reserve can be had. As for scenic areas within the reserve, three main sites are open to the general public. These are:

(1) San-Ca-He in Mengyang Sub-reserve;
(2) the forest and limestone cliffs at Menglun Sub-reserve;
(3) Bubong scenic site in Mengla Sub-reserve.

Entrance fees are charged to visitors at each of these sites.

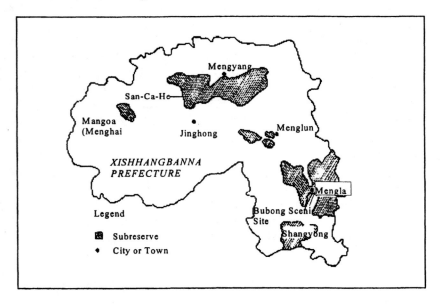

Figure 12.2   Location of the sub-reserves of Xishuangbanna State Nature Reserve in Xishuangbanna Prefecture

San-Ca-He is the closest ecotourist site to Jinghong for visitors and the road from Kunming to Jinghong passes by it. It is located about 18 kilometres from Mengyang town, the nearest small township. Passing travellers from Kunming sometimes visit the site and tours are available from Jinghong.

In 1993, Menyang Sub-reserve earned about ¥10,000 from fee-paying visitors and appears to have had fewer than 10,000 fee-paying visitors in 1993. It was reported by the Director of Ecotourism Development for Mengyang Sub-reserve (personal communication, October, 1994) that most local tour operators do not include this sub-reserve in their itinerary because they say that it does not have enough to offer. Nevertheless, small tourist groups do come and most seem to be well satisfied by sitting on the back of an elephant and having their photographs taken. San-Ca-He is the principal tourist site in this sub-reserve and a domesticated elephant (originally from Burma) is kept there.

While walks along constructed paths into the rainforest are available, none of these are exceptionally long. Wild animals are very rarely seen as is usual in rainforests, although the calls of many birds can be heard. Wild elephants are present in this area but they are not often seen by visitors although there are visible signs of their presence, such as their droppings, their impact on vegetation and, during the wet season, their footprints. Near a pond or a waterhole sometimes used by elephants for bathing and drinking, a set of viewing platforms has been erected, and it is possible to stay there overnight in a small treetop 'hotel'.

The fees charged to Chinese domestic visitors to San-Ca-He in Mengyang Sub-reserve in 1994 were:

- ¥3 for a visit to the site;
- ¥10 for a photograph to be taken on the back of the elephant;
- ¥60 for a ride on the elephant into the forest;
- ¥10 for a guide;
- ¥20 to stay overnight in the canopy 'hotel'.

The number of visitors to San-Ca-He varies seasonally. July, August and September are relatively unsuitable for visits because of heavy rain, floods and transportation problems. Predictably, most visitors find walking in a wet rainforest fairly unpleasant.

The site at San-Ca-He is being developed with a view to increasing the number of visitors. A strong concrete access road to amenities has been built, and foot paths into the forest have been constructed, making use of concrete bricks. These paths have been laid so as to minimize damage to vegetation. However, no funds have been made available for the maintenance of such facilities and this is considered to be a problem by the management of the sub-reserve because their internal maintenance funds are very low. The path has already been damaged slightly by elephants and some trees have fallen across it.

By providing infrastructure at the San-Ca-He site, the management of this sub-reserve hopes to attract joint ventures or independent businesses to supply other tourist facilities. By 1994, however, such a possibility had not materialized. The sub-reserve was constructing a small hotel/guest house at the site, which was to contain 20 beds. It is believed that this may mainly be used by foreigners. The building of this hotel has been financed by a soft loan from the Provincial Tourism Development Company. It seems that the overall loan from this company is about RMB 5 million. Income from the hotel will not be sufficient to repay the loan, even if the hotel achieves a high occupancy rate. Repayment will depend upon other tourism ventures materialising, such as joint ventures at the site.

One of the problems of concern to the management of the sub-reserve is the remote chance of visitors seeing wild animals. The possibility of keeping a small zoo at the San-Ca-He site, to display some of the wild animals present in Mengyang Sub-reserve, has been considered. However, this will add to costs and, for some, it will conflict with the ideal of conservation under natural conditions. A small attraction already in existence at the San-Ca-He site is the butterfly farm. With adequate guidance and interpretation, its significance as a tourism attraction could be upgraded.

The management of the sub-reserve stated that apart from the difficulties mentioned above, they faced other problems in attracting more visitors. These included:

(1) Transport difficulties – at least a two-day road journey from Kunming is needed to reach the site. While there are flights from Kunming to Jinghong, a shortage of seats limits visitors by air. The route in 1994 was a monopoly of Yunnan Airlines.
(2) Tourists departing from Kunming have a choice of other destinations in Yunnan, many of which also have significant cultural and natural assets (Cf. Wen, 1997). For example, the area around Dali, west of Kunming, has such attractions, and can be reached relatively quickly by road from Kunming. (See Table 12.2).

The site of the so-called forest curtain and limestone cliffs in the

Menglun Sub-reserve provides a contrasting ecotourism development to that at San-Ca-He. Whereas that at San-Ca-He is relatively capital-using and 'top-down' in conception, that at the Forest/Limestone Cliffs seems to be less capital-intensive (as far as it had developed at October 1994), and it involves a joint venture between a local farming co-operative and the management of the nature reserve.

THE MASTER PLAN FOR TOURISM DEVELOPMENT IN XISHUANGBANNA STATE NATURE RESERVE

In June 1993, a 'Master Plan for Tourism Development in Xishuangbanna State Nature Reserve' was completed by the Yunnan Forestry Investigation and Planning Institute as a part of the planning process for the development of tourism in Xishuangbanna Prefecture. This background document outlines plans for tourism development in the reserve for the next decade or so. The document lists 11 development sites for the State Nature Reserve and these are set out in Table 12.4 with their characteristics indicated. However, as at October 1994, only three of these sites had been opened for tourism within the reserve; namely, San-Ca-He, Menglun Forest/Limestone Cliffs, and Bubong, all of which have been discussed above. In addition, a museum and displays dealing with nature conservation, exist at the Jinghong headquarters of the Bureau for the Protection of Xishuangbanna State Nature Reserve. This museum is primarily used for educational purposes and is mostly utilized by schools.

As shown in Table 12.4, the largest investment for tourism development is planned at the Menglun Forest/Limestone site and at San-Ca-He in Mengyan Sub-reserve. A visit to these sites in October 1994 indicated that the amount of capital construction completed or underway at San-Ca-He was much greater than at the Menglun Forest/Limestone Cliffs.

Although the list in Table 12.4 is described as 'planned' tourism developments, it would be more realistic to describe these as 'possible' tourism developments; most do not involve firm plans.

The overall 'plans' for tourism development by the Bureau for Xishuangbanna State Nature Reserve are quite ambitious. Hotels are 'planned' for construction at San-Ca-He, Bubong and Mengla Forest, Limestone Cliffs. Together, these hotels are expected to have 1274 beds. In addition, it is suggested that the reserve should have a transport company located in Jinghong, equipped with 4 large bus coaches (40–60 seats), 8 of modern size (10–20 seats) and four motor vehicles with 3 or 4 seats. Two cruising vessels with 30–35 seats each are recommended and ten small speed craft. A travel agency is also envisaged, with 30 employees. In general, a large increase in staff numbers associated with the reserve is planned in accord with expansion of its ecotourism activities.

Table 12.4   Planned scenic sites for tourism development in Xishuangbanna State Nature Reserve as at mid-1993. Planned size of capital investment by sites, planned length of walking tracks, main attractions

Name of scenic site	Planned size of investment		Length of planned walking tracks in kms	Main attractions or activities
	¥m	% of total at scenic sites		
1. San-Ca-He	11.56	22.35	8.5	Tropical forests, wildlife, butterfly farm
2. Menglun	12.95	25.04	9.6	Forests, limestone cliffs
3. Bubong	3.24	6.26	0.5	Forest, treetop walk
4. Huang-Shan-Tang Natural Zoo	5.4	10.44	8.5	Elephants, peacocks, deer
5. Lancang River	2.39	4.62	33.0	River scenery, cruising
6. Meng Yuang Peak and Cave Area	—(a)	–	TBA	Cave
7. Nan-San Reservoir	4.7	9.09	TBA	Water-based recreation
8. Nan-Gong Mt.	3.08	5.95	58.0	Climbing, scientific research
9. Mengyang River	2.31	4.47	37.0	Adventure sports, research
10. Xi-Cao-Tang Hunting Area	5.09	9.84	–	Hunting
11. Jinghong Forest Museum	1.00	1.93	–	Education, marketing
Total	51.72	100.00(b)	155.1+	

Source: Based on Yunnan Forestry Investigation and Planning Institute (1993), Ch. 4.
Notes: (a) No details available
           (b) May not exactly add due to rounding

When all tourism-related capital investment is taken into account, the 'planned' investment by the reserve amounts to ¥77.05m. (about US$11m) a part of which is accounted for in Table 12.3. The proposed breakdown of this total investment by categories is set out in Table 12.5. Expenditure on hotels and related housing is the main category (47.44 per cent), followed by road construction and transport equipment (24.7 per cent), scenic area construction (9.1 per cent), auxiliary construction (9.1

per cent), 'necessary' construction (7.7 per cent), and forestation (1.2 per cent). Infrastructure expenditure is clearly a high-priority component.

Table 12.5 Proposed or 'planned' capital expenditure on ecotourism expansion by the Bureau of Xishuangbanna State Nature Reserve

Category	¥	%
Hotels and related housing	36,557,300	47.44
Road construction and transportation equipment	18,991,000	24.7
Scenic site construction	7,659,800	9.9
Auxiliary construction	7,018,700	9.1
Other necessary construction	5,905,900	7.7
Forestation	911,700	1.2
Total	77,054,400	100.0[a]

Source: Based on Yunnan Forestry Investigation and Planning Institute (1993, Ch. 11).
Note: (a) Does not add exactly due to rounding

No detailed analysis of the economic returns from the above investment is provided, but in the Master Plan for Tourism Development in Xishuangbanna State Nature Reserve, extremely optimistic figures are given for predicted growth in a number of visitors to the reserve. As a result of discussion with leaders of the sub-reserves in October 1994, it seems that the number of visitors to sites in the reserve in 1993 was between 30 000 to 50 000. This Master Plan (Yunnan Forestry Investigation and Planning Institute, 1993, Ch. 5) forecasts that in 2000, there will be 30 000 foreign tourist arrivals in Xishuangbanna Nature Reserve and 600 000 domestic arrivals, rising to 60 000 and 800 000 respectively in 2005. Unfortunately, there appears to be little basis for such optimistic predictions. It seems possible that enthusiasm has resulted in exaggeration of the prospects for tourism growth in the reserve and likely receipts from tourists. Certainly more analysis would be necessary, to determine whether financial and social economic returns from the proposed investments for the expansion of tourism are likely to be positive. There is a danger of infrastructure being expanded beyond a level that can be supported by demand.

CONCLUDING COMMENTS

Tourism is growing rapidly in Xishuangbanna Prefecture and tourism has been designated as a leading industry for the purpose of stimulating economic development of the prefecture. Consequently, the industry is receiving economic priority and some concessions, for example, favourable terms for loans. Restrictions on travel and tourism are being reduced and plans are being prepared to make it possible for foreign tourists to enter China directly though Xishuangbanna. A number of improvements in transport systems and supply of services have been proposed to assist the growth of tourism in this prefecture. The situation has been discussed for the prefecture as a whole, and with particular reference to Mengla County.

Xishuangbanna is an area with high species biodiversity, contains one of the few remaining areas of tropical forests in China, and is the only part of China that still contains Asian elephants. The 'greenery' of Xishuangbanna State Nature Reserve plays an important role in helping preserve biodiversity in China. However, at the present time, it seems that only a small fraction of Chinese tourists actually visit sites in the reserve, though many more may enjoy it from main roads which pass through parts of it. As discussed, the Bureau for the Protection of Xishuangbanna State Nature Reserve has plans to expand ecotourism in the reserve and has already embarked on an expansion programme. While economic opportunities exist for such plans, caution is required in undertaking this investment if a financial or economic loss is to be avoided. Joint ventures with the local community, such as the development at Menglun Forest/Limestone Cliffs, will probably increase the likelihood of a positive financial return being earned on investment in these tourism facilities. There is a need for further analysis of the economic opportunities for expansion of ecotourism in the reserve, bearing in mind the general considerations mentioned in Chapter 8.

REFERENCES

Tisdell, C.A. (1996), 'Tourism development in China: its nature, the changing market and business opportunities', *Journal of Vacation Marketing*, 2(2), 123–36.

Tisdell, C.A. (1997), 'Tourism development in India and Bangladesh: general issues illustrated by ecotourism in the Sunderbans', *Tourism Recreation Research*, 22(1), 26–33.

Wen, J. (1997), 'Tourism in Regional Development: the Case of Yunnan Province in China', in C.A. Tisdell and J.C.H. Chai (eds), *China's Economic Growth and Transition*, Brisbane: Department of Economics, The University of Queensland, pp. 225–313.

Wen, J. and C.A. Tisdell (1996), 'The spatial distribution of tourism in China: economic and other influences', *Tourism Economics*, 2(3), pp. 235–50.

Wen, J. and C.A. Tisdell (forthcoming), 'Regional inequality and tourism distribution in China; *Pacific Tourism Review*.

Yunnan Forestry Investigation and Planning Institute (1993), *Master Plan for Tourism Development in Xishuangbanna State Nature Reserve*, Kunming: Xishuangbanna State Nature Reserve.

13. Agricultural Pests and Protected Areas: Experiences in Xishuangbanna

INTRODUCTION

Protected areas are often the source of what the farming community regard as agricultural pests, and Xishuangbanna State Nature Reserve in Yunnan is no exception. This chapter discusses problems, including economic problems, associated with agricultural pests and their incidental protection by nature reserves, taking Xishuangbanna Nature Reserve as an example. The main pest associated with the reserve is the Asian elephant *Elephas maximus*, which causes damage to agriculture outside as well as within the reserve. However, these elephants are also an important attraction for tourists visiting Xishuangbanna which contains the only remaining wild elephants in China. The present economic value of tourism within the reserve is much less than the economic damage caused by elephants and other species protected by it. So whether the net economic value of protecting this species in Xishuangbanna is positive depends on other factors discussed, and future tourism prospects. Methods of controlling 'pests' from the reserve are examined, as is the scheme for compensating agriculturalists for damages caused. In this chapter, the task of achieving an equitable solution to the pest problem is given considerable attention, and the economics of reconciling the conflicting interests of those who regard a species as either a pest or as an asset, is considered.

At present, it is popular to emphasize the benefits of protected areas and the conservation of species. While this is reasonable, sight should not be lost of the fact that protected areas can be a source of negative spillovers to nearby farmers. Protected areas may, for example, increase fire risks to nearby farms, or be a source of agricultural pests such as weeds and animal agricultural pests such as elephants and wild pigs (Tisdell, 1982). When animal species are protected in a nature reserve

195

and cause agricultural damage on nearby farms, the economic loss incurred results in grievance against the reserve if farmers are not adequately compensated. Their dissatisfaction is further heightened if the animal species involved are completely protected both inside and outside the nature reserve, as they are in Xishuangbanna Prefecture.

The prefecture is located in the far south of Yunnan and is bordered by Laos and Myanmar (Burma). It has been classified as an area of megadiversity (Myers, 1988, Mittermaier and Werner, 1990) and consequently nature conservation in this prefecture is of worldwide interest. Xishuangbanna not only contains the last remnants of China's population of Asian elephants, *Elephas maximus*, but also a very high degree of botanic diversity. Tourism is a rapidly developing and important industry in this prefecture and Chinese authorities would like to reap economic benefits from the further development of nature-based tourism in the area.

There are two important nature reserves in the prefecture: Xishuangbanna State Nature Reserve and Nangunhe Nature Reserve. In 1989, Sukumar (1989, pp. 18, 30) indicated that probably 100–230 head of elephant exist in these reserves. In 1994, Zhu Xiang estimated the numbers of elephants in Xishuangbanna to be on average around 150–250, and that their population had shown an increase in recent years. Nevertheless, this elephant population is very low and their distribution has been seriously reduced in comparison to that throughout China in historical times, when the range of *Elephas maximus* extended to the Yantze (Chang) River.

While nature reserves in Xishuangbanna help conserve species with some positive economic values, at the same time, several of these species cause damage to the crops of local farmers. Consequently, this is a source of social conflict and, as evidenced below, the agricultural damage caused by elephants is the most severe. On the other hand, elephants are one of the most important tourist drawcards for Xishuangbanna nature reserves, and have other economic values. This social conflict cannot be ignored from a conservation viewpoint because as Sukumar (1989, p. 202) observes, 'any grandiose plan for conservation without adequate provision for human interests is bound to fail'.

This chapter considers animal pests emanating from nature reserves in Xishuangbanna, in terms of their total economic value. In practice, this means concentrating on the Asian elephant. However, the conservation and appropriate management of endemic vertebrate species requires social conflicts to be resolved and therefore policy-makers, in seeking practical solutions to conservation issues, must go well beyond the total economic evaluation of such species.

The case material used here was collected in Xishuangbanna, but the problems observed are placed in a general context since they are not peculiar to this reserve. First, the total economic evaluation of an agricultural pest species such as *Elephas maximus* is discussed, along with broad issues involved in conflict resolution and management of the species. It is observed that while much attention has been given to the economic evaluation of the African elephant *Loxodonta africana*, (Barbier *et al.*, 1990), much less has been given to the Asian elephant, *Elephas maximus*. While both species have some common economic values and cause similar damages, there are differences, as highlighted below.

The status of animal pests from Xishuangbanna State Nature Reserve, especially the elephant, is outlined. The control and management of vertebrate pests from the reserve is then considered, including the measures which local farmers take to protect their property against these pests. Even when populations of wild animals are managed optimally from a social viewpoint, farmers are still liable to incur economic damage from such animals. The question then arises of whether farmers should be compensated, and how. Considerable attention is given to compensation and social security schemes in relation to protected animal 'pests'. The scope for local farmers to gain economic benefits from the conservation of such animals is discussed, and the compensation scheme currently operating in Xishuangbanna Prefecture is critically analysed.

TOTAL ECONOMIC EVALUATION OF THE SPECIES, CONFLICT RESOLUTION AND CONTROL

Protected animals, regarded as assets by some, are often agricultural pests and this dichotomy creates difficulties for their conservation and economic evaluation. Sometimes one individual may even see the same species as a pest in some contexts and as an asset in others. For example, elephants may be regarded as pests by farmers and villagers in areas near nature reserves, if they roam to their farms and cause damage. Nevertheless, these same farmers and villagers may not object to the elephants if they remain in the nature reserve or do very little agricultural damage. On the other hand, tourists and those valuing the existence of such animals regard them only as a positive asset. Given this conflict, how is a species to be valued from an economic viewpoint?

In cost-benefit analysis, economists have traditionally determined social benefits resulting from variations in the availability of resources, by using the Kaldor-Hicks principle. This principle, which is sometimes called 'the potential Paretian improvement principle', implies that social benefits are to be determined by adding the benefits or losses experienced by individuals or groups from the variation in the availability of a resource. This means that the effects of this variation on income distribution are ignored. For example, suppose that the resource is the level of population, P, of a species, and let $R(P)$ represent the total value placed on it by those who see the species as an asset, and let $L(P)$ specify the economic loss suffered by those who see the species as a pest. Applying the Kaldor-Hicks principle, the social economic benefit from the population of the species can be expressed as

$$V(P) = R(P) - L(P). \qquad (13.1)$$

As a rule the population of a species can be varied by human intervention, at a cost. The level of population of a species may be reduced below its 'natural' level at a cost, or can even be increased by expenditure designed to improve the habitat or other conditions experienced by the species. If $\bar{P}$ represents the natural level of population of a species, the cost of varying its population may be of the form $C(P, \bar{P})$. Hence, extending the above view of economic welfare, social net benefit from the availability of the species is

$$B(P) = R(P) - L(P) - C(P, \bar{P}) \qquad (13.2)$$

and the socially optimal level of population of the species is the one which maximises this expression.

Note that this model incorporates similar assumptions to those of the pest control model of Headley (1972) as discussed in Tisdell (1982, Ch. 9). It is a simple model because it does not take account of the dynamics, of management of a species. The calculus of variations and dynamic programming may be applied to model dynamics, as has been done by Clark (1990) and by Conrad and Clark (1987) but at the expense of much greater complexity.

According to the Kaldor-Hicks principle, a change is a social improvement if those gaining from the change could compensate and be better off than before the change. Usually, application of the Kaldor-Hicks principle results in some degree of compromise between the parties with conflicting interests. For example, if some individuals regard the species as an asset and others see it as a pest, the socially optimal level of population of the species, based on the maximisation of expression (2), will normally result (i) in a smaller population of the species than is optimal for those viewing the species positively, and (ii) a higher level of population of the species than is desirable from the point of view of those who regard the species negatively (Tisdell and Zhu, 1995, Appendix). In this socially 'ideal' situation, conflict will continue to exist between the parties and will have to be 'managed' by regulators. As part of such management, compensation schemes for economic damage by a species may be introduced, as has been done in Xishuangbanna.

The whole question of the social value to place on the population of a species is an extremely complex one, but it is now more widely appreciated that economic values must include not only direct, but indirect, values. The notion of total economic value, consisting of direct and indirect use and non-use values, has been popularised for instance by Pearce *et al.,* (1989) and has been applied to valuation of the African elephant (Barbier *et al.*, 1990, pp. 17–21) in a general way.

Barbier *et al.*, (1990, p. 18) suggest that the greatest direct economic use value of the African elephant is for tourism, ivory, meat and hides. In terms of export earnings, tourism may be the most important economic benefit from the African elephant. In terms of its natural ecological functions, the African elephant also has indirect use value because it has 'the ability to diversify savanna and forest ecosystems, and as seed dispensers, reduce bushlands, expand grasslands and reduce the incidence of the tsetse fly' (Barbier *et al.*, 1990, p. 19). This may improve conditions for grazers and other species. The Asian elephant may perform similar functions. Furthermore, the African elephant was considered to have significant non-use values, such as existence value, bequest and option value.

In comparison, the Asian elephant also has significant tourism value but no studies of the type undertaken by Brown and Henry (1989) for the non-consumptive value of elephants for tourism purposes in Kenya, appear to have been undertaken in Asia. In this respect, however, it should be noted that in some parts of Asia, such as Xishuangbanna, it is difficult to see elephants because there are fewer of them and, in comparison to the savannah areas of Africa, they are confined as a rule to tropical rainforests or similar vegetation, thereby reducing their visibility. This may therefore provide the animals with smaller economic tourism potential than in Africa. Furthermore, the eating of elephant meat is no longer practised in most of Asia, and the Asian elephant is less valuable than the African for ivory. This is because female Asian elephants, and a proportion of male Asian elephants, are without tusks. Consequently, the direct value of the Asian elephant could be lower than that of the African elephant, especially in areas such as Xishuangbanna.

On the other hand, the Asian elephant can be domesticated and is still used in some countries, such as Myanmar, for logging. However, their domestic use is declining.

The fact that the Asian elephant can be domesticated makes it an extra tourist attraction, since it can be used for transporting tourists safely within national parks; and elephant 'schools', such as the one north of Lampang in Thailand, draw many visitors. In addition, the non-use value of the Asian elephant is probably very high, given the standing of the elephant in Asian history, culture, religion and folklore. Unfortunately, no hard-and-fast estimates of these values are available. Nevertheless, case material from Xishuangbanna throws some additional light on the matter.

THE STATUS OF ANIMAL PESTS FROM XISHUANGBANNA STATE NATURE RESERVE, ESPECIALLY ELEPHANTS, AND ECONOMIC CONSEQUENCES

Xishuangbanna State Nature Reserve in Yunnan consists of five separate sub-reserves and is a source of agricultural pests like many other nature reserves. The main problem is the Asian elephant *Elephas maximus*, which is thought to be responsible for about 90 per cent of the agricultural economic damage caused by pests roaming from the reserve. Other animal pests include monkeys, for example Rhesus monkeys *Macaca mulatta*, bears, gaur *Bos gaurus*, spotted or Sambar deer *Cervus unicolor* and wild pigs *Sus scrofa*, but on the whole these are not considered to be serious agricultural pests.

On average, it is estimated (October, 1994) that pests straying from Xishuangbanna Nature Reserve cause ¥1 million in agricultural damage and that agricultural damage in the whole of Xishuangbanna Prefecture from wild animals, is approximately ¥2 million annually (personal comment, Director, Xishuangbanna State Nature Reserve). (In October, 1994 ¥8.3 = US$1.00.) As mentioned above, 90 per cent of this agricultural damage is attributed to elephants.

In Xishuangbanna, elephants eat crops such as rice, corn and bananas. Many damage the embankments of paddy fields, and break fences. Even within the reserve they may cause some damage. For example, walking tracks may be broken up by the movement of elephants and they sometimes push trees across them. This has already happened along one of the important newly constructed walking tracks at the San-Ca-He site in the Mengyang Sub-reserve. Substantial portions of the track are constructed of concrete bricks and are located along a route frequently used by elephants. Especially in the wet season, elephants slide off the track and sometimes travel down the embankment on which it is built, thereby undermining the track. Trees are also pushed across the track by elephants, so adding to the maintenance costs. This is a source of concern for the management of the sub-reserve because it has scant funds of its own for maintenance.

In large numbers, elephants seriously damage forest vegetation in order to satisfy their food requirements. They also use trees and shrubs as scratching posts, and knock them down 'to let off steam' or test their strength. However, when disturbing rainforest, Asian elephants may be performing a normal important ecological function, as noted earlier in relation to the African elephant.

Elephant populations in the sub-reserves of Xishuangbanna State Nature Reserve are unevenly distributed. The main concentration is in Shangyong and Mengla Sub-reserves in the far south of the prefecture. The elephant population moves between these sub-reserves. The first mentioned sub-reserve is on the Laotian border. Elephants often cross the Lancang (Mekong) River and so move between Laos and Xishuangbanna Prefecture. The managers of the sub-reserves report that due mainly to heavy hunting pressure on elephants in Laos, there has been a net migration of elephants to the Chinese side of the border. In general, the population of elephants in the reserve is increasing, and numbers in the whole reserve are estimated to be 150–200 head.

There are probably around 50 head of elephants in Mengyang Sub-reserve but only 3–4 in the smallest, Menglun, which in fact is a fragmented sub-reserve. The main concentrations of elephants are in the Shangyong and Mengla Sub-reserves where numbers fluctuate due to migrations. On average 150–200 head occur here.

Due to economic development, the elephant population in Mengyang Sub-reserve has become isolated from the population further to the south. Economic development now impedes migration of elephants to and from Mengyang. It has been suggested that land corridors be established between the sub-reserves, to assist the migration of elephants and to ensure genetic mixing of populations. Plans have been drawn up for the creation of such corridors but these are very tentative, and in fact may never be established, because the cost of land acquisition is likely to be very high. Furthermore, the corridors would add to the pest problem for agriculture from the reserve. In addition, the corridor proposed at present is dissected by at least one major road and this adds to the problems.

The Asian elephants in Xishuangbanna are the only remaining wild elephants in China. There are several historical reasons for the major decline of populations of wild elephants in China. These include past open-access to the species (Tisdell, 1991; Clark, 1990; Repetto and Gillis, 1988; Hardin, 1968) and particularly the conversion of land from natural vegetation cover to other forms, such as agriculture (Swanson, 1994, pp. 10–11; Hardin, 1960). Sukumar (1989, pp. 32–38) lists several specific factors that have resulted in the decline of elephant population throughout Asia. These are:

(1) exploitation of the habitats of elephants by humans, e.g., competition from humans for plant resources, change in vegetation cover such as the establishment of forest plantations (often of monocultures), logging;
(2) land and vegetation degradation caused by shortened cycles in shifting agriculture;
(3) the spread of permanent agriculture;
(4) the construction of hydro-electric and irrigation dams which displace elephants and deprive them of valuable food resources located in the valleys;
(5) the capture of elephants legally and illegally;
(6) the hunting of elephants for ivory, meat and hides, and for pest control purposes.

Most of these adverse factors have operated in Xishuangbanna in recent times. For example, some of the areas in Xishuangbanna frequented by elephants were converted to rubber plantations. Xishuangbanna also contains a number of tribal minorities who still practise shifting agriculture. Due to population pressures, cycles of shifting cultivation have been reduced in length, so reducing the area of forested land at any one time, and the extent to which disturbed forest communities are able to recover after cultivation. This has reduced available food resources for elephants and increased their vulnerability to hunting. Furthermore, the area brought under agricultural cultivation has been extended, sometimes illegally, into the Xishuangbanna State Nature Reserve. While no major dams had been built in Xishuangbanna in 1994, one on the Lancang (Mekong) River, was contemplated for the purposes of electricity generation and irrigation, and for location in the Mengyang Sub-reserve of Xishuangbanna State Nature Reserve.

In the past, the Asian elephants in Xishuangbanna were heavily poached. As a result, a high proportion of the elephants at present are without tusks, or have very small ones, due to selection processes.

Economic development in Xishuangbanna can be expected to place increasing pressure on elephant populations outside reserves, even though hunting of these elephants is illegal. From the viewpoint of China as a whole, maintaining the existence of the Asian elephant population may have a reasonably high value. However, this indirect value has not been measured, nor has the value of elephants in attracting tourists to Xishuangbanna or to the reserve. The local tourist industry does use wild elephants for promotional purposes, and wooden carved elephants are produced for sale in Xishuangbanna. A multi-sided relief of elephants decorates the centrepiece of a main road intersection in Jinghong, the capital of Xishuangbanna Prefecture. On the other hand, the chances of tourists seeing wild elephants in Xishuangbanna are relatively low, and the majority of Chinese tourists to Xishuangbanna never venture into the reserve or look for elephants there.

At San-Ca-He, there is an elephant-viewing treetop lookout which can be reached by about a half an hour's walk from the entrance to the site. It overlooks a favourite watering and bathing area of wild elephants, however, elephants do not always frequent it. To increase the chance of seeing elephants, it is possible to stay the night there in the treetop 'hotel'.

In October 1994, there was one domesticated elephant at the San-Ca-He site. This fed locally in the sub-reserve and was mainly used by tourists for rides and photographing. It was brought from Myanmar and was in fact, the only elephant seen by most visitors to this site or the reserve. The possibility of having an extra domestic elephant was discussed with the managers of the sub-reserve. This would help to compensate visitors for not seeing wild elephants or other animals. Wild animals are not easily seen in tropical forests such as those in Xishuangbanna State Nature Reserve, in contrast to the situation on plains or open woodland in Africa and in parts of North America, for example, where visibility is high. This reduces the appeal of tropical forests to many ecotourists.

The management of the sub-reserve felt that the main difficulty in increasing the number of domesticated elephants at San-Ca-He would be that they would feed locally and damage the vegetation of the sub-reserve, and that supplementary feeding might be costly.

The possibility that visitors to the San-Ca-He could be encouraged to buy corn and sugar-cane pieces to feed to the elephants was discussed.

This is done in Thailand at the elephant training school to the north of Lampang, where such activities are popular with visiting tourists. A similar practice occurs at the Lone Pine Koala Sanctuary in Brisbane, where visitors can buy pellets to feed kangaroos. However, those managing San-Ca-He said that they had tried a scheme whereby visitors could buy concentrated food to feed to their domesticated elephant, but that the Chinese were not inclined to make such purchases and so this approach was discontinued.

Furthermore, domesticated elephants have to be protected from wild elephants. At night, the domesticated elephant at San-Ca-He was housed in a building with thick steel pipes as side walls to protect it from wild elephants. Extra costs could be involved in adding to such enclosures.

To have a definite quantitative measure of the total economic value of wild elephants in Xishuangbanna would be useful for management purposes. Unfortunately, data is not available to provide this. Nevertheless, a number of relevant observations can be made. The direct use for tourism is low, since only a small proportion of visitors to Xishuangbanna actually visit the reserves inhabited by elephants. Furthermore, the chances of seeing them in the rainforest are very low. In fact, only about ¥30,000 is collected in visitors fees annually from visitors to Xishuangbanna Nature Reserve. So currently, this reserve generates little direct income. The tourists' or consumers' surplus [for further discussion about such measurement see Driml and Common (1995)] obtained from visitors, has not been measured, and it is impossible at this stage to say to what extent visits are motivated by the possibility of seeing a wild Asian elephant.

On the other hand, the indirect and economic non-use values of the elephant in Xishuangbanna may be high. The Asian elephant probably performs an important role in maintaining botanic diversity in the reserve, and it is a publicised tourist feature in the major towns such as Jinghong, where tourists to Xishuangbanna spend much of their time. The local elephant-carving industry, involved in production for the tourist market, probably owes its continuing existence to the presence of elephants in the locality. It seems that some tourists visit an area because of an image-factor, and elephants add to the natural image of Xishuangbanna. It might also be observed that there are other species that are rarely seen, such as the tiger, but still visitors come to nature reserves and national parks, such as the Sundabarns in India and Bangladesh, on the chance that they may see them. They add 'character' to the tourist destination and therefore draw tourists to the neighbourhood.

Using the terminology of Barbier *et al.,* (5) introduced previously, the non-use value of the Asian elephant in Xishuangbanna from the Chinese perspective is likely to be relatively high, because it is the only remaining population in China. Even if not all Chinese place an economic value on conserving the Asian elephant in China, and even if the value placed on this by individual Chinese is relatively low, China's population of 1.2 billion can be expected to place a substantial total value on the continuing existence of the Asian elephant in Xishuangbanna. If 400 million Chinese were willing to pay the equivalent of 1 cent per year to retain the Asian elephant in China, this would amount to $4 million annually. Option and bequest values would add to the total economic non-use value of the elephant in Xishuangbanna.

Against the total benefits of the Asian elephant one has to offset its economic damages, plus expenditure involved in deterring the elephant from doing such damage, and all the other costs associated with the management of the elephant. The economic damages involved appear to be ¥0.9 million to ¥1.8 million annually for the whole of Xishuangbanna, according to the Director of the Xishuangbanna Nature Reserve. The other costs probably amount to not more than ¥0.2 million annually. So, on indirect evidence, the total net economic value of the Asian elephant population in Xishuangbanna is highly positive. However, there must be some doubt as to whether the population of elephants in Xishuangbanna is viable in the long-run, given the fragmentation of Xishuangbanna State Nature Reserve, and the available home areas for elephants. Compare Sukumar, (1989), p. 206.

CONTROLLING VERTEBRATE PESTS FROM PROTECTED AREAS

As observed above, protected areas are often the source of agricultural vertebrate pests, or important to their survival, as is Xishuangbanna. The animals concerned are often mixed goods – assets from the point of view of the protected area and the general public, but pests from the standpoint of agriculturalists. Because of their mobility, they can also be regarded as transboundary resources (Clark, 1990, pp. 158–168). Sometimes, it is economic to implement management strategies for the control of such species, taking into account the economic damage which they cause to agriculturalists.

Agricultural damages caused by vertebrate pests straying from protected areas can be controlled in at least three different ways:

(1) enclosure of the animals in the nature reserve;
(2) their exclusion from agricultural land or from agricultural areas likely to be damaged by such animals, for example, by appropriate fencing;
(3) through reduction of their populations (possibly selectively) by human action.

Each of these options can be costly.

The sub-reserves of Xishuangbanna State Nature Reserve appear mainly unfenced. So its wild animals are not enclosed. Furthermore, to build fences or barriers to enclose elephants effectively in its sub-reserves would be very difficult and costly. It would also interfere with the movement of elephants between sub-reserves and therefore reduce genetic mixing.

As for exclosures, some villagers in Xishuangbanna have erected short lengths of electric fence at points where elephants are likely to enter farmed land and cause damage. These single-strand fences are set relatively high on wooden posts and the electrified wire is held by porcelain insulators. Power is supplied by a battery unit recharged by solar energy. These units have been supplied by WWF (The Worldwide Fund for Nature) Europe, and are maintained by the Bureau for the Protection of Xishuangbanna State Nature Reserve.

Such a unit is located at Zhong Tian Ba village which adjoins Mengyang Sub-reserve. The fence is several metres in length and is stretched across a slight gully which extends from this sub-reserve. At the time of inspection, corn (maize) had been grown in this area. With only slight difficulty, an 'intelligent' elephant could have walked around the fence, since it formed a barrier rather than an enclosure either for crops or for the elephants.

Villagers reported that initially electric fences are a relatively effective deterrent. However, in time, some elephants learn how to disable electric fences. They pull out the wooden posts holding the electrified wire, thereby knocking the fence to the ground, and then walk over it. The opinion of the villagers was that the fence was of some value but was not completely effective.

Zhong Tian Ba has suffered loss of rice to elephants. When the animals begin raiding the rice fields and the electric fence is not fully effective, the villagers stay up at night to guard the fields, camp there and light fires to frighten the elephants away. Yet, most villagers appear to want more electric fencing.

This method is in fact widely used in many countries as a barrier to prevent movement by elephants (Thouless and Sakwa, 1995). Thouless and Sakwa (1995, p. 99) state that 'in the past a variety of barriers were constructed to exclude elephants from farming areas, but electrified fences are now considered to be the best solution to the problem'. While electric fences appear to vary in their effectiveness, this appears not to be related closely to their design, construction and voltage, but may depend on the previous experience of elephants with such fences, and the nature of the elephant population involved. Thouless and Sakwa (1995) suggest that they should be regarded as signals for 'no-go' areas rather than real barriers to the animals. This may require the shooting of rogue elephants which make it a habit to break through electric fences. This would be a more suitable approach than unselectively reducing the population of elephants.

Electric fences appear to be more effective for the control of the Asian elephant than the African. Thouless and Sakwa (1995, p. 105) indicate that this may be because many Asian elephants are tuskless and African elephants make considerable use of their tusks for breaking electric fences.

As for the strategy of reducing animal populations as a pest control measure, this policy is not favoured in Xishuangbanna State Nature Reserve. There is no culling programme for elephants, as was the case in the Kruger National Park in South Africa. Elephant populations in Xishuangbanna are still considered to be relatively low and their conservation is the main goal.

Reducing the total population of these large mammals may be an unnecessary and costly strategy for the control of damage to agricultural crops. Sometimes it is sufficient to remove 'rogue' animals or to reduce the male population of the species for control purposes. Sukumar (1989, p. 93) points out that 'adult male elephants are far more prone than a member of a female-based family herd to raid agricultural crops and kill people'.

Whatever control policies are adopted to manage vertebrate pests protected by nature reserves, these should ideally be devised and implemented with co-operation between managers of the nature reserves and local landholders. The management problem should be approached in an integrated manner. This is not to say that control of 'pest' species is always desirable or economic, and this leaves open the question of payment of compensation to agriculturalists suffering damage through wildlife movements from protected areas.

In fact, four broad strategies exist to deal with the protected wildlife pest problem:

(1) no control and no compensation to landholders damaged by the wildlife;
(2) control but no compensation;
(3) no control but compensation;
(4) control and compensation.

In the case of Xishuangbanna State Nature Reserve, there is no control of wildlife populations but some compensation is paid to agriculturists who suffer damages from such wildlife. Let us consider this compensation.

COMPENSATION PAID TO AGRICULTURALISTS FOR DAMAGES CAUSED BY WILDLIFE FROM XISHUANGBANNA STATE NATURE RESERVE

Compensation paid by the Bureau for the Protection of Xishuangbanna State Nature Reserve to villagers, for damages caused by animals straying from Xishuangbanna State Nature Reserve, amounts to about ¥100,000 per year. This compensation comes from a fund provided annually from government sources, the exact amount being determined each year. However, it seems to be relatively stationary at ¥100,000. The budgeted amount is allocated to villagers in proportion to the amount of pest damage estimated by the Bureau for each claim. This proportion is found by dividing the total compensation fund by the total agreed damages. Currently, this is around 10 per cent of estimated economic damage.

When damage by animal pests from the reserve occurs in a village, the village, in order to make a claim, must report this damage to the management of the relevant local sub-reserve, who will send their own assessors to assess the damage. In the past, the damage could be certified by any local government officer but this was found to be unreliable. At the end of the year, all allowed claims are added up and the available compensation funds distributed in proportion to the total compensation fund available. Most of the compensation is paid for the damage caused by elephants.

Disadvantages observed for this compensation scheme are:

(1) the proportionate compensation is low;
(2) the proportionate compensation for damage is the same whether the farmer loses his whole crop or just a small fraction of it;
(3) there is a long delay before any compensation is paid;
(4) transaction costs are involved – the villagers must report and confirm the damage and it must be assessed by sub-reserve staff.

Proportionate compensation is low presumably because, given low incomes in China, little surplus is available to fund income security schemes. In essence, the scheme involves co-insurance but the proportionate burden carried by villagers is very high at 90 per cent. This is not to suggest that it would be desirable to pay 100 per cent compensation even if it were feasible. To do so (or to compensate to a high degree) would increase moral hazards. For example, villagers may take little or no action to prevent marauding animals from destroying their crops.

The question has been raised whether proportionate payment of compensation in relation to the value of estimated damages is equitable. For example, a farmer who loses the whole of his crop would end up with 10 per cent of its value after compensation, whereas one who loses 20 per cent would end up with 82 per cent of its value after compensation. If the farmers had the same income and the same amount of cropped land this would seem inequitable. This could, in principle, be allowed for by paying compensation on a sliding scale, with the compensation rising in proportion to the percentage of damage sustained by the farmer in relation to his/her income. This, however, still leaves open the question of whether poorer farmers should receive greater proportionate compensation for the same percentage of damage sustained. In relative utility terms, the proportionate loss of the poorer farmers is higher.

It would be of considerable assistance to those affected by pest damage, if the period for processing claims and paying compensation was reduced. The possibility of doing this needs to be explored. Care should also be taken to reduce transaction costs to the lowest practical level.

If the protection of animals located in the reserve becomes more effective and their populations increase (this is currently an objective), the extent of agricultural damage is likely to increase. Furthermore, as agricultural yields and the intensification of agriculture in Xishuangbanna increases, the extent of pest damage is liable to do the same. This is bound to have implications for future relationships between the reserve and local farming communities.

CONCLUDING COMMENTS

Nearly all nature reserves are a source of pests for neighbouring agricultural properties and this has to be taken into account in establishing and managing the reserves. The problem of achieving optimal levels of population of species is complicated by many factors. For example, the species may be an agricultural pest but regarded as an asset by non-agricultural members of the community. Furthermore, varying the level of population of a species or reducing its propensity to cause agricultural damage, is often only possible at an economic cost. So several economic problems arise in managing populations of wild species. Some of these issues have been illustrated for Xishuangbanna Prefecture, Yunnan. Apart from these management questions, economics also has relevance to schemes designed to compensate villagers for damage caused by protected wild animals. Again this has been illustrated for Xishuangbanna Prefecture.

An issue that has not been discussed is who should pay into the pool of funds available for compensation. Economists often argue that beneficiaries should pay. If the general community benefits, then this provides some rationale for the government to contribute to the compensation fund. Possibly, most of China's population sees some value in conserving elephants in Xishuangbanna and in protecting biodiversity there; hence, it seems not unreasonable for the Chinese government to contribute. Even the international community may benefit, so some contribution from it would also be justified. As yet, there is no formal scheme for this contribution. The only international contribution so far has been the voluntary one of WWF, in providing facilities for electric fencing to exclude elephants from farming property. If tourists or the tourism industry benefit from the preservation of a pest species, as in Xishuangbanna, then possibly they should also contribute some funds to the compensation fund.

The 'equitable' solution depends on how one believes rights should be assigned. If it is believed that farmers should have a right to protect themselves against pests and are prevented by some laws from doing so, compensation to farmers seems justified. On the other hand, if it is believed that wild animals have a right to life and ought to be conserved, no compensation might be paid to farmers for damages.

In the latter circumstance, if farmers bear the full cost of agricultural damage, they may still find it worthwhile to set up a co-operative insurance fund, as suggested by Sukumar (1989, p. 218). If pest damage is not predictable and involves a random element, such a fund could be used for compensation. However, farmers would need to be divided into classes, to determine the appropriate insurance premiums. It would also be possible, in principle, to establish a compensation fund financed partially by the insurance contributions of farmers, and by contributions from the government and other parties benefiting from the conservation of the pest species. Ethically, such an approach would be based upon the idea that property rights do not belong exclusively to any single party having an economic interest in the populations of a particular species. *De facto* shared rights in the environment and in natural resources have, in fact, become commonplace. The solutions to problems involving such joint rights often involve compromise, and cannot always be precisely specified in advance. This case provides an example of a limitation to the 'property rights' solution to environmental problems, (advocated, for example, by Coase, 1960) which traditionally involves the allocation of exclusive property rights to a single person or entity.

REFERENCES

Barbier, E.B., J.C. Burgess, T.M. Swanson and D.W. Pearce 1990, *Elephants, Economics and Ivory*, London: Earthscan.

Brown, G. and W. Henry 1989, 'The economic value of elephants' in *LEEC Discussion Paper 89–12*, London: London Environmental Economics Centre.

Clark, C.W. 1990, *Mathematical Bioeconomics: The Optimal Management of Renewable Resources*, 3rd edn, New York: Wiley.

Coase, R. 1960, 'The problem of social cost', *The Journal of Law and Economics*, 3, 1–44.

Conrad, J.N. and C.W. Clark 1987, *Natural Resource Economics: Notes and Problems*. Cambridge: Cambridge University Press.

Driml, S. and M. Common 1995, 'Economic and financial benefits of tourism in major protected areas', Australian Journal of Environmental Management, 2(1), 19–29.

Hardin, G. 1960, 'The competitive exclusion principle', *Science*, 141, 1291–97.

Hardin, G. 1968, 'The tragedy of the commons', *Science*, 162, 1243–47.

Headley, J.C. 1972, 'Defining the Economic Threshold', in Agricultural Board, Division of Biology and Agriculture, National Research Council, *Pest Control Strategies for the Future*, Washington, DC: National Academy of Sciences, pp. 100–8.

Mittermaier, R.A. and T.B. Werner 1990, 'World of plants and animals in megadiversity countries', *Tropicus*, 4(1), 4–5.

Myers, N. 1988, 'Threatened biota: hotspots in tropical forests', *The Environmentalist*, 8(8), 1–20.

Pearce, D.W., A. Markandya, and E.B. Barbier 1989, *Blueprint for a Green Economy*. London: Earthscan Publications.

Repetto R. and M. Gillis 1988, *Public Policies and the Misuse of Forest Resources*. Cambridge: Cambridge University Press.

Sukumar, R. 1989, *The Asian Elephant: Ecology and Management*, Cambridge: Cambridge University Press.

Sukumar, R. 1991, 'The management of large mammals in relation to male strategies and conflict with people', *Biological Conservation*, **55**, 93–102.

Swanson, T.M. 1994, *The International Regulation of Extinction*, New York: New York University Press.

Thouless, C.R. and J. Sakwa 1995, 'Shocking elephants: fences and crop raiders in the Laikipia District, Kenya', *Biological Conservation*, **72**, 92–107.

Tisdell, C.A. 1982, *Wild Pigs: Environmental Pest or Economic Resource?* Sydney: Pergamon.

Tisdell, C.A. 1991, *Economics of Environmental Conservation*, Amsterdam: Elsevier.

Tisdell, C.A. and X. Zhu 1995, 'Protected areas, agricultural pests and economic damages' *Biodiversity Conservation Working Paper No. 16*, Brisbane: Department of Economics, The University of Queensland.

14. Financing Nature Reserves in China: The Case of Xishuangbanna State Nature Reserve

INTRODUCTION

Available funds for protecting and managing nature reserves are extremely limited in developing countries, including China. This chapter considers the financing and management of Xishuangbanna State Nature Reserve in Yunnan, as a case study. This reserve is under the overall management of the Bureau for the Protection of Xishuangbanna State Nature Reserve but there is considerable decentralization in the management of its five sub-reserves. These are managed from four stations, one for each of the sub-reserves except for Mengla and Shangyong Sub-reserves which share the same station. The source of funds for the reserve and sub-reserves are listed and the nature of outlays are specified. Almost all available funds are spent on salaries, wages and pensions for staff of the reserve, leaving few funds for overheads, transport and other items, especially capital items. Government is the principal source of funding, but some income is obtained from ecotourism, from a butterfly farm and factory for processing butterflies, from multiple-use operations, such as rental income from concessions to growing passionfruit in parts of the reserve, and from resource management fees, such as fines imposed for illegal use of the reserve, and payments for the controlled removal of timber and wood from the reserve.

Political influences on financing are discussed. It is suggested that the high ratio of expenditure on staffing to total expenditure, can be partly explained by political considerations. It is, however, observed that actual salaries paid to employees of the reserve are very low, even by Chinese standards. Given the shortage of discretionary funds available to the reserve, especially for capital goods and investment, substantial progress with the latter items is dependent on foreign aid. In this respect WWF(Europe) has been one of the most important donors to date. Some funds for such purposes have also become available from the Global Environmental Facility.

Because funds for protecting and managing nature reserves are very limited in all developing countries, the usual situation seems to be that the funds available for administering nature reserves are barely sufficient to maintain the staff employed by the authorities responsible for this administration, and that additional funds for transport and items other than salaries are severely limited. As an example of financing and related issues, this chapter considers the financing of the State Nature Reserve of Xishuangbanna located in Yunnan in south-west China. Much of the data reported here were collected during a visit in October 1994.

Xishuangbanna State Nature Reserve consists of five sub-reserves:

(1) Mengyang
(2) Menglun
(3) Mengla
(4) Shangyong
(5) Mangoa (or Menghai) (see Figure 14.1).

Overall responsibility for the protection of these sub-reserves lies with the Bureau for the Protection of Xishuangbanna Nature Reserve, located in Jinghong, the capital of Xishuangbanna Prefecture. The day-to-day operations of the sub-reserves and a substantial amount of decision-making affecting their operations, lies with their individual field stations or offices, located in towns near the individual sub-reserves. The administration station for Mengyang Sub-reserve is located in Mengyang township, and that for Menglun in Menglun township. The administration of Shangyong and Mengla is combined, and the station is located in Mengla township. That for Mangoa Sub-reserve appears to be located at Menghai township. Most of the staff are located at these stations rather than in the sub-reserves themselves.

SOME FINANCIAL DETAILS

Most of the funding for the Xishuangbanna State Nature Reserve is obtained from the central government. The Bureau obtains these funds through the Forestry Department of Yunnan and then divides this sum into one portion for administration of the Bureau and another portion for the sub-reserve administration. In 1993, the Bureau was allocated ¥1.74m by the government for its operations, of which ¥1.13m was allocated to the administration carried out by the stations of the sub-reserves. The Bureau obtains a very limited amount of income from other sources, such as its butterfly factory located at Jinghong which processes butterflies for sale as souvenirs. Some of the butterflies used come from its butterfly farm located at San-Ca-He in the Mengyang Sub-reserve. The Bureau also obtains a small income from the administration of the sub-reserves, for example, a fraction of income from entrance fees to scenic sites.

The amount of funding available from the government for the administration of Xishuangbanna State Nature Reserve is usually adjusted in line with the rate of inflation. For 1994, it increased to ¥2.54m to reflect the then high rate of price inflation in China. Funds available show little or no growth in real terms.

In October 1994, 235 staff were employed in the administration of Xishuangbanna State Nature Reserve. Of these, 67 were employed by the Bureau in Jinghong, and 158 were employed in the administration of the sub-reserves. In relation to the sub-reserves, 68 staff were engaged at Mengla (for the administration of Mengla and Shangyong combined), 50 at Mengyang, 23 at Menglun and 17 at Menghai. The first-mentioned two sub-reserves are the largest in the system. These staff numbers do not include villagers who were paid a retainer to help with nature protection.

The income and expenditure for Mengyang Sub-reserve was reported to be as shown in Table 14.1. This indicates that ¥240,000 in 1993 was obtained from the Bureau (government funds). Of this, ¥200,000 was spent on salaries, ¥28,000 on protection expenses, and ¥1,500 on security, leaving only ¥10,000 for the running of vehicles, communication costs, propaganda and so on. Virtually no funds were available for investment purposes and in the view of the officers of the nature reserve, their funds were inadequate to provide support services.

In addition, a small amount of net income, ¥40,000, was obtained from other sources. This included approximately ¥10,000 from the entrance fee to San-Ca-He scenic site in Mengyang Sub-reserve, ¥10,000 from multiple operations (such as payments for the growing of wild ginger in the forest), rent for land used for growing crops such as passionfruit, and income from the guest house in Mengyang. It also includes net income from the butterfly farm at San-Ca-He of ¥10,000 and ¥10,000 from resource management fees, such as fees for collection of fallen timber, and fines for violation of the nature protection laws. This amounts to just over 14 per cent of the income of the sub-reserve. However, half of this income is paid to the Bureau with the sub-reserve administration retaining the remaining half. So this reduces the extra income obtained by the sub-reserve to ¥20,000.

Table 14.1 Some income and expenditure information for Mengyang Sub-reserve for 1993

Income from Government Budget	¥240,000
Expenditure (Main Items)	
Salaries	¥200,000
Protection expenses	¥1,500
Security	¥1,500
Available for other expenses such as running of vehicles, communication and so on	¥10,500
Other Net Income	
Mainly entrance fee to San-Ca-He scenic site	¥10,000
Multiple operations[a]	¥10,000
Net income from the butterfly farm at San-Can-He	¥10,000
Resource Management Fees[b]	¥10,000
	¥40,000

[a] Includes income from cultivation rights in the sub-reserves and ¥4000 from Sub-reserve Guest House in Mengyang township. This latter sum pays the salary of the person in charge of the guest house.
[b] Includes fines for poaching etc. and fees for collection of firewood and timber for local village construction.

Menglun sub-reserve station was allocated ¥210,000 from the government budget in 1993, of which 60 per cent was spent on the salary of its existing staff and ¥60,000 was used to pay the annual pensions of 10 retired staff. After these payments, only about ¥24,000 was left from government funds for remaining expenses. Of this, approximately

¥10,000 was spent on forest protection and most of the remainder was allocated for field work. Approximately ¥20,000 – ¥30,000 is obtained as income from other sources. This extra income is mostly used for protection work and to improve the standard of living of employees. The main sources of this income are:

(1) entry fees to scenic sites, for example income from the Limestone/Forest Cliffs site;
(2) income from the guest house in Menglun township;
(3) rental income from reserve land used for fruit growing, for example passionfruit;
(4) resource management fees such as fines for poaching, charges for firewood collection.

After meeting its salary and pension commitments, the sub-reserve only has ¥40,000 – ¥50,000 (US4,200 – 5,200) of funds available to it.

For 1993, the sub-reserve station for Mengla and Shangyong had an income of ¥510,00 from the government, of which the lion's share was spent on salaries and pensions. It received an income of approximately ¥20,000 from other sources. The main sources were income from tourists (visitor fees) to Bubong scenic site and from resource management fees, mostly fines. Its proportionate income from other than direct government grants is lower than at Mengyang and Mengla. Although the administration of the sub-reserve has given some concessions for the growing of rubber trees, no income has been received from this source as yet.

In 1993, the overall distribution of government funds between the sub-reserves appears to have been as set out in Table 14.2.

Table 14.2 Distribution of government funds between the sub-reserves of Xishuangbanna State Nature Reserve, 1993

Sub-reserve	Amount (¥)
Mengyang	240,000
Menglun	210,000
Mengla/Shangyong	510,000
Mangoa	170,000
Total	1,130,000

DISCUSSION OF FINANCIAL ISSUES

Lack of available finance seriously constrains the management of the sub-reserves. The average salary rate of employees is only ¥4,000 per year (around US$470), which is a low subsistence level. However, housing is provided free and food supplies are supplemented in some cases from gardens and fruit trees grown in a limited area. Nevertheless, low incomes (even by comparative Chinese standards) are a fact of life for employees of the reserve, so it is not surprising that pressures to expand standards of living are strongly felt. There is some interest (because of the shortage of government funding) in earning income from other sources, a number of which have already been indicated.

Income from ecotourism

Ecotourism is one such income source. Income is earned from entrance fees to three different sites in the sub-reserves. The Bubong site (Mengla) and the Limestone/Forest Cliffs (Menglun) site appear to be profitable if only tourism operations are considered.

The Bubong site has about 10,000 visitors per year and appears to earn ¥10,000–15,000 per year from visitors' fees. However, it was originally planned as part of Bubong Ecological Research Station, which was a joint venture of the Xishuangbanna Nature Reserve Bureau and the Yunnan Ecological Institute, and was intended for scientific research with an expectation of earning some income from visiting scientists paying fees to use the research facilities. However, this use has not materialized. The accommodation and research facilities built in Bubong village are virtually unused by scientists. Scientists from the Yunnan Ecological Institute consider the area to be too remote and find it difficult to obtain supplies there, so now the building in Bubong village is mainly rented for general accommodation, and the scenic site is basically used only for tourism.

The treetop walk in Bubong scenic site was financed by an American wildlife group. It is likely to need major repairs in the future for tourism purposes. Possibly a future joint venture could be considered, to finance repairs and improvements.

A joint venture arrangement has been entered into for development of the Limestone/Forest Cliffs site in Menglun Sub-reserve, for ecotourism. The joint venture is between the sub-reserve and a local farming co-operative. The sub-reserve is assured of an annual payment for five years from the venture (paid by the farming co-operative) increasing year by year. After the fifth year, the sub-reserve and farming co-operative will share receipts equally. In return, the farming co-operative has carried out capital works at the site, for example, the construction of a substantial foot bridge across a river, to provide access to the site, and foot paths. Thus, the administration of the sub-reserve has not been obliged to meet any capital costs and the development is virtually riskless from its point of view.

This is not the situation at San-Ca-He in Mengyang Sub-reserve. An attempt is being made here to expand the number of paying visitors at the site, and increase income obtained from ecotourism. The theory is, that by providing improved infrastructure and facilities at the site, joint venturers or sole venturers will be attracted to set up tourism-related enterprises there. A substantial concrete road has been constructed, and a small hotel/guest house is being built. Walking tracks, using concrete bricks, have been constructed. For this purpose, the Bureau has borrowed about Rmb 5m. from the Yunnan Tourist Development Corporation. In 1994, no joint ventures had been attracted. The economic viability of the project depends on joint or sole ventures interested in tourism being attracted to the site. If the administration of the sub-reserve is forced to operate the new hotel/guest house and no other tourist ventures are attracted to the site, income will be insufficient to repay the loan. Without other participants, the development will result in an economic loss for Xishuangbanna Nature Reserve Bureau (Cf. Chapters 8 and 12) and will be a financial drain. In this case, the risk is being carried by the Bureau and the capital sum is relatively large. In contrast with the previous example of ecotourism development in Menglun Sub-reserve, the development at San-Ca-He involves considerable financial risk for the Xishuangbanna Nature Reserve Bureau. While tourism ventures can add to the financial resources of the reserve, they become a financial drain if they are not a business success.

It was also mentioned that while financial assistance for capital works from various donors is always welcome, that problems arise in many cases (for example GEF funds) because no provision is made for expenditure on maintenance. Local funds are often insufficient for this purpose.

Income from the butterfly farm

Mengyang Sub-reserve operates a butterfly farm at its San-Ca-He site.

Butterflies are bred and reared there and then processed in Jinghong at the Bureau's headquarters for sale as souvenirs. The farm is partially an initiative of the WWF to increase the finances available to the sub-reserve. Facilities consist of a small building containing displays, and a nursery and an outdoor meshed dome into which butterflies can be released.

Three people are employed at San-Ca-He to operate the butterfly farm of whom only one is funded from the sub-reserve's budget. The remainder are paid from actual income from butterfly sales. The butterfly farm is said to be profitable, earning a net income of about ¥10,000 annually.

Eight people are employed at the Bureau's headquarters in Jinghong, processing butterflies and producing various products incorporating butterflies. This is also a profitable operation.

However, the 'butterfly factory' at the Bureau's headquarters does not rely solely on supplies from the San-Ca-He butterfly farm, but purchases a substantial quantity of butterflies from those who collect them along the roadways. This appears necessary to meet the competition because there are a number of independent operators producing products from butterflies collected in the wild. Whether or not this 'open-access' collection is endangering populations of some species of butterflies, is unknown. While it has been reported that WWF has some concern about this, Chinese authorities are of the view that the practice is not currently endangering any particular species. A greater danger to butterfly populations would be loss of the food sources used by different species. Within the reserve, these are relatively secure but this is not so outside the reserve, where satellite imagery indicates that vegetation cover has declined considerably in recent years in Xishuangbanna Prefecture.

The butterfly processing factory at the Bureau's headquarters operates basically in two large rooms. In one room, butterflies are sorted by species and according to their condition. In the second room, any detailed work on the butterflies is done and they are incorporated into products, for example put in glass display frames, mounted on display plates etc. Although there is considerable competition with independent operators, according to the Director of the Bureau, the butterfly enterprise of the reserve is profitable.

Income from multiple operations

Within the sub-reserves of Xishuangbanna State Nature Reserve, so-called multiple-use projects are undertaken. For instance, villagers pay a fee to grow local wild ginger in the forest. This ginger is used for medical purposes and requires tree cover. This activity may have little adverse effect on the forest.

Concessions have also been allowed for the growing of passionfruit, pomelo (also known as shaddock *Citrus grandis*) and rubber trees in Xishuangbanna State Nature Reserve. Clearly, such operations substantially replace natural vegetation and exhibit some conflict with biodiversity conservation, even though the extra funds are said to be used to protect the sub-reserves. In those sub-reserves that are especially short of finance, there is a temptation to extend these 'multiple uses' because they involve no capital outlays, by the administration of the sub-reserves and provide a relatively assured source of income in terms of annual rent or fees. The manager of one sub-reserve thought that more 'wasteland' in his area could be used in this way to generate income. However, at least one of the discussants present raised the point that there is rarely such a thing as wasteland in a forest ecosystem, and suggested that great caution be exercised, on biodiversity grounds, in allocating such land to 'multiple projects'. While multiple projects may help to gain local support for a sub-reserve, it is not clear whether they are all allocated to local villagers with low-to-moderate income.

Extension of multiple use needs to be carefully monitored so as to not compromise the biodiversity objective of the Nature Reserve. Already existing villages encompassed by the reserve and their immediate surrounds, are excluded from the Xishuangbanna State Nature Reserve. The areas around these villages, usually located along streams, are intensively cultivated in most cases. Many of them were already cultivated before the establishment of the reserve.

Another small source of income is derived from the guest houses of the sub-reserves, located at their main stations in the towns. They are in the same area as the general accommodation provided for many of the staff of the sub-reserve, and some rooms appear to be occupied by permanent staff. Priority for accommodation is given to visiting staff of the Bureau or to officials involved in business connected with the Nature Reserve. However, other tourists may also be accommodated. The charge is very low, at ¥20 for a room per night. Facilities are quite reasonable by Chinese standards but maintenance, because of lack of funds, appears to be a problem. There is probably scope to increase income from these facilities by spending a small sum on fixtures and fittings. Currently, the income from these guest houses is only enough to pay the salary of one person who maintains them. If capital and other items were included, then these operations would run at a loss, using Western accounting methods. However, with small outlay, there would be good prospects for increasing income from this source.

Resource management fees

Income from resource management fees cover two basic items:

(1) income from rights to take resources from the reserve;
(2) income from fines for violation of the law, for example, illegal poaching and removal of timber.

Local villagers arepermitted to collect firewood in the reserve and may also be permitted to fell some trees for limited local use, such as house construction. By permitting some legal use of the resources of the sub-reserves, local people may be more sympathetic to its existence and have less excuse for illegally using such resources. Fines are levied on those caught for illegal hunting or use of the resources of these sub-reserves and these may be retained by administration.

Concluding comment on finances

The scope for the management of the Xishuangbanna State Nature Reserve to earn income is relatively limited, particularly as it does not want to compromise its biodiversity conservation objectives. The Bureau seems likely to be dependent on government funds for the major part of its finance for some time to come. While some ecotourism projects in the reserve are bound to be net income earners, others involve considerable business risks. Concessions for multiple projects involve little financial risk for the administrators of the sub-reserves, whereas some types of multiple project can have major adverse environmental impacts on natural ecosystems. Therefore caution is needed in increasing financial reliance on these.

POLITICAL ECONOMY ASPECTS

The Bureau for the Protection of the Xishuangbanna State Nature Reserve has been established under the regulations of the

Xishuangbanna Dai Autonomous Prefecture. Therefore, its operation is, to some extent, influenced by the administration of this prefecture. However, the major part of its funding is from the Ministry of Forestry through the Yunnan Provincial Forest Service, so it has several bodies that can exert an influence on the Bureau.

As for the administration of the sub-reserves, the Bureau has to approve all appointments, and allocates funds to them. However, the county government or administration can also have an influence, for example, in relation to appointment of leaders of the sub-reserves and may also issue instructions to the administrators of the sub-reserves.

The political system therefore allows for multiple influences on policies pursued by the administration of Xishuangbanna State Nature Reserve. Because multiple bodies can have an influence, there is a possibility of conflict between these and such conflict has to be resolved by political means. Lines of command are by no means as hard-and-fast or definite as one might imagine. While this allows the interplay of a variety of social forces, it also provides scope for slackness and inefficiency in the administrative system.

The sustainability of the nature reserve depends to some extent on political perceptions about its role. Politically, it is desirable to have the support of local communities or at least not to have them hostile to the reserve. Therefore, local communities should obtain some benefits from its existence, and have any of its adverse impacts (such as caused by straying elephants) mitigated. The challenge is how to provide benefits to local communities without compromising the conservation goals of the reserve. Apart from the use (mentioned above) of some of the resources of the nature reserve by local villagers, the Bureau is interested in supporting economic development projects for local communities. In this respect, agroforestry (social forestry) projects are being explored, and rapid rural appraisal (RRA) will be used in an attempt to identify community projects which are wanted by local communities, and which may raise their income (Cf. Chapter 11). The theory is that by increasing the productivity of the land outside the reserve, and improving economic opportunities in Xishuangbanna Prefecture, this will ease pressures to use the resources of sub-reserves unsustainably for economic gain.

CONCLUDING COMMENTS

Even in developed countries, funds for the management of national parks and nature reserves always appear to be in short supply, but the situation in developing countries is more acute. The State Nature Reserve of Xishuangbanna provides a practical example of the financial difficulties faced by administrators of nature reserves in developing countries, and in particular, is representative of the financial and political difficulties faced by such administrators in China. Given the constraints mentioned, international aid can play an important role in financing initiatives for supporting biodiversity conservation in China. This is because few funds are available to administrators of nature reserves to fund biodiversity conservation initiatives, after meeting operating expenses. While, technically, there may be scope for economising on the use of funds for administration of nature reserves, for example, by reducing the number of staff employed, politically, scope for this may be limited. Furthermore, any reduction in employment in nature protection is liable to add to China's rural labour surplus, and may do little to bolster local political support for nature reserves. In addition, most administrators are aware that public funds are less likely to be reduced if they are required for salaries of employed staff than if they are needed for 'discretionary' purposes. Thus, for sound political reasons, there is an upward bias in the employment of labour in relation to other purchased inputs for administration.

In the case of Xishuangbanna State Nature Reserve, overseas funds have played a useful role in enabling development initiatives to be taken. Funds from the World Wide Fund for Nature have been used to establish the butterfly farm at San-Ca-He, for the provision of electric fences to exclude elephants from farms, and for experimental agroforestry. Construction of the treetop walk at the Bubong scenic site was financed by an American wildlife organization. Capital works seem to be heavily dependent on outside funding. Joint business ventures have been used recently to tap outside capital for the reserve, for example, the Limestone/Forest Cliffs development at Menglun. One of the problems raised about international aid, however, is that no funds are made available for maintenance and operating costs as a rule. Finance is usually provided only for the establishment of projects, not their maintenance. It is very difficult for the administrators of nature reserves in China to find sufficient funds from their own sources to take care of such items.

15. Sustainable Development and Biodiversity Conservation in North-east India in Context

INTRODUCTION AND BACKGROUND

Chapters 10–14 have concentrated on management issues involving nature conservation in Xishuangbanna Prefecture in China, especially in relation to its State Nature Reserve. While the issues were discussed, analysed and illustrated for a particular locality, they are of wider relevance to China and to Asia. This is not to say that problems of conserving biodiversity, and of attaining sustainable development, are the same in all parts of Asia. Nevertheless, there is a considerable degree of similarity between these problems encountered throughout Asia and in many developed countries. For example, the situation in north-east India, as far as sustainable development and nature conservation is concerned, has similarities with Yunnan.

Although this chapter concentrates on sustainable development and conservation of biodiversity in north-east India, they are placed in a broad context which enlarges the discussion in Chapter 9. Furthermore, given the low-level provision of protected areas in most states of north-east India, it is necessary to give greater consideration to conservation outside such areas. Therefore, agricultural and forest sustainability in this part of India is given a significant amount of attention. To some extent, the Asian situation mirrors global developments, brought about by economic expansion and growth of human population.

Increases in population and in the intensity and breadth of human activities, are making ever mounting inroads into natural environments, and reducing biodiversity. Some of the environmental effects are now being felt on a global scale; for example, depletion of the ozone layer and the build up of greenhouse gases such as carbon dioxide. Of course, humankind's transformation of nature has been going on for thousands of years (Goudie,

1990; Cunliffe, 1994) but the difference now is its accelerating scale and intensity, made possible in large measure by new technologies and capital accumulation. The question more frequently asked is how much further this process can go without threatening the life-support systems of *homo sapiens*. We have been alerted to the possibility that the strategy of economic growth (by means of capital accumulation and technological progress), which has been touted by many for so long as the answer to reducing economic scarcity, could itself become a source of scarcity for future generations, or even cause ruin for present ones. This can happen if the resource-depletion and environmental consequences of such a strategy are ignored.

In addition, it has become clear that if sustainable development is to be achieved, development projects must be assessed on a holistic basis. This involves taking account not only of their external economic consequences, but their wider environmental and socio-economic implications, including those in the longer term. The biophysical, social and economic dimensions must all be taken into account, and this requires a multidisciplinary approach to project evaluation.

The sustainability issue also raises another question: namely, the ethical one of whether mankind is justified in continuing to eliminate other species solely for its own economic gain. In particular, in high-income countries, can the elimination of a species be justified for the sake of an extremely small increase in incomes which are already high? An example of this occurred in 1995 in Queensland. The mahogany-glider possum is a rare species, dependent on mahogany trees, and is confined to a small geographical area in Queensland. In 1995, part of its habitat began to be cleared for sugar-cane production. But Australia is already a major exporter of sugar, and any increase in Australian incomes (already high) as a result of growing sugar-cane in the area presently occupied by this glider, would be minuscule. Many Australians were of the view that further invasion of this habitat could not be ethically justified, and its clearance has now stopped.

In this chapter, I shall consider the global historical, intellectual and policy context to which biodiversity, conservation and sustainable development in north-east India needs to be related, and consider these matters within Asia, especially south Asia. Attention will then be turned to specific sustainability issues in north-east India, including agricultural sustainability and that of forests and of communities. Comparisons will be made with some localities in south Asia which face, or have faced, similar challenges and problems. This is followed by a discussion of nature conservation within protected areas in north-east India.

THE HISTORICAL AND POLICY CONTEXT

Interest in sustainable development was, it seems, first sparked by the non-aligned countries, including India, in the early 1970s, and was an issue at the 1972 United Nations Conference on Development, held in Stockholm. Pandit Nehru was anxious to make it an international issue, and concern about sustainability was enhanced by the oil crisis of the 1970s. Both pollution and depletion of non-renewable resources, such as oil, as a result of economic growth and population increases, became a major concern (for example Meadows *et al*, 1972). However, most economists rejected the neo-Malthusian point of view that limits to economic growth set by the environment and natural resources, were being rapidly approached, and remained growth optimists. Most believed that technological progress would overcome any apparent limits to economic growth, that (with economic growth) self-regulation of population would occur, that most environmental failures within economic systems can be overcome by appropriate market reforms, and argued that if all else fails, mankind has tremendous capacity to respond socially to environmental dangers (Cf. Tisdell, 1990, Ch. 3). While such optimism may prove justified, it can breed apathy about environmental change and there is the problem that although society may respond to environmental deterioration, it may do so when the damage done is irreversible. Furthermore, there is no guarantee that technological progress will continue at a rapid rate or even continue at all.

While earliest concerns about the sustainability of economic development were based on the occurrence of pollution from economic activity, and the depletion of non-renewable inanimate resources such as minerals, concerns in the 1980s began shifting to the consequences of degradation and depletion of living natural resources, and loss of biodiversity. *The World Conservation Strategy* (IUCN, 1980) appears to have been a turning point. The importance of the conservation of natural biological resources and of biodiversity, for human welfare and sustaining economic activity, came to be stressed. This focus strengthened and is apparent in *Our Common Future* (World Commission on Environment and Development, 1987); it was also a major theme of the United Nations Conference on Environment and Development, held in Rio de Janeiro in 1992. This Conference adopted *Agenda 21*, which calls upon all nations to develop strategies for sustainable development for the 21st Century. China has been one of the first developing nations to draw up such a strategy (State Council, 1994) but it is doubtful if its strategy, as currently stated, is operational.

Agenda 21, amongst other things, requires attention to be paid to the conservation of biodiversity. While countries could not obtain agreement on an international convention for conservation of biodiversity at Rio de Janeiro, mainly because of the disagreement of the United States, the American position subsequently altered with the change of its President. An international convention, the Convention on Biodiversity Conservation, has now come into effect, and places obligations on its signatories to conserve biodiversity in their own countries.

SUSTAINABILITY IN THE INTELLECTUAL CONTEXT OF ECONOMICS

From the early 1970s onwards, a growing group of economists became interested in concepts of sustainability and sustainable development. The interest of virtually all was purely an anthropocentric one. The focus was on how conservation of natural resources and the environment might help satisfy the needs or wants of mankind. All of the value of conservation was to be determined by reference to humans, with willingness to pay (or to accept payment) being an important part of the process of valuing nature; and the concept of total economic value was introduced by Pearce and others (1989). It includes items such as existence value of species in the evaluation of conservation, thereby signalling that economic evaluation need not be based solely on materialistic considerations. However, other species are provided with no rights in themselves, but depend solely for their valuation on the total economic evaluation placed upon them by human beings.

On the question of sustainable development, economists have been engaged in two broad areas of debate. These involve (1) the ethical or normative basis for sustainable development and (2) the conditions that need to be satisfied in order to achieve sustainable development; a matter involving positivism. Debate is ongoing about both issues.

Most economists argue that the income of future generations (of human beings) should not be made less than that of the present generation(s) as a consequence of actions taken by present generations. It is believed that present generations have an economic moral obligation to future ones. This is given some ethical underpinning by the Rawlsian principle of justice, namely that inequality in the income of individuals can only be justified if the inequality is to the detriment of none (Rawls, 1971). The principle relies on the 'veil of ignorance' assumption, namely that any individual could have been born into the shoes of any other and that if an original contract before birth could have been entered into, all would agree to this principle of equality. I have pointed out its shortcomings elsewhere (Tisdell, 1993, Ch. 9). In addition, note that it would require everyone to take a risk-averse attitude; furthermore, it is purely man-centred. Also, if carried to its logical conclusion, Rawls' principle requires equality between individuals in the current generation, unless inequality disadvantages no one.

The second contentious matter involves the conditions required to satisfy the above mentioned aim, that the income of future generations be not less than that of present generations. At least two schools of thought have emerged in economics:

(1) those who argue that weak sustainability conditions are sufficient;
(2) those who argue that strong sustainability conditions are required.

The basic argument is about what constitutes suitable bequests to future generations for the purpose of maintaining incomes (Pearce, 1993, Ch. 2).

Advocates of weak sustainability conditions are optimistic about the future, and suggest that substitution of man-made capital for natural resources, and for environmental quality, is acceptable and that accumulation of man-made capital (especially if combined with efforts to sustain technological progress and improve human capital through education) is a suitable bequest for maintaining the income of future generations. On the other hand, those favouring weak sustainability conditions claim that continuing substitution of man-made capital for natural environmental resources is no longer a suitable bequest for future generations. Man-made capital eventually perishes. Furthermore, natural resources and environmental stocks have already been severely reduced by economic growth. They may have been reduced to a core essential for the maintenance of life-support systems and economic production. Additional reduction is likely to imperil economic production, because natural and environmental resources are essential ingredients of most production processes, and directly provide services to human beings. In the view of those recommending strong sustainability conditions, considerable effort should be made to maintain the existing natural resource/environmental stock. This does not mean that no economic change is permitted which uses natural environments, but that environmental offset policies should be instituted. For example, if a new coal-using power station is opened that would add to carbon dioxide emissions, these emissions may be required to be offset by planting trees, to act as sinks for the additional carbon dioxide. Or again, conversion of forested land to agriculture may only be permitted if additional forest is planted to act as an offset. Naturally, there is room for argument about what constitutes a suitable offset.

The above arguments are about what is necessary to sustain the welfare of human beings. However, some believe that a wider ethical perspective is needed. Aldo Leopold (1966) argued that man has a responsibility to respect the 'web of life'. Tisdell (1991, Ch. 11) has suggested that some weight should be afforded to the conservation of other species, independently of their value to humankind. Aspects of Hinduism and of Buddhism appear to support this view, and it may be that features of Taoism and the traditional emphasis of the Chinese on harmony and balance between mankind and nature, provide additional support for this point of view. In any case, holders of this conservation ethic will be less inclined than economic man (as typically portrayed by economists) to forgo nature conservation, even if it might benefit future generations of humans economically.

DEVELOPMENT OF ASIA, ESPECIALLY SOUTH ASIA, AND THE RURAL ENVIRONMENT

Unlike sub-Saharan Africa, Asia showed considerable economic growth, at least in east Asia, until the Asian economic crisis began in August, 1997. While international emphasis, for example by the World Bank, has been on the so-called miraculous economic growth of east Asia, this should not be allowed to detract from the substantial growth achieved by south Asian countries. The GDP of the major south Asian economies grew at annual rates in excess of four per cent in the period 1980 – 95 (see Table 15.1). However, rapid rates of population increase, but declining rates in most south Asian countries (see Table 15.1), meant that the rate of increase in the income per head of their population was slower (see Table 15.2).

With the exception of Sri Lanka, south Asian countries still seem to be a considerable distance away from completing their demographic transition to a stationary level of population. The population levels of Bangladesh, India and Pakistan are expected to double at least before they stabilise (see Table 15.3). Thus, population increases plus aspirations for higher per capita increases, can be expected to put great strain on natural environments in south Asia in the foreseeable future.

Already, in rural areas in south Asia, land-use patterns have been affected. Between 1979 and 1991, forest and woodland areas in Bangladesh decreased by 13 per cent and in India by 0.7 per cent. The percentage of land allocated to crops increased in all south Asian countries in this period, and that for land used for permanent pasture either declined slightly or remained stationary. These are all signs of intensification of rural land use

Table 15.1 Rates of growth of production and population in selected South and East Asian economies

	GDP Annual percentage change			Population Annual percentage change		
	1970–80	1980–90	1990–95	1970–80	1980–90	1990–95
South Asia						
Bangladesh	2.3	4.3	4.1	2.6	2.4	1.6
India	3.4	5.8	4.6	2.3	2.1	1.8
Pakistan	4.9	6.3	4.6	3.1	3.1	2.9
Sri Lanka	4.1	4.2	4.8	1.6	1.4	1.3
East Asia						
China	-	10.2	12.8	1.8	1.5	1.1
Indonesia	7.2	6.1	7.6	2.3	1.8	1.6
The Philippines	6.0	1.0	2.3	2.5	2.4	2.2
Thailand	7.1	7.6	8.4	2.7	1.7	0.9

Source: Based on World Bank (1994, 1997).

Table 15.2 GNP per capita in US dollars 1995 for selected South and East Asian eonomies and their growth rates of GNP per capita, 1985–95.

	GNP per capita 1995	Average annual growth (%) 1985–95
South Asia		
Bangladesh	240	2.1
India	340	3.2
Pakistan	460	1.2
Sri Lanka	700	2.6
East Asia		
China	620	8.3
Indonesia	980	6.0
The Philippines	1,050	1.5
Thailand	2,740	8.4

Source: Based on World Bank (1997) Table 1.

for economic purposes. Actually, the degree of intensification of such use (which normally has adverse consequences for biodiversity and the natural environment) is much greater than is apparent from the above figures, because they do not factor in developments such as the increased incidence of multiple-cropping, and the rising use of artificial fertilisers, pesticides and irrigation.

Table 15.3   Estimates and predictions of population levels for selected Asian countries: totals in millions

	1992	2000	2025	Hypothetical stationary level
South Asia				
Bangladesh	114	132	182	263
India	884	1,016	1,370	1,888
Pakistan	119	148	243	400
Sri Lanka	17	19	24	29
East Asia				
China	1,162	1,255	1,471	1,680
Indonesia	184	206	265	355
The Philippines	64	77	115	172
Thailand	58	65	81	104

Source: Based on World Bank (1994), Table 25.

As for biodiversity, south Asian countries are extremely well endowed. However, a large number of their higher plants, birds and mammals are threatened with extinction. In Bangladesh and India respectively, over 2000 species of higher plants are believed to be threatened with extinction (World Resources Institute *et al*, 1994, Table 20.4). A large part and source of the unique biodiversity of India is located in north-east India. The area of India under (nature) protection is 4 per cent, slightly below the Asian average of 4.4 per cent, and well below that of Europe at 9.3 per cent and the USA at 10.5 per cent (World Resources Institute *et al*, 1994, Table 20.1). However, the situation in Bangladesh is much worse from a conservation point of view because only 0.7 per cent of its land area is afforded protected status; nor is any of its area afforded total nature protection.

NORTH-EAST INDIA – GENERAL OBSERVATIONS

North-east India is a region of tremendous biological and cultural diversity.

It consists of seven states; Arunachal Pradesh, Nagaland, Manipur, Mizoram, Tripura, Meghalaya and Assam, as shown in Figure 15.1. It is an asset not only to India but to the whole world. However, as in many other areas in Asia, socio-economic change is threatening this diversity.

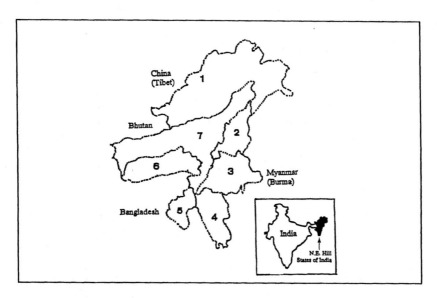

Figure 15.1 The seven north-east hill states of India. They are Arunachal Pradesh (1), Nagaland (2), Manipur (3), Mizoram (4), Tripura (5), Meghalaya (6) and Assam (7)

In general, the levels of per capita income in the north-east Indian states are lower than elsewhere in India but compare favourably with those of some other Indian states, for example Bihar. It is estimated (Ministry of Finance, 1994, Table 1.8, p. S – 12) that for 1990–91 the per capita net state domestic product for Bihar was 2,650 Rupees, whereas for Manipur it was 3,893 Rupees, for Mizoram (in 1989–90) 4,135 Rupees, for Meghalaya 4,190 Rupees for Assam 3,932, for Arunachal Pradesh 5,046 and for Tripura 3,328. By contrast however, Delhi recorded a figure of 10,638 Rupees. Per capita incomes in the north-east are still considered low but are not dramatically below the overall level in India.

The rate of population growth in north-east India is rapid and overall is above the Indian average. It ranged in 1981–91 from an average exponential growth rate of 2.17 per cent for Assam to 4.45 per cent for Nagaland. Mizoram recorded a 3.34 per cent growth rate (Ministry of

Finance, 1994, Table 9, p. S – 115). Population densities in the north-east are low by Indian standards and range from 10 people per square km in Arunchal Pradesh to 286 in Assam. Mizoram had a low density in 1991 of 33 people per square km (Ministry of Finance, 1994, Table 9. p. S – 115). Nevertheless, with such rapid rates of increase, population density is rising rapidly and continuing to affect the region's natural environment.

Consequences for Agricultural Sustainability

Agriculture and forests are important for economic welfare in north-east India, where the vast majority of the people are engaged in rural pursuits. However, a number of the agricultural practices used in the region are becoming increasingly unsustainable. They will continue to do so as population densities increase there and demands for higher incomes result in activities intensifying economic production.

As pointed out by Ramakrishnan (1992) and others, shifting agriculture (slash-and-burn or *jhum* agriculture), which is practised by a number of tribal groups is becoming less sustainable as cultivation cycles are shortened due to population pressures. Once this cycle goes below 10–12 years, it seems that it is no longer an economic form of agriculture, compared to other possible types of settled agriculture. This raises the question of just how sustainable settled agriculture is in the north-east, taking into account the monsoonal nature of the area, the prevalence of sloping lands and the nature of soils. Certainly, modified forms of settled agriculture are likely to be called for in this region to improve agricultural sustainability; for example, mixed systems of cultivation as in permacultures, use of hedgerows for soil erosion control, and so on. These are all matters worthy of investigation.

All this underlines the point that strategies for sustainable development must be based upon anticipation, and that flexibility is needed. Given that population levels are going to increase in the north-east of India, then policies for sustainable development, including sustainable agricultural development, need to be designed taking this into account. A dynamic approach to planning for sustainability is required.

A reduction in the length of *jhum* cycles has a number of adverse environmental consequences. It reduces biodiversity and it increases the rate of soil erosion, apart from its unfavourable economic consequences for the cultivator. While the slash-and-burn technique appears to be relatively sustainable, and not a major environmental danger when population densities are low or economic demands on this system are low, this is not the case for higher population densities.

With increasing population and increased agricultural demand on land:

(1) the fallow period is usually reduced when slash-and-burn is in use;
(2) the technique is extended to new areas, which may be marginal from an agricultural point of view.

Agriculture is intensified and extended using this technique.

The consequences are that:

(1) a greater area of land is under cultivation at any one time, which allows greater soil erosion, and water run-off; factors of particular concern in hilly areas;
(2) shorter fallow periods result in falling levels of soil nutrients, and in many cases, reduced soil depth, so crop yields decline.

Furthermore, there are serious consequences for nature conservation. First, the larger area of land under agricultural cultivation means that refuges for wild animals are reduced, and so is their area of habitat. Second, reduced fallow periods result in shortening of the period for biological succession of species. This means botanical species requiring longer periods to re-establish themselves, may disappear. Pre-existing patterns of symbiosis between the economic activities of humans and nature are broken. The total result (of the cultivation of virgin land and of intensification of cultivation, as evidenced by shorter fallow periods) is reduced variety of wildlife habitats and landscapes, and loss of biodiversity.

When slash-and-burn is on a limited scale and of low intensity, it is compatible with the conservation of a high degree of biodiversity. Indeed, by adding habitat variety, it may well add to biodiversity in a region. But this is not so when it is on an extensive scale and intensified. In this latter stage, public or collective measures are necessary to conserve biodiversity. This may be achieved, in part, by increasing the area afforded nature protection and/or in some areas, trying to preserve slash-and-burn at 'traditional' intensities and scales. However, the latter may only be possible if the communities affected are given economic assistance.

In certain cases, it may be worthwhile encouraging settled agriculture, if reasonably sustainable forms are available or can be discovered. If these forms are more productive than shifting agriculture, an economic bonus may be that marginal agricultural lands can be assigned to areas for nature protection. As discussed later, the proportion of land afforded nature protection in most states of north-east India is extremely low. While in the past, this probably did not have a very adverse effect on biodiversity, the situation has changed rapidly and is worsening from the point of view of sustaining biological diversity.

It might be noted that social difficulties or impediments, to changing from various forms of communal property rights in land to private property rights, hamper a switch to settled agriculture in many parts of north-east India (Tisdell, 1998). Unless co-evolution occurs, it is very difficult to achieve transition to settled agriculture, even if this is desirable. Furthermore, one should bear in mind that not all areas in which shifting agriculture is practised are likely to be able to sustain settled agriculture.

Forest Sustainability

Inroads continue to be made into forested and woody areas in north-east India as population pressures and desires for economic development increase.

Ramakrishnan (1992, p. 386) reports:

In north-eastern India, large-scale disturbance of the rain forest ecosystem has resulted in varied levels of degraded, arrested bamboo forests, either with weed take-over or a totally bald landscape. During the last few decades, large-scale timber extraction for industrial purposes has cleared vast areas of land for invasion by exotic weeds (.....) Thus exotic weeds such as *Eupatorium* spp., and *Mikania micrantha* have taken over vast tracts of cleared land, along with native weeds such as *Imperata cylindrica* and *Thysanolaena maxima*. Once this large-scale invasion has occurred, the jhum farmer is even more limited by the land area available for his jhum system of agriculture, as he prefers to avoid sites of high weed density. Because of this and increased population pressure, the jhum cycle has dropped drastically in length, from a more favourable 20 years or more, to an extremely short 5 years, or even less. Having no other option, in the absence of an alternate agricultural technology that is viable from an ecological and social angle, the jhum farmer perforce had to resort to very short jhum cycles, although the system operates below subsistence level and has caused further environmental degradation. Large-scale timber extraction and very short jhum cycles of 4–5 years have resulted in an arrested succession of weeds in north-eastern India.

In some cases, deforestation has led to desertification in north-east India. Ramakrishnan (1992, pp. 386–387) suggests that desertification in

Cherrapunji in Meghalaya has been rapid and sudden, mainly due to past deforestation. Reforestation has been arrested. Furthermore, in other areas, reforestation has been attenuated, for example, by the growth of bamboo. Forested areas are trapped in a bamboo successional stage with 'obvious adverse consequences for biological diversity in the region'. Ramakrishnan, (1992, p. 387) suggests that mixed plantation forests may be needed to re-establish forest succession and help in increasing biological diversity. There are clearly many other issues that need to be investigated as far as the sustainability of forests in north-east India is concerned. Forests are especially important there because they play a substantial role in providing economic support for many tribal groups, and are an important source of fuel. They also play a major role in maintaining biodiversity and in providing environmental services, such as improving waterflows and reducing soil erosion.

Sustainability of Communities in the Northeast

It is often argued that sustainable development is not just a matter of achieving economic sustainability, and that sustainability must be considered in relation to at least three dimensions. These dimensions are:

(1) the biophysical,
(2) the economic,
(3) the social.

For this reason, it is usually recommended that strategies for sustainable development be studied on a holistic basis, employing an interdisciplinary approach. Such strategies should ideally satisfy sustainability conditions for all of the above three dimensions.

Views differ about what constitutes social sustainability, but it generally involves the maintenance of a sense of community and of cohesion in society. It also requires the continuing ability of the society to avoid disintegration and to respond effectively to changes which call for a communal response. Irrespective of the exact definition adopted, it is clear that the social dimension cannot be ignored in planning and implementing development strategies.

Ramakrishnan (1992, Ch. 3) has described social patterns in north-east India as being ones involving economic mutualism between different tribal and ethnic groups, using somewhat different techniques of obtaining a livelihood and utilising different sets of resources, so that competition between them is reduced and they are able to more easily retain their separate identities and communities. While some exchange occurs between groups, subsistence activities play a dominant role in the region. Ramakrishnan (1992, p. 88) points out that although it is difficult to generalise about village organisation and formation in this region, 'diverse communities often coexisting in the same area have evolved ways in which they are able to do so, sharing resources in a highly complementary manner.'

However, the equilibrium of communities can easily be shattered by resource-depletion and increasing resource scarcity, which can render some ways of life and some communities unsustainable. For example, with diminishing forest resources in the north-east, those communities heavily specialised in using these resources could find their communities endangered. Gathering from forests still plays a significant role in the subsistence of some tribal groups. One group, the Sulungs of Arunchal Pradesh, obtains almost half of its food requirements from hunting and gathering (Ramakrishnan, 1992, p. 117). Hill tribes, such as the Garos and the Khasis in Meghalaya, and the Nithis, the Karbis, the Kacharis and the Chackmas, all show significant dependence on forest resources for food and fuel, a dependence that rises during poor seasons. These societies are liable to be disrupted by loss of forest resources.

Comparison with Nearby Regions

Problems of sustainable development being experienced in north-east India are by no means unique. They appear to be widespread throughout the remoter areas of south-east Asia and will become more apparent as economic growth in this region proceeds.

Similar conditions exist, for example, in Burma (Myanmar), although the economic growth there has been slow, also in parts of Thailand, Laos, southern Yunnan (China), Indonesia, Malaysia (for instance, in Sarawak) and in parts of the Philippines. Geographical conditions are similar in all these cases, and a variety of tribal groups are present. This means that any workable strategies for sustainable development discovered for north-east India, are likely to have application in nearby regions.

To some extent, there appears to be a shared historical background with nearby regions. For instance, tribal groups in several nearby regions also have sacred forest groves or holy hills which are conserved in their natural state (Cf. Colding and Folke, 1997). These occur amongst the Dai people in Xishuangbanna Prefecture, Yunnan and in some parts of Sumatra. Slash-

and-burn cultivation is practised by a number of the hill tribes in Xishuangbanna and appears to be quite common in Burma (Myanmar), in Indo-China and other parts of south-east Asia. Most of these areas are subject to population pressures, and increasing demands are being made (or are likely to be) upon their natural resources, to foster economic growth. All of these regions face a common problem: how to permit or even encourage economic development and simultaneously conserve their unique natural and cultural environments.

PROTECTED AREAS AND NATURE CONSERVATION IN NORTH-EAST INDIA

Biodiversity is under threat in several parts of Asia because:

(1) of extension and intensification of land-use outside protected areas;
(2) a low proportion of land area in some regions has been afforded official status for nature protection;
(3) in several cases, areas afforded official protected status can not be effectively protected and are subject to poaching, natural resource extraction and illegal use. On the whole, this is the situation in north-east India.

In most states in north-east India, a very low proportion of the land area is in national parks or sanctuaries according to the *United Nations List of National Parks and Protected Areas: India* (1993). This can be seen from Table 15.4 which indicates the percentage area of each state in north-east India officially afforded the above mentioned protection. This can be compared with the percentage for the whole of India of 4 per cent in 1993. While Arunachal Pradesh is considerably above the Indian averages, most states in north-east India are well below this.

There may be at least two reasons why the proportion of areas assigned for nature protection is low. All or most of the land may be claimed by 'traditional owners' which makes it difficult to divest them of ownership. This is particularly so in areas which have not been fully subjugated by the national dominant group. For instance, Nagaland has been a hotspot of insurgency over a very long period, and an extremely low proportion of Nagaland has been allocated for nature protection. Furthermore, in areas where there is insurgency or lack of law and order, there may seem little point in establishing an officially protected area because this could only be such in name.

Table 15.4 Percentage of area in national parks or sanctuaries in the states of north-east India

State	%
Arunachal Pradesh	11.01
Assam	1.83
Manipur	1.21
Meghalaya	1.36
Mizoram	4.48
Nagaland	1.19
Tripura	5.79
INDIA	4.00

Source: Estimated from Internet data of World Conservation Monitoring Centre (1998e) and data of Government of India on size of states.

The difficulties involved in managing protected areas in north-east India can be best appreciated by taking a few examples. Many of these difficulties occur in other less developed regions of Asia, and elsewhere.

The Namdapha National Park, located in Arunachal Pradesh is in a mountainous area and is relatively large, 198 254 ha. However, its management is complicated by the presence of twenty-eight villages of 58450 people within the park (1984), and the presence of Miao, a town of over 3 000 people, just west of the park. Nearby is a Tibetan refugee settlement, as well as a settlement for Chakma refugees from the Chittagong Hill Tracts. Species diversity is very high and it has been recommended that the park be included in a biosphere reserve (World Conservation Monitoring Centre, 1998a). It seems, however, that the proposed buffer zone is under threat because Chakma refugees who have settled within it are rapidly increasing in population, employing slash-and-burn agriculture, and encroaching on reserve forests and unclassified forests (World Conservation Monitoring Centre, 1998a).

Two very important protected areas exist in Assam, namely Kaziranga National Park and Manas Sanctuary. Both contain considerable diversity of species, including the one-horned Asian rhinoceros and tigers.

Kaziranga National Park is said to be one of the finest and most picturesque wildlife reserves in Asia, but is only 37 822 ha. in size. 'It protects the world's largest Indian rhinoceros population, as well as many other threatened species' (World Conservation Monitoring Centre, 1998b). Management problems include: loss of rhinoceros due to poaching; loss of land area due to the Bhramaputra River changing its course; at times severe flooding, which drowns some wild animals and forces others out of the park where they are prone to human depredation; and illegal presence of domestic buffalo in the park where they spread rinderpest and compete for food resources. Flooding seems to have become more serious, due to loss of vegetation in the watershed of the Bhramaputra. While there are no villages within this park, it is bordered by several (World Conservation Monitoring Centre, 1998b).

Manas Sanctuary is 39 100 ha. in area and contains one forest village with 144 villages in its buffer zone. The buffer zone has become fragmented, posing a threat to many animals. 'Of particular concern is Amtika Village in the midst of the buffer zone, and in an area occupied by the golden langur. As there is no buffer zone to the south, there has been pressure from cultivation, settlement, collection of forest productions and some poaching, as well as from increasing contact between local people and wildlife. Crop-raids by elephant and hog-deer are increasingly common, leading to ill-feeling amongst local residents'. (World Conservation Monitoring Centre, 1998c). WCMC states that 'burning, hunting and extraction of timber and firewood are practised at non-sustainable levels in the buffer zone'. At one stage, the reserve was threatened by the possible building of dams.

Furthermore, insurgency has been a problem. Campaigning for autonomy of the Bodo people, the Bodo Students Union occupied the Sanctuary in 1989. Sanctuary staff were killed and poachers and timber smugglers took advantage of the situation. 'A large number of trees have been felled and the habitat of species, such as golden langur, hispid hare and pygmy hog, has been put at risk. Intervention to protect the sanctuary by either the Assam State Government or Central Government has been delayed by a lack of available manpower and political difficulties' (World Conservation Monitoring Centre, 1998c).

Finally, consider Balphakrom National Park in Meghalaya State. It is only 22 200 ha. in size but supports a great diversity of fauna and flora. Elephants are one of its major management problems. They cause considerable damage to crops during the dry season (World Conservation Monitoring Centre, 1998d).

Thus one sees that a number of the problems which arise in managing protected areas in China also occur in north-east India.

Tourism and particularly ecotourism in north-east India is very underdeveloped. This is partly a consequence of remoteness of this region from the major part of India; the absence of an international airport in the area; restrictions on movements of foreigners (for example, Inner Line permit requirements); and the presence of insurgency in parts. Nevertheless, more could be done to develop ecotourism and cultural tourism in this region (Cf. Barman and Goswami, forthcoming; Mitra, forthcoming).

An interesting question is the extent to which insurgency in north-east India is a consequence of non-sustainable development (Cf. Hall, 1998 and Hall and Hall, 1998, in reference to Rwanda and Burundi). In reality, the causation is probably circular: insurgency adds to economic and environmental problems in the region and this, in turn, gives rise to insurgency. Large numbers of Indian troops appear to be stationed in this region, not only because of the presence of local insurgency, but because it is a border region, and its northern boundaries remain in dispute with China.

CONCLUDING COMMENTS

Globally, concern has been growing about the possibility of not achieving sustainable development. Some argue that this concern represents a new form of imperialism fostered by high-income countries. On the other hand, many in less developed countries believe sustainable development is important from their own viewpoint. Although Pandit Nehru is not likely to be regarded by many as a passionate environmentalist and conserver of nature (Roy and Tisdell, 1995, Ch. 1), he was instrumental in fostering concerns to achieve sustainable development amongst the international community.

Although the environmental agenda of high-income countries, does not always coincide with the wishes of lower-income countries, and that of the centre does not always accord with that of the geographical periphery, it would be dangerous and short-sighted of any region to ignore the environmental consequences of its own socio-economic change. To do so would be a sure recipe for long-term economic and social disaster.

However, the pursuit of sustainable development does not imply that socio-economic systems should remain in a frozen or static state. Ironically, it is often the case that attempts to keep such systems frozen will reduce sustainability. It is probably true to say that the use of a number of agricultural techniques and forestry practices in north-east India are becoming less sustainable today. There is a need, therefore, to search for more sustainable alternatives. It may even be that some communities will no longer be able to survive in their traditional forms because available natural resources will no longer sustainably support these societies. Acceptable ways should be found to enable such communities to adjust to changing environmental circumstances, many of which are not subject to control or easily controlled, for example, those arising from population growth. This does not say that nothing can be controlled, but emphasises the need for realism in planning for sustainable development.

REFERENCES

Colding, J. and C. Folke (1997), 'The relations among threatened species, their protection, and taboos', *Conservation Ecology,* (online), 1(1): 6.

Cunliffe, B. (1994), *The Oxford Illustrated Prehistory of Europe*, Oxford: Oxford University Press.

Barman, K.K. and B. Goswami (forthcoming), 'The Status of the Tourism Industry in North Eastern India', in K. Roy and C. Tisdell (eds) *Tourism in India and India's Economic Development*, Commack, New York: Nova Science Publishers.

Goudie, A. (1990), *The Human Impact on the Natural Environment*, 3rd edition, Cambridge, Mass: The MIT Press.

Hall, J.V. (1998), 'Environmental resource security and violent conflict in Rwanda and Burundi: a natural experiment', a paper presented at the PRAEO Conference held in Bangkok 13–18 January, 1988 and co-ordinated by the Western Economic Association.

Hall, J.V. and D.C. Hall (1998), 'Environmental resource scarcity and violent conflict', a paper presented at the PRAEO Conference held in Bangkok 13–18 January, 1998 and co-ordinated by the Western Economic Association.

IUCN (1980), *World Conservation* Strategy, Switzerland, Glands: IUCN.

Leopold, A. (1966), *A Sand Country Almanac: with Other Essays on Conservation from Round River*, New York: Oxford University Press.

Meadows, D. L., J. Randers, and W. Beherens (1972), *The Limits of Growth: A Report for the Club of Rome's Projection on the Predicament of Mankind*, New York: Oxford University Press.

Mitra, A. (forthcoming), 'Prospects and Problems of Tourism Development in Hilly Regions of North East India: A Study of Arunachal Pradesh', in K. Roy and C. Tisdell (eds) *Tourism in India and India's Economic Development*, Commack, New York: Nova Science Publishers.

Pearce, D., A. Markandya and E.B. Barbier (1989), *Blueprint for a Green Economy*, London: Earthscan Publications.

Pearce, D. (1993), *Blueprint 3: Measuring Sustainable Development*, London: Earthscan.

Ramakrishnan, P.S. (1992), *Shifting Agriculture and Sustainable Development: An Interdisciplinary Study for Northeastern India*, Paris: UNESCO and Carnforth, UK: Parthenon.

Rawls, J. R. (1971), *A Theory of Justice*, Cambridge, Mass.: Harvard University Press.

Roy, K.C. and C.A. Tisdell (1995), 'Gandhi's Concept of Development and Nehru's Centralized Planning', in K.C. Roy, C.A. Tisdell and R.K. Sen, *Economic Development and the Environment: A Case Study of India*, Calcutta: Oxford University Press, pp. 1–16.

State Council of the People's Republic of China (1994), *China's Agenda 21 – White Paper on China's Population, Environment and Development*, Beijing: China Environmental Press.

The Ministry of Finance, Economics Division (1994), *Economic Survey 1993 – 94*, New Delhi: Govt. of India Press.

Tisdell, C. A. (1993), *Environmental* Economics, Aldershot, UK: Edward Elgar.

Tisdell, C. A. (1991), *Economics of Environmental Conservation*, Amsterdam: Elsevier Science Publishers.

Tisdell, C. A. (1990), *Natural Resources, Growth and Development*, New York: Praeger.

Tisdell, C.A. (1998), 'Co-evolution in Asia, markets and globalization', a paper presented at the PRAEO Conference held in Bangkok 13–18 January, 1998 and co-ordinated by the Western Economic Association.

World Bank (1994), *World Development Report 1994*, New York: Oxford University Press.

World Commission on Environment and Development (1987), *Our Common Future*, Oxford: Oxford University Press.

World Conservation Monitoring Centre (1998a), 'Indian–Arunachal Pradesh: Nandapha National Park', http:/www.wcmc.org.uk/igcmc/s_sheets/arunac_p/1039v.html.

World Conservation Monitoring Centre (1998b), 'India–Assam: Kaziranga National Park', http:/www.wcmc.org.uk/igcmc/s_sheets/worldh/kazirang.html.

World Conservation Monitoring Centre (1998c), 'Indian–Assam: Manas Sanctuary', http:/www.wcmc.org.uk/igcmc/s_sheets/worldh/manas.html.

World Conservation Monitoring Centre (1998d), 'India–Meghalaya: Balphakram National Park', http:/www.wcmc.org.uk/igcmc/s_sheets/meghalay/1564v.html.

World Conservation Monitoring Centre (1998e), 'United Nations List of National Parks and Protected Areas: India (1993)', http:/www.wcmc.org.uk/igcmc/parks/un93.html.

World Resources Institute, United Nations Environment Programme and United Nations Environment Programme and United Nations Development Programme (1994), *World Resources 1994 – 95*, New York: Oxford University Press.

PART IV

Concluding Observations

16. Nature Conservation and Development in Retrospect

After providing an overview of links between nature conservation and sustainable development, this book outlined possible roles for environmental and resource economics in planning for sustainable development. Conservation of biodiversity can be an important goal in itself and its maintenance can contribute greatly to the attainment of sustainable development. The significance of biodiversity as a factor making for sustainable development was discussed, taking into account a range of concepts of sustainable development. Biodiversity conservation was found to be of significance in relation to all the concepts of sustainable development considered.

Despite the importance of biodiversity conservation for sustainable development, its significance in this regard and for ecological stability (ecological resilience), has been exaggerated by some authors. Perrings *et al.*, (1995, p. 5) in fact state that findings about the link between biodiversity, or complexity of ecosystems, and their stability are contradictory. A number of authors (Conway, 1985; Holling 1973, 1986; Barbier *et al.*, 1994) associate the resilience of ecological systems with their sustainability. However, many highly diverse ecological systems are not very resilient because the species and the ecosystems within these show little biological tolerance and consequently little adaptability or flexibility in relation to environmental change. Ecological systems containing little biodiversity are likely to be more sustainable than highly diverse systems, if the components of the former systems show much greater biological tolerance (greater tolerance or adaptability in relation to environmental variation) than the latter. It may also be the case that in more diverse ecosystems, greater redundancy or virtual replication of species by ecological function occurs. If so, such systems could withstand the loss of a greater number of species than less diverse systems could and continue to function acceptably. Of course, acceptability involves value judgments. In any case, the sustainability of ecological systems or the maintenance of their function, depends upon much more than their diversity, and in some cases diversity is not the major influence on their sustainability.

It has been argued strongly that resilience is an inadequate indicator of the sustainability characteristics of systems. Factors such as the robustness of systems must also be taken into account, that is the ability of a system to withstand shocks without being deflected from its equilibrium or path, or to show little deflection in such circumstances. Furthermore, the overall performance of most systems, including ecological systems, depends on the functioning of their components. In assessing the sustainability of systems, we must carefully explore their ability to perform their functions if their parts become lost or impaired. Many features of sustainability cannot be captured by the resilience concept alone.

Even if conservation of biodiversity maintains the resilience of ecological systems, (a) humans may not desire to conserve biodiversity purely to obtain this resilience, and (b) they may desire to conserve biodiversity which has little or no impact on the resilience of ecological systems. It may be desirable to maintain the resilience of ecological systems only if this is instrumental in attaining other human objectives, for example, sustaining food supplies for humans. In this case, the desired resilience is a means to an end. Furthermore, from an anthropocentric point of view, those ecological systems which provide no benefits to humans (either directly or indirectly) are dispensable.

Nevertheless, some humans may wish to conserve biodiversity independently of its role in ecological systems. They may want to do so from a utilitarian point of view, or because of perceived moral responsibilities. Examine the utilitarian position first.

Even if one considers utility obtained from material goods (such as food) or direct benefits of biodiversity, maintaining some biological diversity may be important for sustaining utility. Given the law of diminishing marginal utility, a variety of foods is likely to be preferred, and this may call for a range of different food crops. Furthermore, by maintaining a variety of species, it may be possible to better utilize different regional and environmental conditions for production purposes. The market may, but will not always, conserve the variety desired in relation to material goods. It is, however, less likely to do so when the value of indirect benefits of biodiversity are taken into account.

As mentioned in the text, total economic value consists of the value of direct benefits plus indirect benefits of biodiversity. Alternatively, we could divide these benefits into tangible and intangible economic benefits. Market failure is liable to be widespread in relation to the intangible benefits, but may not be absent either in relation to tangible benefits. Biodiversity may be desirable for non-materialistic reasons, namely that it adds to variety to life and gives greater scope to humans to experience novelty. Thus, extended utilitarianism can be used to support the conservation of biodiversity to some extent.

This is not to suggest that extended utilitarianism, made increasingly operational through the concepts of total economic evaluation and the Kaldor-Hicks principle (potential Pareto improvement principle), provides a watertight guide to the social value of biodiversity conservation. Furthermore, not everyone accepts utilitarianism as a guide to social action.

For example, it can be argued that total economic value has no independent standing because such evaluation is partly a product of the total dynamics of the social system (cf. Tisdell, 1997, p. 1374). Individual values are dependent on social processes. Again, many refuse to accept money as a measuring rod of values, or reject the types of social preference orderings obtained by applying principles like the Kaldor-Hicks principle.

It is sometimes argued that humankind has a moral responsibility to conserve biodiversity, irrespective of the wishes of individuals (Leopold, 1966). In such cases, willingness to pay or to take compensation may not be accepted as the final arbiter of desirable social action. In any case, we must bear in mind Pigou's (Pigou, 1932) injunction that economic value is not total value. It is just one possible input into social choice.

It follows that even if total economic value could be fully captured by the extension of market systems, the social outcome may not maximise value in its totality.

The view is sometimes expressed that conservation of biodiversity will be enhanced if the operation of markets is extended and the economic use of nature is enhanced. This, of course, will not be the case if the nature obtaining greater economic use is open-access property. The solution may therefore be one of extending private property rights. But such extension can be costly, and it is likely to be partial and selective. In the latter case, extension of property rights and economic use of species may even reduce biodiversity, as was pointed out in Chapter 5 (Cf. Swanson, 1994). There is, therefore, considerable danger in relying solely on market extension as a mechanism to enhance biodiversity conservation.

Economic growth and the extension of markets through the global economic system, also have implications for the conservation of biodiversity. Globalization and structural adjustment policies seem more likely than not to reduce biodiversity, as was argued in Chapter 6, unless countervailing collective action is taken to provide public (non-market) support for biodiversity conservation. Such support needs to be of both a national and global nature. The fact that environmental quality and performance in conserving nature follows a U-shaped curve as a function of per-capita income (a reverse Kuznets-curve), should not blind us to major problems. For all intents and purposes, biodiversity loss is irreversible. Hence, if the loss occurs during the early stages of a country's economic growth, it cannot be reversed once the country achieves a high level of income. Of course, at a higher level of income the country might be expected to adopt measures which increase the likelihood of its remaining biodiversity being conserved.

Because of market failures in relation to nature conservation, financial support for nature conservation of a non-exchange type is needed. Such assistance may consist of private donations and gifts, and assistance from governments, including those from international bodies. The institutional mechanisms involved may be quite complex and involve NGOs, government bodies, individuals and so on. As a rule, demands for the use of funds for nature protection far exceed the funds available, and this raises questions of how to allocate funds between claimants, and how to increase the amount of available funds. These issues were taken up in Chapter 7.

Nature conservation need not rely entirely on donations and public funds. Managers of protected areas may be able to appropriate some economic benefits from them, for example, by developing ecotourism as an income-earner. However, it is not always easy to reconcile tourism in protected areas with the conservation of biodiversity; nor is ecotourism always profitable. In some cases its development can even become a net drain on the funds available for the management of a protected area. The issues involved were discussed in Chapter 8. It is emphasized that the total economic value of a protected area cannot be assessed purely in terms of the amount of its total economic value appropriated. Some protected areas, for which a high degree of appropriation occurs, are less valuable than others with a low degree.

Part III of this book concentrated on actual problems being encountered in conserving nature in Asia. Asia, especially east Asia, exhibited rapid economic growth, which was already apparent in the 1970s and continued virtually unbroken to August 1997, when the Asian economic crisis began to take hold, as a result of financial and political problems. The resulting slowdown or, in some countries, reversal of economic growth may not last for long, and economic growth will return to high levels once again. Whether that happens remains to be seen. In any case, the Asian economic growth which has already occurred has had major impacts on the natural environment. Asia is experiencing similar environmental impacts (outlined in Chapter 9) to those that occurred in Europe, the USA and Australia during their respective periods of rapid economic growth. One impact is loss of biodiversity as economic growth occurs. An interesting comparison can be made with the British situation in which a number of wild animals either became extinct or became locally extinct in historic times. Harting (1880) suggested that the most important factors in animal extinctions in Britain and Ireland were increased hunting, and clearing and economic development of the land. The latter, involving loss of habitat, was probably of greater significance because Harting (1880, p. 209) concludes his study as follows: 'Lake and moor have become fields of yellow grain; forest has changed into morass, morass into moor, and moor again into forest, until finding nowhere to rest in peace; the bear, the beaver, the reindeer, the wild boar, have become in Britain amongst the things that were'. Similar patterns are in the process of being repeated in Asia. For those who value biodiversity, the issues involved need to be addressed urgently.

Many complex issues are involved in attempting to reconcile economic growth and nature conservation. These can often be best appreciated by means of focused case studies at the regional level. The results of such studies were reported here for Xishuangbanna Prefecture in Yunnan, and for north-east India.

Xishuangbanna is regarded as an area of megadiversity as far as biological diversity is concerned. While there is a strong desire on the part of residents of Xishuangbanna to increase economic growth, there is also a desire to conserve its status as a 'green gem'. The natural environment of Xishuangbanna is a major attraction for tourists and tourism in this prefecture has increased rapidly, thus stimulating economic growth.

A number of development and conservation issues were considered drawing on field experience in Xishuangbanna Prefecture. These included: factors required in making an economic assessment of protected areas such as Xishuangbanna State Nature Reserve, socio-economic means for reconciling nature conservation and economic growth, some of which are being trialled by China; tourism development in Xishuangbanna, including ecotourism development in Xishuangbanna State Nature Reserve, as a means of reconciling nature conservation and economic growth; damage caused by agricultural pests protected by

Xishuangbanna State Nature Reserve and methods, such as compensation schemes, adopted to deal with this problem; consequences (some involving political economy) for conservation of the funding of the management of protected areas. All of these aspects have implications for biodiversity conservation in protected areas, and are not specific to Xishuangbanna.

Like Yunnan, north-east India is another region containing a high degree of biodiversity and considerable cultural diversity. In many of the states the area set aside for nature reserves is extremely small. While in the past, considerable biodiversity could be maintained in the absence of protected areas because the intensity of agricultural and other land-use was low, intensity of land-use has increased greatly in recent years. This increase has become a major threat to the conservation of biodiversity. Furthermore, agriculture using slash-and-burn techniques is becoming increasingly unsustainable, both from an economic and environmental point of view. Urgent action is needed to develop and introduce more sustainable agricultural methods for this region, a task made difficult by existing forms of property rights. In addition, if nature is to be more effectively protected in this region, it seems necessary to increase the amount of land in nature reserves or control slash-and-burn activity (agricultural intensification) in selected areas, that is reduce or control agricultural intensity in designated areas. But to do this, it is necessary to provide the local people either with viable economic alternatives or compensation.

This discussion highlights the need for a holistic approach to nature conservation. It is not realistic to consider protected areas as if they are islands separated from their surrounding communities. Furthermore, political impacts on the future of protected areas cannot be ignored. Effective planning and management of protected areas is possible only if surrounding communities and their interests are taken into account. The management of protected areas should be inclusive rather than exclusive.

REFERENCES

Barbier, E.B., J.C. Burgess, and C. Folke (1994), *Paradise Lost? The Ecological Economics of Biodiversity*, London: Earthscan Publications.

Conway, G.R. (1985), 'Agroecosystems analysis', *Agricultural Administration*, **20**, 31–5.

Harting, J.E. (1880), *British Animals Extinct within Historic Times*, Ludgate Hill, London: Trübner & Co.

Holling, C.S. (1986), 'Resilience of Ecosystems: Local Surprise and Global Change' in E.C. Clark and R.E. Munn (eds), *Sustainable Development of the Biosphere*, Cambridge: Cambridge University Press, pp. 292–317.

Holling, C.S. (1973), 'Resilience and stability of ecological systems', *Annual Review of Ecology and Systematics*, **4**, 124.

Leopold, A. (1996), *Sand Country Almanac*, New York: Oxford University Press.

Perrings, C.A., K-G Mäler, C. Folke, C.S. Holling, and B-O Jansson (1995), *Biodiversity Conservation: Problems and Policies*, Dordrecht: Kluwer.

Pigou, A.C. (1932), *The Economics of Welfare*, London: Macmillan.

Swanson, T. (1994), *The International Regulation of Extinction*, New York: New York University Press.

Tisdell, C.A. (1977), 'Local communities, conservation and sustainability: institutional change, altered governance and Kant's social philosophy', *International Journal of Social Economics*, **24**(12), 1361–75.

Index